Walker's Way

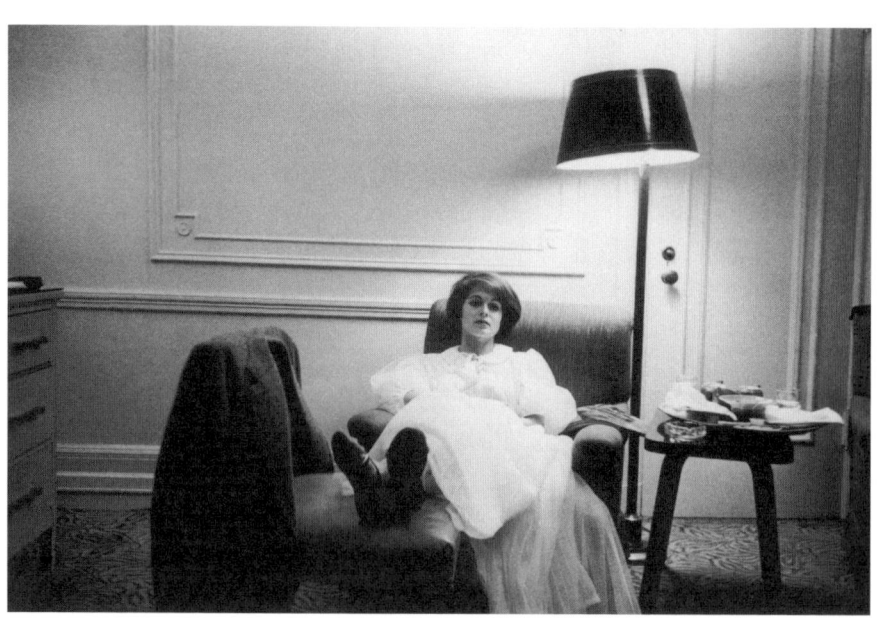

Resting in our room at the Copley Plaza Hotel, 1960. Photographs by Walker Evans

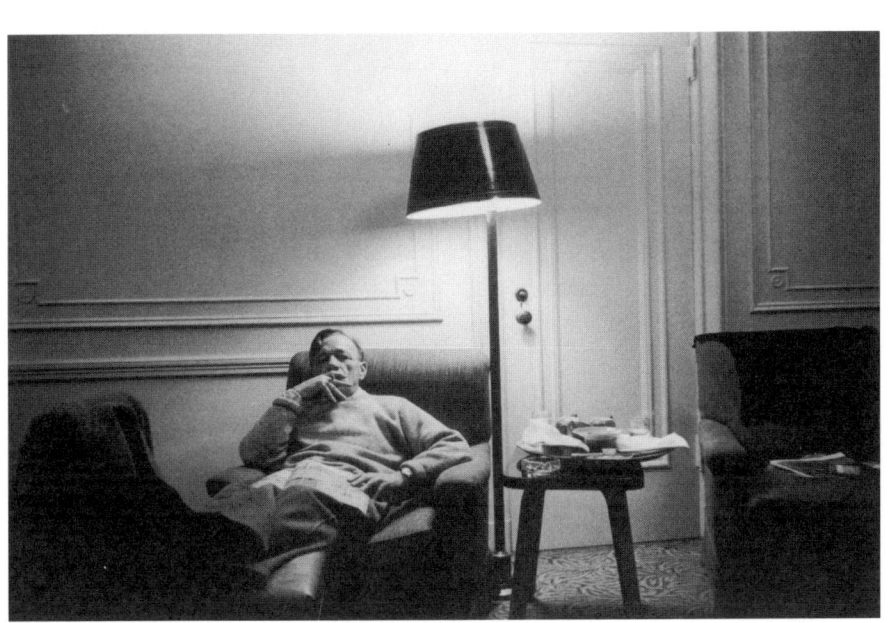

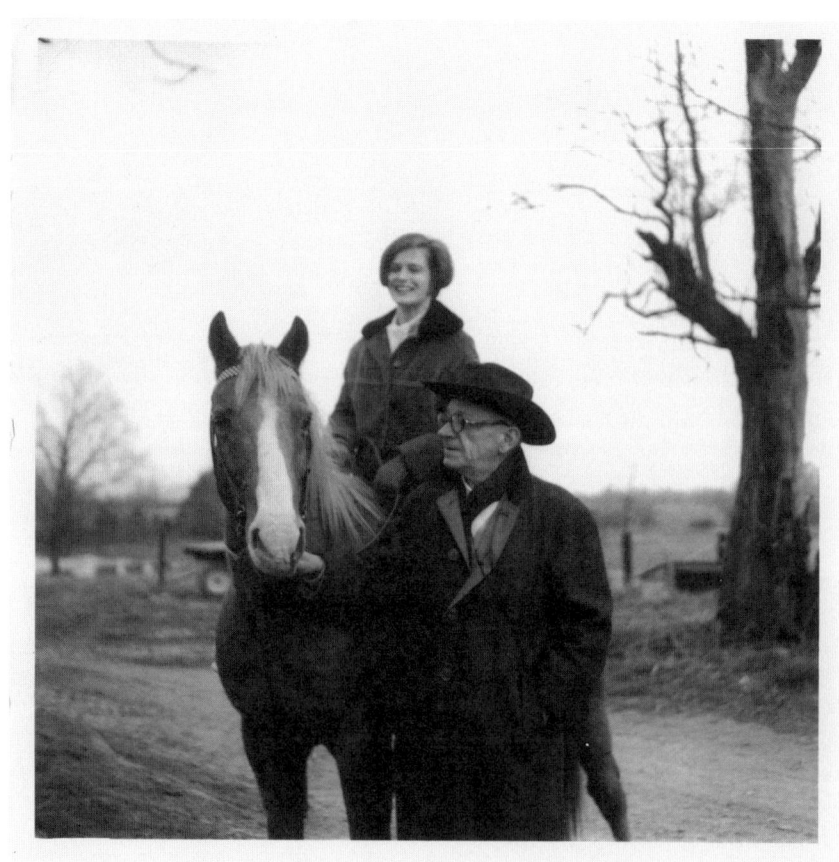

With Walker on a visit to the Mabrys. Photograph by Eliza Mabry

Walker's Way
My Years with Walker Evans

by Isabelle Storey

 powerHouse Books Brooklyn, NY

In memory of

My father
Dorothy Eisner and John McDonald
Tania and Jimmy Stern
Alice Morris
Leslie Katz

Chapter 1: New York City, 1959

Ursula opened the apartment door and I glanced at the slender, gray-haired man reclining on the sofa in the living room. His face was in a cloud of cigarette smoke, and he seemed to pay no attention to Plush, who ran across the room and jumped up into my arms.

Ursula, herself not much taller than Plush, tried to calm the poodle down and led her toward the sofa. "This is the pretty Swiss miss I promised you for the evening," Ursula said as she introduced me.

Walker, as he insisted I call him, raised his head a little, smiled, and took my hand. "Isabelle—la belle Isabelle, you must speak French?"

"*Bien sûr*," I replied, "my first language is French. As a child I lived in Paris for two years."

He sat up and looked at me with a curious intensity. "Where?"

I mentioned the 16ième arrondissement, the Rue de Passy, and our cul-de-sac, named Villa Scheffer, with the black iron gate and the English-looking row houses. How the nosy concierge hated all of us children, especially the ones on bicycles!

He laughed and said he didn't know that part of Paris. "I guess I wasn't rich enough, or I thought it was too bourgeois."

I told him that my best friend at the time was James Joyce's grandson, Stevie, and that from the garden side of our house we could see into the large windows of the Aga Khan's Art Deco villa. He wanted to know if I had a picture of Stevie and me in Paris.

"I do, I do," I said. "It's only a small snapshot, nothing much."

This excited him and he asked me to describe the picture in every detail. He laughed out loud at the thought of my brother Bernard and me in our Paris garden wearing Swiss hats, the kind that look like a yarmulke and are part of the Bernese farmers' regional costume.

During dinner, Ursula and her husband Landshoff (he didn't use his first name) entertained Walker with their own Paris anecdotes. They described the first time they met my parents and us children, all three with a bad case of whooping cough, in a hotel dining room in Switzerland. This was the summer before the war broke out and Landshoff, who had left Nazi Germany earlier, was courting Ursula in Paris. She emphasized how helpful my father had been to Landshoff, who was struggling to obtain permission from the Catholic church to photograph the ancient granite burial chamber belonging to the monastery on the Swiss side of the Saint Bernard mountain pass.

    Walker asked a few questions about the monks and the architecture of the place, and Landshoff, who was more interested in landscape, gave an enthusiastic account of the stark beauty of these high alpine meadows surrounded by snowy peaks. For him and countless émigrés, Switzerland seemed like paradise. Walker, of course, had never set foot in my country. He must have known instinctively that this small, landlocked democracy would not suit his taste or temperament.

Like so many young Swiss after the war I couldn't wait to leave and live elsewhere for a while. As a newcomer I embraced New York with all my senses and soon felt emotionally and physically at home in the city. I missed my family and my close friends from design school in Zurich, but I did not miss Switzerland. I reveled in the spirit of adventure and total anonymity, in much the same way my father had in 1935 when, as a thirty-year-old journalist, he moved his family to Berlin.

Walker was among the first Americans I met in New York. Most of my friends were European. My husband, Alec von Steiger, knew several members of an old Philadelphia family, and with them we experienced a privileged country life. On weekends some of their college-age children and members of a famous hunt often rode through the open land, their pink coats flashing in the gloomy November light. We spent our first Thanksgiving and Christmas in their big stone house and were overwhelmed by their kind and generous hospitality. Yet after floating for a couple of days in a comfortably mindless state, partly due to an abundance of Bloody Marys, martinis, roast beef, and Yorkshire pudding, I was overcome by a sense of acute boredom and emptiness. In the evenings there was little gaiety. I didn't get the jokes, the conversation dragged, and I found no visual pleasures in the muted decor of dusty rose, turquoise, and a dull green.

    In France there would have been unusual antiques and paintings to look at, and in England a library table piled high with new books.

In both countries and in my parents' house in Bern, we would have drunk plenty of good wine during dinner, instead of ice water in heavy crystal goblets.

Walker captured my imagination at the Landshoffs' that evening. He seemed to be endowed with everything I liked: charm, taste, style, an unerring eye, humor, and intelligence. He was a rare bird indeed, in his soft, pale gray tweed plumage and a touch of pink around the neck. And he seemed interested in me—I could hardly believe my luck. New York was doing its magic. I was in the right place at the right time, and I intended to hold on to it all.

Alec was in the Hamptons with his boss, the photographer Hans Namuth, working on location, and I was alone in the city.

A few days later Walker invited me to see *My Fair Lady* with Rex Harrison. I don't remember whether Julie Andrews was still in the show, but in Walker's opinion, Rex was the one to watch.

Walker said we would dine before the theater and asked me to choose a restaurant. Red velvet and gold interiors used to be my favorites for bars and restaurants, so I reserved a table at Romeo Salta on West Fifty-sixth Street.

Before Walker picked me up in a taxi at our apartment on East Fifty-second Street, he telephoned to make sure Alec was still away on his working trip. I assured him that he was.

Once inside the restaurant I noticed a change in Walker's face: the sparkle in his eyes was gone. He seemed annoyed, and his manner was almost rude when the maitre d' showed us to our table.

Something was wrong. What had I done to upset him so? I couldn't ask, I hardly knew him.

Walker ordered an old-fashioned for himself and wine for me. He lit a cigarette and sat back in his chair. "Why did you choose this restaurant?"

"I love Italian food," I said in an offhand tone of voice, hoping he wouldn't detect my nervousness, "and the salad is made at the table with good olive oil and red wine vinegar, not those creamy dressings." It was safer not to mention the decor.

"Good reasons, I suppose. Let's hope the food is better than this God-awful junk," he said and made a sweeping gesture over the whole room.

"I thought it would remind you of Europe, but it is a bit much." I tried to bring back the charm of our first evening, or at least amuse him.

He put his cigarette down, took his glasses off, and smiled. "I'll forgive you this time. You haven't been here long enough to know that this joint is utterly phony, and you don't know me, but I'll teach you about this town and America, if you're willing to learn." He picked up his cigarette and dropped the ashes all over the white tablecloth.

What stuck most in my mind was that he would teach me—and who could possibly know more about America than Walker? All my immigrant friends and the chic Europeans who constantly traveled to and from New York really knew nothing about this vast country.

The catchy, delightful music of *My Fair Lady* changed Walker's mood at once. I was enchanted by the sets and the costumes. So far I had seen only three American musicals in my life. In the early fifties, an all-black troupe toured the major cities of Western Europe with an unforgettable production of *Porgy and Bess*. My father was so enamored of the music, the female singers and tap-dancing men, that he took us all to see it twice.

When Alec and I arrived in New York, we rushed to see *West Side Story*. Later, Ursula and I went to a revival of *On the Town*, the lyrics and tunes of which I can recite and hum today, I love them so.

Walker might have dozed off for a while, but he certainly woke up and paid close attention the minute Rex Harrison appeared on stage in his long cardigan. It fascinated me to watch Rex and Walker simultaneously, and as the story developed I couldn't help thinking that Walker identified with the character of Professor Higgins. I wasn't surprised when I found out later that Walker was an inveterate Anglophile.

Was I meant to be his Eliza? He had already offered to teach me, and my London summer school English was all too basic. Unlike Eliza Doolittle, my wish was to acquire an American accent as soon as possible, so no one would ask me where I came from, not even the taxi drivers. I wanted to become a New Yorker overnight.

Before the music stopped, Walker took my hand and squeezed it.

He was silent in the taxi on the way home, and after I thanked him for the evening, he blew me a kiss and stepped back into the waiting cab.

Chapter 2

By the time Alec returned from the Hamptons, I had fallen in love. It was very different from my previous experiences with boys from home, and later with my fellow design students and artists, or with my husband. In the very beginning my love and feelings for Walker were mostly in my mind and imagination: a euphoric state without any sexual desire, very unlike the past, when I often felt strong physical attraction to men first and only later found out how little else they had to offer. I always measured their intellect against my father's, and most young men fell short.

Alec was different. A gentleman of the heart as well as by birth, he became my chum after a brief infatuation during a skiing vacation just before I turned eighteen. He was always around when I needed him, and my parents approved of him. Our families knew each other, which was important in a provincial town like Bern. At last I was able to look my mother in the eye and stop lying to her.

My early teenage years had been tempestuous. The oldest of three girls, I lived in constant opposition to my mother about everything that mattered to me: boys, friends, clothes, hairstyles, red fingernails and lipstick, jazz, movies, and parties. Sex could not be mentioned in my mother's presence without a long, tedious lecture. Little did she know that on rainy afternoons, when she left the house to have tea with her sister, I spent hours in my room satisfying myself to the music of Sentimental Journey. *Portnoy's Complaint* was a familiar phase in my adolescence. Between sixteen and eighteen I experimented with boys in cars, during après-ski in small chalets heated by wood stoves and on chaperoned trips to Italy, France, and England.

When my father was home (he traveled a great deal after the war), I went on long walks with him and talked about my troubles. We never had enough time together, and his way of cheering me up was to take me to cocktail parties, embassy events, and balls. He loved to dance, and I taught him to jitterbug. Before I turned twenty,

I had developed a taste for champagne and caviar and flirting with worldly gray-haired men.

The Italian tailors and seamstresses in the custom workroom for Sophie at Saks, where I was an assistant, began to wonder why I left early two, three times a week, since I lived within walking distance. They had nicknamed me, by far the youngest in the place, Miss Tiger, and threw in expressions like *bella figura* to make me laugh, or sang "Arrivederci Roma" in unison once I had told them that I understood their language.

Walker had invited me for tea at his place at five o'clock. My heart was pounding as I climbed the five flights to Walker's apartment for the first time. I knew plenty of people who lived in brownstones and walk-ups, but 1666 York Avenue was a tenement. I had no idea what to expect.

Walker stood by the door, dressed in baggy gray flannels and a camel-colored cardigan, just like Rex Harrison. "Come in, come in," he said, gently pulling me by the arm. "Sit down and have some tea." He took my coat and disappeared into the next room.

The first thing I noticed was a small claw-foot bathtub next to a large enamel sink held up by a single shapely pedestal. It was his kitchen! Half the tub was covered with a wooden board—it was the only counter space in the kitchen and too small for all the tea-stained cups and saucers left to be washed. Only the front part of the nice old maple dropleaf table between the two windows was set for tea; the rest had not been touched for days. A stack of newspapers, dirty ashtrays, and unopened mail covered the back of the table near the wall. There, half hidden by all this mess, stood a lovely pair of fluted, polished silver candlesticks.

Walker moved slowly, carrying a bulbous blue and white teapot. He put it down and asked me to pour.

"I love teapots," he said. "As you see, this one's Victorian, but I have discovered one in a little hole-in-the-wall antique shop on upper Third Avenue—a real beauty, all white."

"I would love to buy it for you," I said, feeling myself blush, "a thank-you present for *My Fair Lady*." I went on to tell him of my passion for antiques and unusual objects.

"You're too kind," he said and offered me some Carr's biscuits spread with cream cheese and guava jelly. "So you're a collector too? I

Chapter 2

wonder if we like the same things." He was sipping his tea and eating very slowly, while his cigarette was burning in an ashtray.

I spoke of my uncle in Bern, who had given me several French drawings, and described a nineteenth-century pastel, a girl's head wrapped in a pale blue veil that I had chosen in the Paris flea market when I was thirteen. "My godmother, Grande Isabelle, took me to Paris and gave me the money, but I found the pastel by myself, in one of the stalls. It looks like a Constantin Guys."

"Well, that all sounds very nice, but I collect more or less *objets trouvés*, things that have no real value, that simply speak to me." He got up, walked over to a long shelf above what seemed to have been a space for a coal stove before radiators were put in, and picked up a small ironstone jar. The cover had a spotted blue-black sturgeon in the center against a yellow background, and clear, black lettering around the outer edge. The established name of Fortnum and Mason, purveyor to His Majesty the King, left no doubt that the jar's contents had once been caviar.

I thought it had a spontaneous, almost humorous quality and said so.

"You do, really?" His face and hands became animated, and he began to talk about London, how it was full of original shop-and-tavern signs and boxes of all shapes and sizes with interesting labels still to be found in the specialty shops, the chemists and food halls of Harrod's and Covent Garden market. "Ah—and do you know about printed ephemera? What the word means?"

I hesitated—was he going to help me?

"No? I'll show you, much better than any explanation."

Without delay he went to the back room of the railroad flat, and I heard him rummage around for a long time. It sounded as though a dozen mice were nesting in tissue paper.

He came back carrying a green shoebox. He set it down on a chair and took the cover off.

From where I sat I couldn't see his face, only the box. His head and upper body were turned away and bent over, and his fingers moved very fast sorting through small pieces of paper.

He produced a stack of calling cards, each carefully engraved with names and addresses that he considered either socially impeccable or hilariously funny. "Look," he said, "here's a great one from

Kenilworth, Illinois, where I lived as a child. 'Winslow B. Quick, Attorney-at-Law,' probably turn of the century, and here we have 'Dr. C. Grover Inglefinger,' ha, ha, ha. Friends send them to me from all over."

The next treasures to come out of the box were the colorful little squares of printed tissue paper in which Italian oranges are wrapped. All through my childhood we used to flatten these blue and red tissues and blow them across the dinner table, a game my mother finally stopped by threatening to make us peel potatoes for pommes frites at lunch on Sunday. Some of our Swiss black-and-white chocolate bar wrappers were worthy of Walker's collection. I asked him if he would like me to write to my friends in Zurich and ask them to send special brand labels to him.

"Please do," he said. "Nothing designed, or cute—hate that word. You see, I don't much care for design, it usually bores me, too self-conscious." Purely functional objects, he believed, like well-made tools, were almost always good-looking. "Take a stainless steel hammer, even a simple broom." Boats and automobiles, he continued, were wonderful combinations of function and design. He raved about the Liberté and was disappointed that I had never sailed on her.

After four years at design school studying Bauhaus aesthetics I didn't agree with him entirely. Our teachers' philosophy was that form follows function. I argued that even the shape of a hammer can be improved with design. New American cars, I pointed out, had too much unnecessary decoration. Did he know Italian cars? All curves and elegant lines, and what about the latest, sleek, unadorned Olivetti typewriter that fit into a briefcase?

Walker was getting tired and it was time for me to go home. I was sorry I showed my disagreement and tired him. Poor Walker, he was still recovering from an ulcer operation he had had some months ago.

In the taxi down Second Avenue I reviewed all of Walker's highly subjective pronouncements and marveled at his way of looking at things. His insistence that well-made tools and hardware were things of interest and beauty was part of my school's ideology too, but as he referred to certain everyday objects and chose a few examples to make his point, he also transformed them, gave them a whole new meaning. From then on I observed what was around me more closely and tried not to compare it with Europe all the time.

The afternoon had gone by in a flash. He played with words like a virtuoso juggler. "Printed Ephemera"—what a brilliant title for a photographic essay! I couldn't wait to hunt for ephemera in the thrift shops on Third Avenue and find the perfect treasure for him.

When I got back to our apartment, Alec was waiting. He had set the table with wine glasses and had cooked osso buco for supper. One of his ways of relaxing was to spend time in the kitchen. On Saturday mornings we often set out to explore new neighborhoods and always brought along a net bag. The longer we walked the heavier the bag would get as we stuffed it full of special cheeses, salamis, and pastries. We'd travel as far as Bleecker Street to buy a certain crusty Italian bread.

During dinner, after a glass of wine, I thought about telling him I had met Walker Evans at the Landshoffs. He knew they were friends, and Landshoff often talked to Alec about Walker, whom they worshipped as an artist. I hesitated. My new love was purely platonic, and as far as I could tell, Walker was not sexually interested in me either. I needed more time to think, to be alone with my secret.

On one of my next visits to Walker's apartment, I asked if I could clear the papers off the long shelf in the kitchen and compose a still life using pieces from his collection.

"By all means," he said, amused, "fire away."

I had ventured into his small bedroom off the kitchen once before to pick up my coat and comb my hair. The large gold mirror above the four drawer mahogany chest made the crammed room bearable. There was no space left for a nightstand, or even a shelf to hold the pile of books. A gooseneck reading lamp was fastened to the wall on one side of the bed, and the books and a telephone were on the carpeted floor.

I discovered some of his treasures on top of the chest: round and oval silver boxes for pills and cufflinks; a square, polished wooden box with inlaid brass letters that formed the word HANDKERCHIEFS on the cover; and English hairbrushes and a comb, all neatly laid out on an immaculate white linen bureau scarf. After looking at everything, I chose one of his blue stomach medicine bottles and brought it into the kitchen. Blue and white were my color choices; the new white Empire teapot I had bought for him was placed slightly off-center. Walker had mentioned his strong dislike for centered decorations on tables and mantelpieces, and pairs of lamps, vases, or urns placed symmetrically on both sides of a sofa. He laughed when he told me that he often felt the urge to move things around in his friends' houses.

While I walked back and forth through the four rooms of the apartment, Walker lay on the bed with a book. He complained of a lack of energy.

The front room, which faced York Avenue, had an abandoned look. Originally planned as a sitting room with built-in bookcases and a small, decorative cast-iron and enamel coal stove, it was used for storage. Boxes filled with yellow manila envelopes were stacked in corners and covered with a layer of soot. The dark green window shades were pulled down. I hurried through the second bedroom, which smelled of cigarette smoke and fine leather. Walker used it as a dressing room and a place to display his beautifully shined, custom-made English shoes, all in a neat row.

Back in the kitchen, I made tea and brought it to his bed.

"You're an angel," he said, putting his book down.

I laughed. "That's not what I'm usually called."

He was reading the Olympia Press edition of *Lolita*, which I had given him the other day. I didn't dare ask if he liked it. Instead we talked about Giorgio Morandi. My still life resembled one of his paintings, I said, bottles and bowls; I hoped he'd approve of it.

The telephone rang. I picked it up off the floor, handed him the receiver, and left the room. I overheard fragments of his conversation, a whisper followed by a lull—then explosive laughter that filled the whole place.

"Brilliant, terribly funny, makes me feel naughty, of course—the guy's a genius!" After a long pause I heard him say, "Oh, from a very nice Swiss girl, you wouldn't know her."

He must be talking about *Lolita*, and the woman on the phone must be a girlfriend. He sounded different, secretive, as though he were sexually aroused. Something exciting was going on between them, that's why he had no desire to kiss me. Surely this was an experienced, sophisticated woman worth talking to, and I was just a "very nice Swiss girl," a girl nobody in New York knew.

Walker hung up. Cigarette smoke seeped into the kitchen, and my eyes began to sting. I waited for him to speak, maybe even apologize for his lengthy conversation. The March wind howled through the ailanthus trees in the courtyard. It was dark. The small American gothic shelf clock struck seven. I wished I were already home.

Walker was asleep when I went in to say goodbye. I tiptoed past his bed to get my coat and scarf, but my movements through the narrow rooms woke him up.

"You're going?" he said with an enigmatic look on his face. He checked his watch, searched his pockets for a cigarette, and sat up. "I had a delicious nap."

The matchbox was on the floor, so I picked it up and gave him a light.

"If you wait ten minutes I'll take you down in a taxi." He blew out a lot of smoke. "I'm having dinner with Caroline in some restaurant on Second Avenue, near you."

"Was she the one on the phone?" It took all my courage to ask.

"Yes, indeed, Caroline—actually Lady Caroline, but she doesn't use her title in New York. We talk about books and literary gossip." He seemed pleased with himself. "She knows everybody in London."

"Is she very beautiful?" I imagined a tall, fair, aristocratic-looking English beauty, like the ones I had occasionally seen in the Ritz bar with my father. They seemed to own the world, the way they dashed around town in chauffeur-driven Rolls-Royces.

"Beautiful? No, that's the wrong word. Rather striking. Large gray eyes, an interesting face, and she thinks like a man. Very unconventional, different from most American women." He put on a tie and disappeared into the second bedroom to choose a jacket and the right pair of shoes. He mumbled something in French, like *"femme intellectuelle, un peu folle."*

She sounded fascinating, someone I'd love to meet. Would he introduce her to me?

"Well—hmm, I'm not sure, but we'll see, maybe." He adjusted his knitted black silk tie in front of the mirror, took out a white linen handkerchief and put on his Burberry trench coat. A well-worn brown hat, obviously a favorite among many, made him look quite debonair, and from a distance, in the darkness of the street, hailing a taxi, he seemed much younger.

Where was I going to fit in, I asked myself. His past had so many secret compartments, not surprising for a man his age. All these years he had lived without prosperity, a recognized artist outside society, yet he wanted to belong to some parts of it now. The Century Association, where I had never been, was important to him, and he loved to put on his black tie and dine with the "rich and famous." At times he even seemed to behave like a snob.

I once asked him about his work with James Agee, after I had read *Let Us Now Praise Famous Men*, but he said very little and wouldn't tell me how he really felt in Alabama among the rural poor, or what his friendship with Agee was like. It was impossible for me to piece together this important part of his life with the few fragmented accounts and comments he uttered for my benefit. Always careful to conceal his emotions under a polished veneer of worldly irony, he remained a mystery to me. On the surface it was easy enough to find out what he liked, and as to his dislikes, he had so many they wouldn't fit on a page. But who was the real Walker Evans? Would I ever know?

I decided not to call him for a while and to try to sort out some of my feelings, even question why I had fallen under his spell. Was it that I was more and more stimulated by New York, and that Walker represented America for me, a country I wanted to know better, not drive through superficially, like a tourist, as was Alec's plan for next summer?

The more I tried to forget Walker, the more I wanted to be with him. He seemed to fill all the empty spaces in my mind. On my walks in the city I wrote down what I saw. Every antique shop, every hardware store I passed had something in it for him. I spent hours in second-hand bookshops looking for editions he might like. The Brooklyn Bridge, which Alec and I crossed on foot as a New York ritual; doorways and brownstones; cast-iron columns; signs; lettering in old bars and restaurants; the Algonquin Hotel—most things I loved in the city had Walker's stamp on them, and I was beginning to see them through his eyes.

Chapter 3

There was no word from Walker, and I was getting worried. Then on the first warm April day, the afternoon sun feeling good on my winter bones and every corner of the avenue filled with buckets of tulips and hyacinths, the doorman handed me a bouquet of white and yellow freesias tied with a white ribbon. He said an older man had come by with the flowers.

I tore away the paper and found a little envelope stuck in the flowers. I read the message on the card: "Where are you? I miss you. I need to see you. Call me in the morning around nine. Vôtre cher ami. W."

I went up to my apartment, put the flowers in water, and left at once. Walking a few blocks down Second Avenue calmed me down. There was a certain urgency in his message. Was I reading too much into it? He had not been as specific in the past. I was to call him at nine, which was early for him. All kinds of unrelated thoughts darted in and out of my head. Was he unwell? He had been tired the last time I saw him. Perhaps a new job, an out-of-town assignment for *Fortune*, now that the weather was better? Or did he simply miss me?

Surely, I hoped, this was the beginning of a new phase in our relationship. The platonic teatime visits were no longer enough. Had all my fantasizing at night, my wish for a life by Walker's side in New York, come true? I wasn't prepared for it yet, and Alec, sound asleep next to me through these endless nights, knew nothing. Now I would have to tell him.

It was still light outside when I crossed the avenue and turned west. The setting sun cast a glow over red brick walls and sheets of glass reflecting dark clouds in the orange sky. Even the trees looked unreal in the last moments of twilight, like props, their crowns covered with bright green buds. The wind no longer had any bite, and it was only a matter of days now before leaves would burst open everywhere. How quickly the rush of spring changed the mood of the city. I remembered it from last year, a month after Alec and I had walked off the boat.

The next morning I called Walker from a pay phone in the ladies' room at Saks. He said he wanted to meet Alec, and I should invite him and the Landshoffs for dinner.

"What shall I tell him?" I needed to sit down, hold on to something.

"Oh, tell him the truth—that you met me at their house some time ago. Use your imagination, nothing very obvious, just play it down."

I asked if we could meet beforehand and discuss the evening, but he said no and gave me some dates. He was in a hurry, he said, and mumbled some words of apology. His voice sounded impersonal, almost cold. This wasn't the deep, engaging, cigarette voice I had missed so much.

There was no way out. I had to arrange this dinner for him if I wanted to succeed. Not something I would do for just anybody, but then I wasn't dealing with an ordinary man, and what's more, he was interested in me.

Alec was astonished when I casually mentioned, before supper, while reading the mail over a glass of white wine, that I had met Walker Evans at the Landshoffs. "Why didn't you tell me," he asked and looked at me with pleading eyes, slowly shaking his head. "After all, you know how much I admire his work." He fidgeted with his signet ring. "And this was two months ago? Where was I?"

This was the way it was going to be from now on, I thought, only much worse. I dreaded it. All the old feelings of guilt I had experienced with Maman would be back to haunt me once more, and finally, after I pushed the guilt out of my way, sadness would fill my heart and soul and linger for a very long time. Alec was a man whom nobody wanted to hurt. He was liked for his trusting innocence, his innate decency and kindness. There was still a little time left, but the day when I would have to face him honestly and watch his blue eyes fill with tears from the pain I caused him was soon to come.

Alec could hardly believe that such a famous photographer as Walker would want to come to our house for dinner. "What's he like? Is he approachable, easy to talk to?"

Alec was always a bit nervous with new people, and especially with known artists. In his work for Hans Namuth he had met his share of famous painters and sculptors and he was aware of their occasional eccentric behavior, but Walker Evans, whose pictures in the book *American Photographs* he and many of his fellow students had seriously studied and discussed in the art library of our school in Zurich, was one of his heroes.

I suggested that we keep the conversation light and amusing and avoid the subject of photography, unless Walker brought it up. Since Alec was not a reader, literary talk was out, but cars were one of Walker's special loves and they could certainly talk cars. Alec used to participate in sports car rallies in Switzerland with his jazz band friends. Le Rally des Neiges, Alec's favorite, was one of the more prestigious sporting events held annually during the Swiss winter.

On the day of the dinner, Ursula called to ask if Plush was invited too, and could she bring smoked salmon for our first course. I was delighted to serve salmon, since we had decided on shad roe and asparagus for the main course. As I was setting the table I regretted not being able to use our wedding silver and the tall candlesticks stored in Alec's parents' attic in Bern. Walker especially liked old silver. At least I had linen napkins, thanks to a hurried trip to Bloomingdale's, and Swiss chocolates, the dark, bittersweet Lindt. Alec was going to Sherry Lehmann's for the wine, a Pouilly Fumé or a chablis. Walker's delicate stomach couldn't handle the delicious strawberries I saw in the market around the corner, so I made a crème brûlée for dessert.

A bunch of yellow tulips, new books from the Museum of Modern Art and a Matisse poster printed in France were among the few luxuries in the apartment. The furniture was from the Door Store, plus some odd pieces picked up on trips to country antique shops in Connecticut and Pennsylvania. A small carved French mirror was the only object I really cared about, the rest was temporary, just like our jobs and the apartment and nearly everything in our New York life.

Walker arrived a few minutes early. I answered the door. Seeing him again after his long absence gave me butterflies in my stomach— an expression I had learned from him. I wanted to throw my arms around him, but he drew back a little, took my outstretched hands, and kissed them. *"Bon soir,"* he said, and complimented me on my pale beige spring dress, a Dior copy with a wide suede belt.

Alec came out of the kitchen to meet him. The two men shook hands, and as we made our way into the living room I noticed how much taller Alec was than Walker. Alec made sure Walker had his drink and an ashtray. All my fears that the evening might turn out to be forced, possibly awkward, vanished. When the Landshoffs and Plush joined us, Ursula talked and laughed louder than Plush's joyful barks, and the commotion became too much for any intelligible conversation. Walker began to bark too—"the only way to talk to a dog," he said—and lit his first cigarette.

During dinner Walker and Alec did most of the talking. Alec raved about vintage jazz, Fats Waller and Louis Armstrong, and Walker pointed out how original some of Ira Gershwin's lyrics were, and Cole Porter's—naughty, funny as hell, full of double entendres, nothing in French *chansons* came close.

"'Birds do it, bees do it, even educated fleas do it,' ha, ha, ha," joked Walker.

Since Alec had done the cooking, I served the food, changed the plates for the salad and brought in more bread. Walker ignored Ursula. I was too busy with the dinner to entertain her, and Landshoff said very little—jazz was not part of his life.

Alec was unusually animated, and Walker paid no attention to anyone else in the room. The Landshoffs left early, using Plush as an excuse.

I suggested a small cognac, hoping Walker would stay a while longer and talk to me, but he said he had had a lovely evening and it was past his bedtime. Alec went to the bedroom to get Walker's coat, and, finally alone with him for a few seconds, I asked if I could see him again.

He said anytime, but why didn't Alec and I come up to his place and cook dinner for him there. He'd love to show him some of his things.

After a few short goodbyes Walker was gone, leaving me close to tears. I heard Alec whistling in the kitchen while he was cleaning up. He had obviously made a hit with Walker. Was this a new twist, a ménage à trois? Hardly what I had in mind.

Chapter 4

When the heat cast a stifling haze over the whole city, Walker left town. He had just acquired a 1949 black Buick touring car from his friend Holly Whyte, a writer at *Fortune*. With the chrome polished to perfection, the red leather seats saddle-soaped and the top down, Walker headed for the beach and his sleeping porch in Lyme. Summer was his best time, he said. Alec and I helped him carry his many cases and bags down to the car. His smile was almost childlike, an expression I had not seen before. There was no irony in his voice, just pure pleasure and anticipation and the certainty that the delights of the warm season, a swim in the ocean and a charcoal-grilled steak, would be his for weeks to come.

The first days of hot sun had already tanned his face and bleached his gray hair to light silver. Wearing a cream-colored English shirt and dark glasses, he could easily be taken for a celebrity, even a movie star. People often turned around to look at him in the streets. Once, as we stepped out of the bar at the Waldorf, someone mistook him for the Duke of Windsor. "I'm built like him," Walker said after the stranger pointed to him and whispered the duke's name.

It was my second summer in the city. The heat and humidity slowly drained all my energy and appetite for life. On my way to work, the air conditioners blew hot air onto the sidewalk, like giant hair dryers, and an acid smell rose from the pavement. Nylons stuck to my legs, chafing the damp skin on my inner thighs. As I hurried to the air-cooled store, my toes hurt, pressed together in high heeled black patent leather pumps. Black was this year's favorite summer color in the fashion world, following the spring shades of beige and navy with white. The only people who wore comfortable clothes were the seamstresses in the workroom. In their wrap-around uniforms and flats they seemed to move with ease. They changed into light sleeveless blouses and cotton skirts before commuting home on the train or bus, their bare legs showing.

Gone were my days of camaraderie with the seamstresses. I had been promoted to the team of junior executives, as a liaison between the workroom and the selling floor, where the dress code called for tailored outfits, jewelry, and full makeup. I even wore a girdle, regardless of my small size; everyone did. The head designer for Sophie at Saks found out that I had worked with French couture clothes in Europe. My new job was to take care of custom orders for the most prestigious clients like Claudette Colbert and other special friends of Mrs. Adam Gimbel, and to make sure they got exactly what they wanted. (Mrs. Gimbel had created the custom salon Sophie at Saks.) In the mornings I usually addressed the sales ladies about the day's fittings, appointments, and special undergarments or satin shoes they might need for their customers. It was hard to make them pay attention, since most were twice my age.

From time to time during the summer Alec and I received an old postcard from Walker through the mail with a short message like, "Having a wonderful time, why aren't you here? Come on out, we'll go for a swim." The cards—depicting a shingled summer hotel near Newport, Rhode Island, or a Connecticut River town square with an out-of-scale heroic monument, or a naughty card—remained tacked up on our small bulletin board in the kitchen for months. Walker was delighted to point out the erotic charm of the scantily dressed young girl pressing her body against a tree, her arms embracing the trunk. He had hundreds of old postcards, which he kept in sturdy file boxes, classified by subject: graveyards, post offices, train stations, churches, and many more. He prided himself on never having paid more than a nickel, except for the really dirty ones. "This will all be part of my Museum for Comparative Trivia," he once said, only half joking, after a hilarious session with Alec and me in his apartment.

By mid-August I had lost weight. I wasn't sleeping well, and during my afternoon break I felt like putting my head on the cafeteria table and taking a long nap. In Zurich an espresso kept me going until closing time. At Saks, the coffee was so weak I had to resort to No-Doz, the over-the-counter caffeinated candy Walker introduced me to. He had every possible pill in a leather case the size of a book, zipped on three sides. When he first opened it for me, I counted at least twenty clear plastic tubes filled with pink, yellow, and white pills. Some were supposed to change his mood, "pepper-uppers" and "downers," he called them; others were pain killers like Demarol, stomach relaxers, and vitamins. He kept his prescriptions going in New York and Connecticut, for fear he would run out. His enthusiastic belief in the magic of pills was such that he gladly shared them with whomever was around.

Alec made an appointment for me to see a Park Avenue doctor whom Ursula had highly recommended. Ursula was convinced I was anemic.

The doctor found nothing wrong with me. After a thorough examination, I sat facing him across a polished partners' desk. There was a large photograph in a silver frame next to a Harvard paperweight. In the photo, a blond woman in Bermuda shorts stood at the wheel of a gleaming yawl, her long brown legs resembling those of tennis champions I had seen at Wimbledon. Two teenage boys tended the winches. The boat was under full sail, moving through dark blue waters on a cloudless summer day. Flawless—just like the tall, blue-eyed doctor himself. He smiled and said: "What you need is a two-week vacation. The heat's got to you." An efficient-looking secretary came in and handed him some papers. "Tell your husband," he continued, "to take you up north—Maine—have you been to Maine?"

I shook my head. "First I need to get some sleep or I won't be able to enjoy it," I said. If I couldn't sleep at home, how was I going to fall asleep in strange beds on the road? "Just in case, do you think I could get some sleeping pills?"

He looked annoyed; he answered with an emphatic NO, as though he were denying candy to a spoiled child. "You'll sleep very well up north. The nights are cool. There's nothing the matter with you that a good sea breeze, rest, and healthy food won't cure." He said he'd be glad to talk to Alec on the phone if he had any questions.

Walker would have been more sympathetic, I thought. He paid attention to his friends when they were sick. On several occasions he had visited a close friend in the hospital and looked worried when he returned. One of his doctors, he said, was truly exceptional, a wonderful man and a great diagnostician. And he smokes! Walker's face would light up when he described Jim Leland. He would gladly introduce me to him if I needed a doctor.

He sounded like a humanist, not like the doctor I had just seen. Doctors were a very personal matter for me and next time I'd be sure to choose my own.

Alec suggested we visit Walker in his "rustic establishment," as he called it, on our way to Maine.

"Spend the day and bring your bathing suits," Walker said, sounding relaxed and pleased. "We'll go for a late afternoon swim." He couldn't put us up for the night, but the Bee and Thistle in Old Lyme was just the place, and he might join us there for dinner. They served honest, home-cooked food and wonderful desserts.

I was feeling weak in my stomach as we crossed the Connecticut River. Alec handed me the sheet of paper with the map he had drawn and Walker's directions. He loved maps and had a good sense of direction. In cities my visual memory for buildings and monuments served me well—I rarely got lost in London and Paris, and New York was easy—but in the countryside I needed an ocean or a sunset to orient myself.

The wide main street of Old Lyme had several grand, early-nineteenth-century houses and well-tended flower gardens. Set back from the road, and shaded by old trees, stood the Bee and Thistle. A friendly, tall woman with dark graying hair greeted us. Mr. Evans had phoned, she told us, and made dinner reservations for seven o'clock this evening; he asked her to take good care of us. She showed us to our cabbage-rose wallpapered room. In spite of the noonday sun it felt airy and cool. Maybe the mint green and white quilt on the maple spool bed had something to do with it. Whiffs of fragrant roses and sweet-scented heliotrope came through the open windows every time the soft breeze blew the sheer white curtains into the room.

"It's quieter on this side, away from the road," said the nice woman. "Keep the shades down. The afternoon sun is hot, but you'll be all right at night. Make yourselves at home. I'll see you all for dinner. Tonight we have salmon and steak."

Alec was busy with his cameras. I looked out at the garden. The perennial flower beds were laid out in old-fashioned symmetry around a garlanded birdbath. Tree-size rhododendrons formed a dark screen, a background that seemed to intensify the colors of the summer flowers. At home in Bern, my younger sister Christine and I used to venture into the shady, moist spaces of our garden and climb around in the tall yews. We had our favorite branches to sit on and spy on our neighbor, old and thin Mrs. Weber, always in black because she was a widow, and her maid Rosa.

Chapter 4

The half-shuttered room and the garden's stillness reminded me of the first summer of the war. We had stayed at home. Papa went away dressed in his uniform; the boccie balls were packed up in their box along with all the laughter and shouts of outdoor games; on Sunday afternoons Maman no longer sang with us, French songs like *"Sur le pont d'Avignon on y danse, on y danse."* The only sound from the piano came from my brother Bernard practicing scales and playing serious music. Maman lived by the telephone and the radio. The house was dark. All the windows were covered with opaque blackout cloth. At night, when we heard the sirens, we'd go down to what used to be our wine cellar and listen to the bombers fly over our city. Our garden had become an empty, lonely place.

Alec and I drove along a winding country road to Hamburg Cove. My eye caught an old red barn surrounded by grazing cows, halfway up a sloping meadow. Below it, closer to the water, a white church steeple rose through a stand of maple trees. The hillside shimmered in the strong sunlight. "Calendar art," Walker called it one evening when he was discussing landscape photography with Alec. This was generally the trouble, he thought, with a pretty view: you can paint it but you can't photograph it. He mocked nature photography. "Leave the sunsets and moonrises to Ansel Adams, the master of cliché."

At the first turn-off Alec started to count the mileage. We spotted the "perfect saltbox" Walker had mentioned in his directions; we took a right and drove along an uninhabited stretch of wooded road. The trees blocked out the last bit of sky. It felt like a leafy tunnel to nowhere. Only Walker would settle in such a remote spot. Finally, bright sunlight at the other end brought relief. We found the farm house and mailbox with the name Voorhees on it and drove through the wide intersection in low gear. We were just a few yards from Walker's place.

Alec stopped the car and we got out. The cabin was supposed to be on the left, but all we could see were more trees and tangled underbrush. Tumbling-down stone walls outlined the narrow road. We crossed the road and climbed over the wall. What a surprise: instead of serene countryside, we had stumbled into a Walker Evans photograph. The only difference was the intense color. An indigo blue car, circa 1930s, seemed to grow out of the tall grass in the scruffy field. Further down, close to a swamp, were a few more half submerged wrecks. The faded blue of the box-shaped car, its rusty bottom against the burnt grasses mixed in with goldenrod and the bright green skunk cabbage on the edge of the swamp were colors and textures we did not expect. For us the untamed vegetation slowly chewing up the decaying car was much more stimulating than the picturesque views of the Connecticut River. Alec was snapping away, just for the record, he said. He wanted to go back and photograph later, when the sun was less bright. This indigo could only get better.

Exploring on the uneven ground near the swamp we disturbed some bullfrogs; first only a couple croaked, then a few more, until the whole swamp came alive with their comical sounds. Pleased with our discovery, we returned to the car and made a U-turn. Off the road, in the shade of a large dogwood tree, we finally spotted Walker's shiny black Buick and pulled up alongside.

Walker appeared from behind an overgrown lilac bush. He must have heard the car doors slam shut, I thought. But where did he come from? I wasn't aware of any dwelling nearby. Again I felt this overwhelming urge to throw myself into his arms and give up everything in my present life to be with him. I couldn't see his eyes, he wore his dark glasses, but his deep tan and faded blue work shirt spoke of a relaxed, pleasurable summer. And he seemed to have regained his energy, the way he stood up straight, hands on his narrow hips; "full of beans," as he had described himself on a good day.

"You found it. Bravo." He smiled and led the way. "Welcome to the Evans compound."

I was amused by the little retreat Walker had created for himself in a postage stamp–sized clearing. It looked like an American primitive, as though he had asked an unskilled local to duplicate a shed with a lean-to from one of his photographs. What used to be a chicken coop, moved from an abandoned farm down the road, was the only closed-in structure on the place. An added-on twelve-by-sixteen screened porch provided space for two bunks, an old dropleaf table for working and eating, and four blue canvas boat chairs. The porch was painted white and had a slant roof, resembling an artist's studio; the board-and-batten siding of the chicken coop was barn red with white battens. Whoever did the paint job, a friend or Walker himself, must have had a few drinks and lots of fun with the stripes.

The porch table was set for three. Walker had cheese, salami, home-baked bread, and a perfect melon for dessert. I was asked to make a salad. Ripe tomatoes were lined up on a narrow sill in the sun. Alec opened the wine, Walker brought in some ice, and we sat down.

I was distracted and not able to take part in the conversation. I half wished I were outside under the trees, left alone to observe Walker through the screens. It was clear he had not missed me. He talked about golf. He loved the game but wasn't very good at it. It saved his life in Florida when he visited his sister, kept him from utter boredom. The courses down there were very different from the ones he knew in New England, especially the rough, which was pruned and mowed. The little nine-holer in Old Lyme was really cowpatch golf—ha—the third hole, what a charmer. Did Alec know the game?

Alec smiled and crumpled his paper napkin. Neither of us played golf. As a child, Alec had spent his summers at his grandmother's place on the Lake of Thun. His favorite fair-weather sport was sailing. Of course in the winter everyone skied.

I detected a slightly superior tone in Alec's voice, quite unusual for him. It was obvious he preferred sailors to golfers. Golf was a safe club sport, whereas sailing meant adventure, self-reliance under difficult, or at times even life threatening, circumstances. I myself had no idea of golf; very few friends of my family played the game. In Bern it was mostly diplomats who praised the region's only course, an expensive private club on a high plateau with views of the Alps. It was hard for me to imagine a golf-playing artist, yet in Walker's case I found it believable. He sometimes had the air of a sportsman, especially at the wheel of his touring car when he wore a London tweed cap.

After lunch, Walker loosened his belt, curled up on one of the porch bunks and took a nap. Alec stepped outside with his cameras, and I carried the plates and glasses into the cabin. It was dark and I almost bumped into the old enamel sink, which was the same kind Walker had in his apartment on York Avenue. A two-burner butane camp stove sat on a counter next to a regular size icebox. Walker had left the empty ice trays in the sink. I filled them and opened the freezer, which, full of steaks and Bird's Eye peas, was badly in need of defrosting. Bachelor housekeeping, I thought, feeling a little sorry for him.

In the living space he had a steamer chair, a Franklin stove, and a crowded book case. Through the small back windows I noticed an outdoor shower. At least the boxed-in flush toilet was inside, off the kitchen area. What more did anyone need during hot summers when the beach was a short ride away? This was the perfect sweep-out: no clutter, no room for guests. I wondered where Walker slept during a thunderstorm when the wind drove the rain through the screens and the bunks got damp. The flattened orange canvas cushion on the steamer chair was hardly enough support for a whole night.

I put the kettle on. It took a few tries to light the stove. The water for the dishes needed to be heated. How would I feel if I had to keep house for Walker and do without hot water and a proper kitchen all summer long? A lot would depend on his moods, I thought. If he really loved me, I could do anything.

In midafternoon we changed into our bathing suits and accepted Walker's invitation to go to the beach in his car. We all rode in front on the smooth red leather, with the top down. Walker showed us his favorite old barn. He had his eye on it, he said, mostly for the Depression-era Coca-Cola sign, but also for the wide, faded red boards. He wanted to buy it and use the lumber to build a small studio. Alec asked if he had photographed it.

"Many times," Walker said. He stopped the car and led us around the sturdy structure. "When we come back around six, half of this wall will be in the shade, divided diagonally by a sharp line. That's not the right light for my pictures." He walked toward the car and waved his hands.

Mothers in station wagons full of sunburnt children sucking on popsicles were leaving the Niantic public beach parking lot. Walker checked his watch and congratulated himself on his perfect timing: four-thirty. Now we wouldn't be hit by a nasty beach ball and crowded out of the best places to swim. We walked to one end of the beach and Walker spread out an old army blanket. Minutes later he was in the water, swimming parallel to the shore in a smooth crawl.

I was surprised he didn't swim out, like my father, who was always the farthest away from the shore and had crossed Lake Geneva as a young man. There was no undertow in this populated bay, and the lifeguard was still on duty. I tested the water. Walker swam by, raised his head, and called for me to join him. Back and forth we swam in shoulder-deep water, he slightly ahead of me, never touching each other. A few times he came up for air, turned and smiled, and I smiled back. Moving in the warm ocean so close to him stirred up new feelings in me. I fantasized that he would take me and we would make love on the beach under the stars, all night long. Was he unaware of my desire for him? I thought I had let him know how ready I was. Shyness was not part of his nature. Or was he worried about Alec? Ursula had recently told me, in her gossipy way, that Walker had taken his former wife away from her husband. All I wanted from him now was a clear sign, a long, passionate kiss—then nothing could stop me. If only he'd choose me, I would go with him.

The shrill whistle of the lifeguard gave me a jolt. I looked for Walker, who had come out of the water and signaled me to follow him. I was still a few steps behind when I noticed the scars on his back. He had once mentioned the removal of his vagus nerve. It was the first time I had seen him without a shirt. If his back looked like a road map, what would his stomach be like after the last ulcer operation? His legs and body were thin, but he was much stronger than last winter. In the water he seemed years younger, almost boyish and full of play. I could have kissed his scars, now that he was paying attention to me once again.

Chapter 5

There was a stack of mail on the hall table when Alec and I returned from our vacation. He quickly leafed through it. I spotted a registered letter with the pretty Swiss stamps. This was the letter he had been waiting for all these weeks.

I went into the bedroom so he could read it alone, and started to unpack the bags. I folded and unfolded the same clean T-shirts, too nervous to pay attention to what I was doing.

"Good news," he said after a long while, standing in the door with the letter in hand. "They want me to start in Basel a year from now, September 1960."

I barely looked up, I was so undone.

"What's the matter? You seem upset," he said.

"I am. I don't want to leave New York."

"But you always knew we'd eventually go back." Alec often appeared helpless, almost apologetic, when I disagreed with him. At times I would have welcomed a good fight, but Alec seldom raised his voice or argued—he withdrew.

The rest of the day was spent doing chores. I went to the dry cleaner and shopped for supper. It was still very humid outside. The trees on our street had turned a sooty gray. Everything—hair, clothes, leaves, even the well-loved neighborhood dogs—was limp and tired from the heat, and there was no relief in sight. I longed for a thunderstorm with high winds and spaghetti rain, as we used to call heavy rain in Switzerland. Like a jet from a gigantic hose it would wash the grimy sidewalks clean, and if we were lucky there might even be a rainbow over the East River. Whenever I saw a rainbow, the moon, or an exceptionally brilliant star in the Manhattan sky, it looked as though someone had put it there like a decoration.

I hardly knew a soul in Basel. All my close friends were in Zurich, but even Zurich couldn't touch New York. And Walker—I had to see him soon—this week—and tell him the news. He had seemed more affectionate on the beach, and I thought I might be closer to a miraculous breakthrough. He might even help me do something worthwhile; my life could expand and have meaning. He was unpredictable though. Nothing escaped him, but he revealed little of himself. With the greatest ease he moved in and out of different worlds and always seemed to know the principal characters in the fields of literature and the arts, the *chefs d'école*, among whom he counted himself. What was I supposed to do to make him bare his emotions?

With Alec as chief staff photographer and in due time partner in one of the first Swiss advertising agencies, my life would be safe and secure. We would live in town, in an old house remodeled by one of our architect friends, we'd collect antiques and modern art, take trips to France, Italy, and England, entertain old friends with gourmet meals and wines, drive a snappy car, like a Lancia, ski, sail, and get an Airedale terrier, Alec's favorite breed of dog.

We never thought of having children. Some of our friends' children, whom Alec photographed and played with for hours, were especially drawn to him, but he often said he would be too worried to bring up a son. His rather arrogant, successful father had lacked warmth and compassion for him and set unreasonable standards for his two sons. Alec's mother was loved by all, and especially by children, for her playful sense of humor. Alec, the younger of two sons, was her favorite. A daughter, who became her father's darling, was born much later. It was hard to tell whether Alec's mother had purposely over the years removed herself from her husband's civic and social life or had always preferred to live in her own world of comfortable, old-fashioned houses surrounded by familiar faces. She seldom spoke up in front of her husband, but to get even with him she'd indulge her children behind his back with a triumphant smile on her round face.

I was the designated leader in our marriage, a role I wasn't sure I wanted for the rest of my life. Alec would even have allowed me to have affairs and would have tried his best to ignore them. I hated what I was doing now, cheating on him in my thoughts and feelings, but I was not in love with him. The future looked all too predictable. I foresaw an uneventful life without intellectual stimulation. What had bound us together until now was mostly our shared visual training and old friends in Zurich and Bern, with whom we had spent every moment of our free time. Since I had met Walker I longed for more than that, and my mind was in a perpetual turmoil. I could barely face the long, awkward silences between Alec and me when we were alone. Back home, in Switzerland, there would be even less excitement and fewer conversations, since Alec was neither a party-goer nor a reader. Rather than meet new people he preferred to take his car engine apart or fix the rigging on a boat. I could see us in the not-so-distant future sitting across a well appointed table in a romantic auberge, like so many French couples in three-star restaurants, doing serious eating without saying a word to each other.

On my way home from the supermarket I called Walker from a pay phone. No answer. Where was he, now that I needed him most? No doubt he'd delay his departure from Lyme for as long as he could and continue to play in the waves, feeling deliciously cool.

Every day I came closer to a decision to stay in New York, with or without Walker. I was grateful to have a routine job, a stage where I could play a part, smile and be charming behind my mask of makeup, a place where no one knew my thoughts. In the evenings I scheduled as many outings as I could. I accepted every invitation to cocktail parties and gallery openings, sought out small jazz clubs and obscure cabaret performers downtown, and if nothing appealed to me there were always plenty of good movies playing all over the city. Alec tagged along.

I lay awake worrying about my life if I were to live alone in the city. In my mind I saw the same pictures over and over again, changing quickly, like slides in a carousel. I was in an empty room, standing on a ladder, painting the dirty walls of my one-room apartment. The color kept changing. Sometimes it was a warm yellow, then a pale terra cotta with white trim. I was in a hurry to get it done, preparing for something, a special event, but I was always alone.

Another recurring image was a dark green plaid suitcase with tan leather straps and trim, the one I had on the boat over. I carefully folded and packed some of my best clothes and shoes, not knowing where I was headed. I doubted if I would be welcome in my friends' houses once they knew I had left Alec, and I didn't know people in San Francisco and Chicago, two cities I was curious to visit. I couldn't get rid of the suitcase. This time it was bigger. I stuffed it full of ski clothes, warm mittens, and woolen hats. In the picture it was snowing. Ever since my childhood winters during the war, snow had been a comfort to me. The sound of crunchy snow underfoot and the gradual silence that descended over towns and villages and even cities like New York during a heavy snowfall filled me with anticipation of pleasures to come. What pleasures? I couldn't go home and ski in the Swiss mountains any longer. Nobody wanted me now that I had caused pain to my family. "The first divorce in our family," my mother would lament to her sister on the telephone when she broke the news after receiving my letter.

The last slide was the Christmas tree. I loved my mother's tall tree with real candles and the handmade, familiar ornaments, like the German *papier-mâché* angels with golden hair and pink cheeks. The tree became smaller as I grew more anxious during these nights, until it was only a sad, bare little tree, and I was no longer in the room. There was no place for me at Christmas. Ursula and Landshoff always left town. I had felt depressed during my first Christmas season in New York. The whole city had turned into a kitschy display of materialism, and the Christmas spirit as I knew it was lost in all this tinsel. I had longed for a snowy village in Vermont.

It was close to Thanksgiving when I heard from Walker again. He sounded tired on the telephone and mentioned that his doctor, Jim Leland, was going to put him in the hospital for some tests, but he wanted to see me first. Could I meet him toward the end of the week after work in the bar of the St. Regis?

I knew he had a history of ulcers and chronic bronchitis during the winter months, but a hospital stay seemed to indicate something more urgent. Of course smoking was the worst for his health, both for his stomach and chest. Perhaps I might be able to help him give up smoking, although I knew from my father that journalists, writers, and artists, whose work depended on long periods of time spent in monastic solitude to think and pursue new ideas, needed their cigarettes almost as much as food.

I didn't know what to expect. If the raw air and dusky light on the avenue was an omen, our meeting might be melancholy. Nothing that the first drink couldn't change. The thought of seeing him and cheering him up if he felt blue was enough to make me hurry around the corner, run past the doorman and into the hotel.

The bar was dark and it took me a moment to find Walker. He looked a little rumpled in an old gray suit and he needed a haircut.

His summer tan was gone. I kissed him on the cheek, and he held my hand until I sat down opposite him at the small table. The usual cigarette was burning in the ashtray. Walker ordered me a sherry. We looked at each other without saying much for a long time. I felt his compassion and warmth the way I hadn't since *My Fair Lady*, when he put his hand over mine. I knew he cared. Words would only spoil this moment—I wanted it to last.

Walker picked up his cigarette and described Doctor's Hospital and how lucky he was to be Jim's patient. "He knows what I need. The place is like a hotel," he said, puffing away, "mahogany furniture and rugs in the lobby, and friends can visit any time of day, until late. I even keep a bottle for them." He coughed and took out his white linen handkerchief. "Will you come and see me?" He gave me a faint smile.

I promised I would. He really needed me. I'd do anything for him in the hospital, bring chicken sandwiches and rice pudding and lots of books.

We left after one drink. It was dark outside. Walker said he wanted to walk me home, a little fresh air would do him good. He'd ask our doorman to get him a taxi. Slowly we walked east. I told him about Alec's job and that I had made up my mind to stay in New York.

Walker turned to me and stopped in front of a row of brownstones. "Have you told him your plans?" he asked.

"More or less. He realizes I want to stay here, but he doesn't talk to me much."

"And what do you want to do with me?"

I climbed up the stoop of the nearest brownstone, waited for him to face me, and said in a clear voice, "I want to marry you." I stood there a few moments and then jumped into his arms. I buried my head on his shoulder and hugged him. He put his arms around me for the first time. It was a long embrace, through too many layers of clothes. When I lifted my head to look into his eyes, I saw tears on his cheeks. This was the real Walker—the side of him I had not known before. He was capable of true emotions. I loved what I saw, and I no longer had any doubts that he loved me.

Three days later Walker surprised me after work, waiting in a taxi by the employees' door. My hair was stiff with hairspray and I didn't feel pretty wrapped in the old storm coat I had worn to work because of the cold drizzle earlier in the day. As we rode down Fifth Avenue, he presented me with a beautiful shiny white box. I should open it later, he said, when I was alone. There was a note in it. He kissed my forehead, just barely brushed it with pursed lips, a fatherly kiss that made me feel like a deserving child on her birthday. "I'm taking you to the Century for tea. You'll meet some of my closest friends." He asked the driver to stop on the corner of Forty-third Street.

I had no time to prepare for this important occasion, my first introduction to the Century, this place of distinction, not just a social club like the Knickerbocker, as Walker had emphasized when he first told me about it. "And wait until you see the building—a perfect gem." He had even given me a history of the club to browse through and mentioned its architect, Stanford White. Someday, Walker was quite certain, I would meet some of White's many grandchildren at parties and weddings around town.

At the door, Daniel, a gentle black man with a discreet manner, greeted Walker and kindly took my coat to be checked. The grand staircase led directly to the art gallery, the only place in the club where women were allowed. From the floor above came laughter, the clinking of glasses, and the smell of cigar smoke, but the gallery was empty.

We sat on a long sofa and Walker ordered tea and cinnamon toast. The Century was not a place where tea was normally served, but the staff knew Walker's habits. Walker sprinkled sugar on the toast and offered me a piece. He said that lately he had to eat six times a day, small amounts, and that he did not get enough energy from his food, but Jim would soon find out if there was something wrong. "Maybe it's nerves," he said. I asked about the art on the walls, an exhibit of architectural drawings.

Some of the exhibits had to do with prints, book illustrations and such. He thought it boring at times, but once a year, the members' show was great fun. "I had a painting in it, just to surprise the committee, and Louis Bouché of course, my friend Bob Osborne, and Bob Hale submitted a large abstract one year, ha, ha, he doesn't paint all that much."

Later *Newsweek* editor Wilder Hobson and his wife Verna joined us for a drink before taking the train back to their home in Princeton. Verna, years younger than Wilder, smiled warmly and came to sit next to me to talk about Europe. Her animated oval face and pink cheeks, so rare in New York during the winter, made her a natural beauty, as though she had just flown in from the English countryside in June with dew drops on her skin. She wore her dark hair pulled softly back in a knot at the nape of her neck and appeared to feel perfectly at ease in a men's club. Wilder instantly bombarded me with personal questions, and in a teasing, amicable way asked if I really knew Walker, his old chum, and was I up to him? Observing these two old friends, so skilled in the game of repartee, joke and talk of books, editors, and writers they knew was just as entertaining as watching a play in London.

After they hugged me and said their goodbyes, I felt I had done all right by Walker too. He seemed pleased and said that his friends would all like me.

Back in my apartment I rushed to the bedroom and hid Walker's present in my lingerie drawer before Alec came to find me. He had poured two glasses of wine for us in the living room, and there was a stack of new maps and guidebooks on the coffee table.

"Sit down," he said and pushed a little plate with olives and celery sticks in front of my glass. "I have a great plan for next year. See if you like it." He unfolded a map of the East Coast. He had circled several cities in red pen: Baltimore, Charlottesville, Richmond, Charleston, Beaufort, and Savannah, all the way down to Key West and around the Gulf coast to New Orleans. Walker had photographed in many of these towns, but there was no way I could see what he saw unless he showed it to me. One of my favorites of his interior photographs, the breakfast hall of the Belle Grove Plantation in Louisiana, told me more about Southern grandeur than any house museum, with the dining room table set for Sunday luncheon and fake flowers in the parlor, possibly could. I had visited a few such houses in New England. Walker's pictures left room for one's own imagination to fill in the details.

Alec did all the talking as his hands traveled over highways and mountain ranges, and when he was done outlining our three-month trip, he said that toward the end of July he would book passage on a freighter for himself and the car. "You could stay in New York—take your time to say goodbye to the city and your friends and fly back to Basel for Christmas."

I poured myself another glass of wine and stared straight ahead. "But I'll never go back."

"Is it because of Walker?"

"Yes."

"When did you see him?"

"This afternoon." I looked away.

"I see." He slapped the maps and guidebooks off the coffee table, stood up, and said, "In that case I'm no longer needed." His voice sounded flat and lifeless, I hardly recognized it. Moments later the front door slammed shut.

I did it, I changed my whole life, was my immediate reaction. And nobody told me what to do, I did it alone. This was the first time I had made such a weighty decision. When I married Alec, I had been encouraged by family and friends, all wishing me well. It was the right thing to do at the time. Now I knew more about myself. Alec was better off without me. Maybe I should have been gentler, prepared him for the blow, but there is no kind way to end a marriage.

Hours must have passed and I was still sitting in the same spot. When I finally got up and went to the kitchen for a glass of water, I saw the cold, untouched eggplant parmigiano Alec had cooked for our supper. Soon, very soon, these everyday comforts would be gone, along with many other things I liked. Better not think about the past; I had to be brave. My future was much bigger, a large canvas already filled with Walker's work and professional life, his friends, and now his love for me. There were so many unknowns it was frightening, but, I reassured myself, every worthwhile beginning was that way. The element of chance made life exciting, and I had missed that with Alec. If I stayed with him, I would always be looking for somebody or something else.

Alec did not return that night. He must have decided to sleep in the studio, I guessed, as he did once in a while when he worked very late. It was close to midnight, and I saw no reason to set the alarm clock. Tomorrow was my day off. I took the phone off the hook and turned the lights out. The only sound was the hum of the city. In the dark, the empty bed felt colder. I pulled my nightgown over my knees, reached over to Alec's side for more pillows, and cried myself to sleep.

The next morning I remembered Walker's present. Now was the time to open it, to read the note. I made some coffee and retrieved it from the drawer. I pulled up the Venetian blinds in the bedroom. The wet pavement below promised another dark November day. In spite of it I felt lighthearted and calm. To be rid of the heavy coat of lies gave me back my freedom. At last I could come out of hiding and move forward.

I untied the white satin ribbon and opened the box. Walker loved white—black, white, and gray were his colors. The note inside was written on engraved Century Association paper.

Nov. 29 1959

Dearest Isabelle,

This is your declaration from me, of love, of devotion, respect, admiration and burning excitement. I write because I want to mark the time, I want you to have something from me as a sign. This is your engagement ring, from Cartier.

I plight our troth.

Walker

Over and over I read the note. It was just like Walker to write with such style. Not a superfluous word, and the meaning was as clear as I had hoped for. His handwriting showed his strength and generous character. Written with a fountain pen in black ink, the note was as visual as it was timeless.

How charming to mention Cartier—yet the box was far too large for a jewel. The present came from Scully & Scully, on Park Avenue. I peeled away countless layers of tissue paper to find the most feminine oval mirror for a young woman's dressing table. Its softly padded mauve velvet frame, the pink satin rose and pale green bow suggested French interiors of the Belle Époque, a reflection of Renoir's women pinning up their long reddish hair. I held the mirror in my hand and turned it over. The back was lined in a lighter shade of mauve moiré and it had its own little stand. I couldn't wait to set it up on top of my bureau opposite an opaline vase. Today I would buy a bouquet of fresh violets—the mirror deserved it. Walker seemed to know what I liked. Bless him, nothing he did or said was sentimental or heavy-handed.

In my euphoric state the exact dates of Walker's hospital stay slipped my mind. I was anxious to hear from him. A few days later he called from Doctor's Hospital and said he was ready to receive me tomorrow, by late afternoon. He thought he'd be through with most of the tests. He sounded quite exuberant on the phone, as if being in the hospital agreed with him. So far, he said, they hadn't found anything wrong. Not to worry, Jim was going to give him new miracle pills.

To cheer him up I wore a red dress and my black velvet hat with the upturned brim. At lunchtime I hurried to the Women's Exchange on Madison Avenue and ordered tea sandwiches with the crusts cut off, to take out. Walker loved custards, so I added two for his dessert and put it all in the Saks cafeteria's refrigerator until closing time.

The entrance hall at Doctors' Hospital gave the impression of a genteel Upper East Side hotel lobby. There was no hospital smell. The soothing green walls made a proper background for a pair of mahogany console tables with matching Chinese lamps and a stiff, upright settee. The fresh flowers were arranged in such a symmetrical manner that they almost looked fake.

The friendly, dark-suited lady behind the desk told me Walker's room number and directed me to the elevator. Few New York City hospitals had this air of quiet, well-mannered elegance. Leave it to Walker to find it and use it when he felt in desperate need of a rest.

Walker's door was ajar. He was deep in conversation with a couple of friends, each holding a drink. "*Ravissant, tout à fait charmant,*" he exclaimed as he took my hand and kissed it. "Meet my friends John and Dorothy McDonald."

John was a gentle-humored man in his fifties, whose straight black hair had not yet turned gray. He looked into my eyes when he greeted me. He seemed to say, "She's quite a girl, good for you to find her." This gave me confidence. A man who appreciated women for qualities other than their looks was easy to talk to—I could be myself. He brought a chair for me and came around with a glass and the bottle of Scotch. In seconds he made me part of the group, and our age difference of nearly thirty years was of no importance to him or Dorothy. Her husky, laughing voice was much bigger than her petite figure and slender legs. She became even more talkative when I told her I had gone to art school in Zurich. In the twenties, she said, she had accompanied her best friend on her honeymoon to Switzerland and her friend's husband admired Lenin. They had spent the night in the old part of Zurich where Lenin had lived, and only realized later that they had slept in a whorehouse. We all laughed, though I could tell that John and Walker had heard the story many times. She looked at me from different angles and asked if I would like to come down to her studio on Cornelia Street, she'd like to draw me.

If Walker had few kind words for his mother and sister, I quickly saw that John and Dorothy represented everything he would have liked in a family: unconditional love, good brains, imagination, true understanding of his work as an artist, and above all, humor. They were his chosen family. He put away the bravado and sarcasm and listened to what they had to say, which made me love him all the more.

Seeing Walker in his hospital bed, dressed in new white Brooks Brothers pajamas, talking and smoking, completely relaxed with his closest friends, as though he were in a favorite living room, almost took away my worries about his health. In this benign, peaceful state of mind, he welcomed these safe, ordered surroundings and kidded the shy nurses' aids who brought him his trays and new pills. The conventional art and bourgeois interiors that he so abhorred in the outside world seemed not to bother him here at all.

Chapter 6

In January 1960, Walker left for Florida to stay with his sister and brother-in-law, Jane and Tal Brewer.

In his opinion Florida was a cultural wasteland. The only good things there for him were the hot sun and beaches with their fishing and bait shacks.

Every night I wrote to him and read the Henry James books he had given me for Christmas. Thoughts and desires for him, and the characters and places in *Daisy Miller*, *Washington Square*, *The Americans*, *Portrait of a Lady*, and *The Aspern Papers*, one of my favorite novels, kept me awake night after night.

With rare exceptions I no longer went out with Alec, though he was still living in the apartment. In the bedroom, where I spent most of my time, I moved the twin beds to opposite walls to give each of us more privacy. I felt awkward with this temporary arrangement, but the living room sofa was too narrow to sleep on.

After a few days of writing to Walker in the evening, I felt freer to mention the conversation we had had recently about confidence.

"By talking to me seriously and letting me know that you had found out about my lack of confidence, you almost gave it back to me," I wrote.

"Through the last year I lost all my self-confidence, and now you give me so much of it that I have to learn again how to use it and to keep it. I promise you, I will work on it while you are away.

"This little separation is very good; you are getting a rest and I have time to think about us and all I want to give you and do for you, beside exciting and satisfying you. This too is important and so wonderful! All this is almost more than I can take right now, because I have to keep my mind on many other things, I don't like at all."

In the same long letter I described Grenville Emmet's visit to our apartment, and how I had the martini ready for him and what a nice, sympathetic lawyer he was. Naturally Alec and I found the divorce fees high, but I thought I could work all summer and pay Walker back for my share and for the lawyer in Mexico.

Alec was so worried about money. He had just called a few freighter lines for his trip back, but they all wanted two hundred dollars for the car. Though he was pleased with Emmet, he said with tears in his eyes: "I am overcome and terribly sad."

Walker was very quick with his answer concerning my confidence and confidence in general. He said it came and went by degrees, for him, as well as for everybody else, but that I should not hide my loss of it in the future. If I talked to him about it, he could probably help.

I read Walker's letters again and again, and when he telephoned early one morning and woke me his voice sounded strong and he seemed to be in a light-hearted mood. His call was especially welcome, since I had had a scary, Kafkaesque dream during the night. He urged me to write it down for him and mail it right away.

"I had felt dizzy and dopey during the evening and without remembering how I got undressed and into bed, I fell heavily asleep.

"In the middle of the night I half woke and had terrible desires; I wanted to satisfy myself and as I started it and was excited, I fainted. I guess I had a little temperature and the violent excitement was too much for me. I came to gasping, and Alec got up and wanted to know what happened. I could not explain it to him, it was rather embarrassing; all my blankets were on the floor and I found myself half naked. Alec remade my bed, and I fell asleep right away.

"Then came the dream. I was climbing up the stairs to your apartment to meet you. The door was locked and I had to use my key. I opened the door, walked in, and the place was abandoned. All the furniture in the kitchen was there, in the same place, but none of your personal objects. The table and the mantelpiece were completely empty, even the smell of leather and smoke was gone. The light was on, but all your lamps had disappeared. I walked around and was scared to death. Oversized bugs and spiders were creeping along the walls and over the sink. The bugs were brown and about three inches long.

"I wanted to open the icebox. Termites had gotten hold of it and it was caved in and full of mysterious holes. It looked like a huge, white, abstract sculpture, and through the ice and the holes I could see some food, mainly endives. I wanted to go into your bedroom and then you called, bless your heart. I think this dream has something to do with my previous unsuccessful self-satisfaction; I am not going to analyze it, too morbid, anyway."

I was surprised when I received another letter the following day. The small blue envelope was covered with stamps and had an overnight mail sticker across the top.

"I'm on the beach. Your wonderful letter just arrived, the one about the Kafka dream. What horror, you're right not to try to analyze it. I don't believe much in dream analysis anyway, it's Jewish to the core: and to hell with it. But you described it so well: my apartment, the icebox—remarkable. At least I was there in the end for you—you may at least let that symbolize my constancy.

"Let that dream of yours be a lesson: finish all pleasures you start. I'll finish my pleasures, too, just for you."

Time flew with our letters going back and forth, and when Walker sent me a telegram with his date and time of arrival, I was elated and danced alone in the apartment until the music stopped for the news. Three more days and we would be in each other's arms.

Walker's train was due mid-afternoon on Saturday. I was alone. Alec had gone away for the weekend with friends. All morning I spent grooming myself. After a long bath and shampoo I covered my body with lotions and scented powder, painted my toenails a pretty coral and put my hair up in large curlers. The hours passed quickly with Ella Fitzgerald on my favorite jazz station and countless cups of coffee.

Different versions of my rendezvous with Walker later in the day raced through my mind. I wasn't able to read or concentrate. In his letters he so often hinted about his desire for me, and I openly wrote about mine—I was sure that our first passionate love-making would happen tonight. As I tried to imagine it I became more and more anxious. What if I disappointed him, such an experienced man? I didn't know what to expect. Short of little kisses on my cheeks and forehead, much the way an uncle kisses his favorite niece, he had barely touched me.

Alec was a shy, conventional lover, and my father's view on the subject was that sexual pleasure was seldom found in marriage. My mother preferred not to think about sex.

It was nearly dark when Walker called. He said he was glad to be back and could I bring supper and cook it for him, he didn't feel like going out. His voice sounded strong, and he seemed to be in a good mood. The long train ride had not exhausted him. "I have a pre-birthday present for you, from the best shop in Sarasota. Can't wait to see you wear it."

In a great hurry I put on my new black skirt and a black cashmere sweater—no buttons, no zipper, easy to take off. A last glance in the mirror and I was out the door.

I shopped on the way and bought veal scallopini and endives at the fancy market near me, bread and meringues at the French patisserie and a bunch of small white roses, the only affordable white flowers I could find.

Walker glowed with his winter tan and new well-being. I held him close and waited for a kiss on the mouth, but he quickly pulled away and walked over to the ashtray. "I feel so well," he joked, "I might even give up smoking." He said his sister still smoked, in spite of her emphysema and asthma. "Poor thing, Tal has to do everything for her, she's almost an invalid." When I turned to face him, he was already puffing on a cigarette.

I felt let down as I prepared our dinner. I had expected a warmer response to my embrace. This, after all, was our reunion, but he seemed more interested in himself. In his letters he mentioned excitement whenever he thought of me; ways to make our marriage a success and to please me. Did he really know how to please a woman?

Walker lit the candles well before dinner and opened a bottle of Château Margaux, which he took out of his sock drawer. "I have to hide it," he said, *"entre nous,"* and he drew the cork under his nose, mimicking the gestures of connoisseurs. He waited half an hour to taste it, and then poured the wine into the two Baccarat goblets I had given him for Christmas. "Here's to you, to us, to your wonderful letters." He lightly touched my glass and gazed deeply into my eyes until the clear bell-like sound faded away.

What a magician he was: the wine, the soft candle-light and his animated talk about Nabokov's *Dozen*, the book that had kept him from utter boredom in Anna Maria, were enough to transform my low mood into high spirits. All through dinner we laughed, spoke French and played with words. Before dessert, he disappeared with-

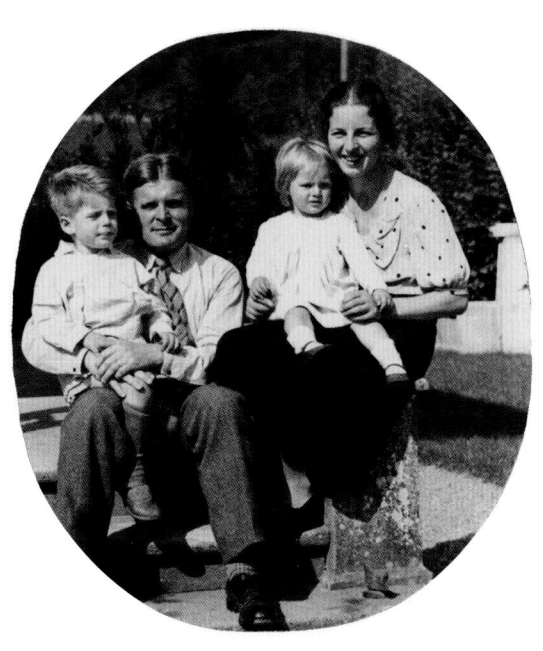
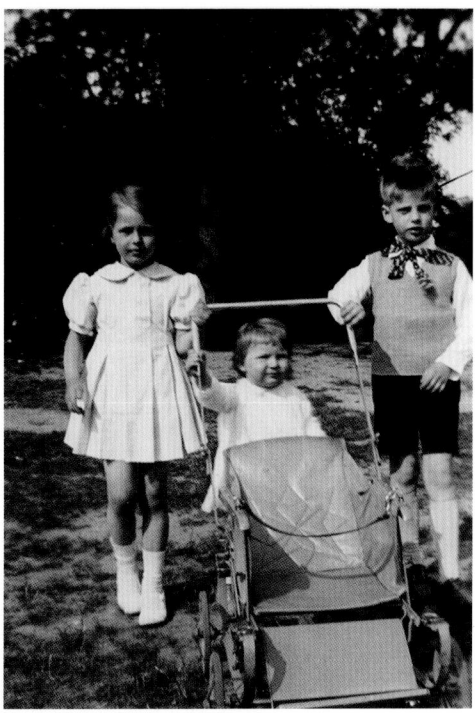
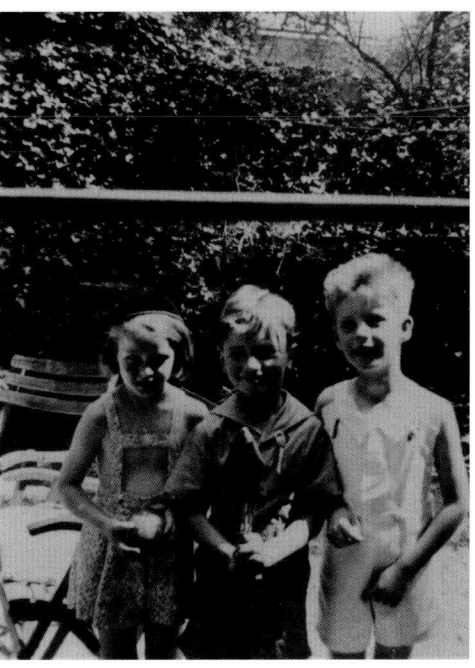
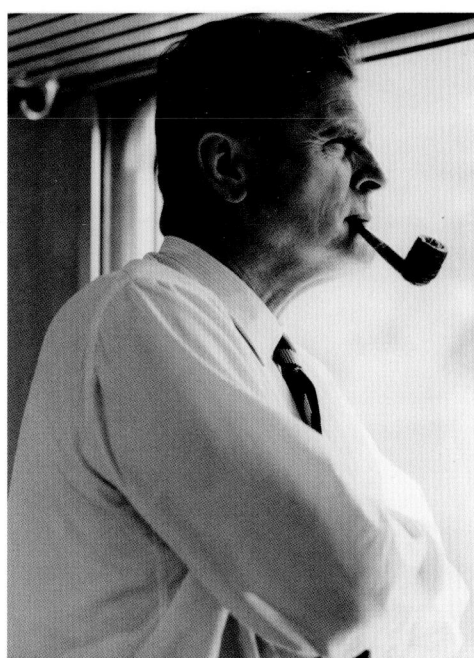

Our young family in 1934, a year before my father moved us to Berlin, where he was a correspondent for a Swiss newspaper.
In Paris with my siblings Bernard and Christine (born in Berlin), on an outing in the Bois de Boulogne, 1938. Photograph by Herman Landshoff
Stevie Joyce (grandson of James Joyce, center), Bernard, and me in our garden in Paris, 1938.
My father on a Swiss train, 1960s. Press photo

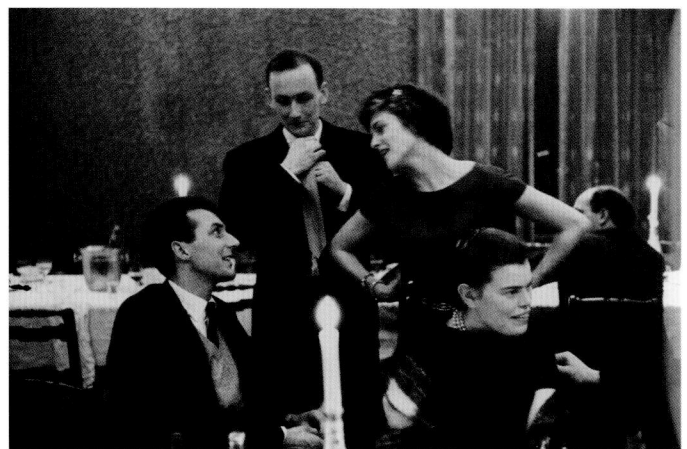

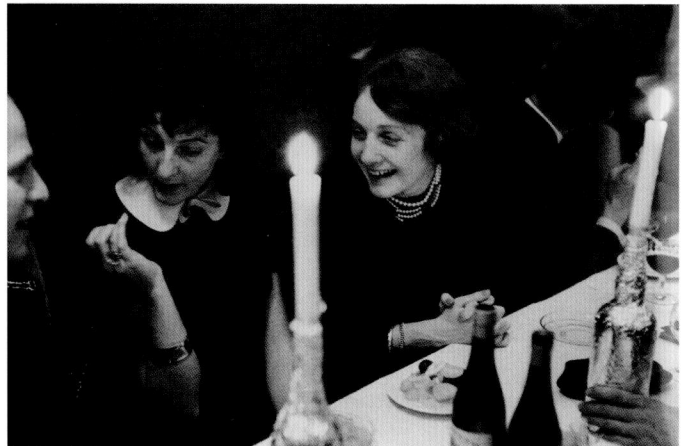

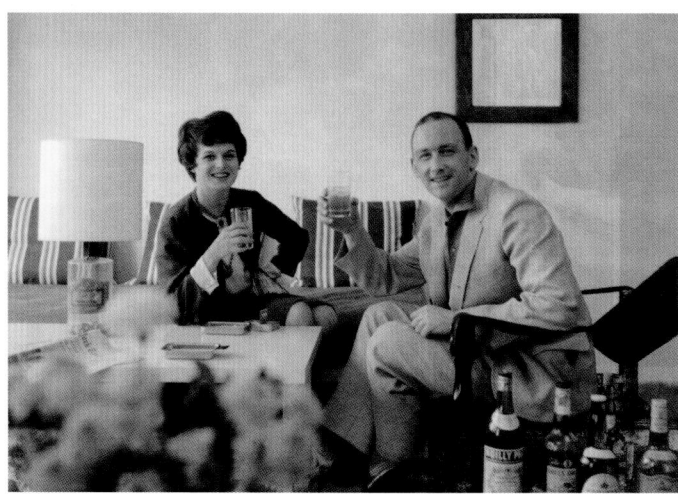

Alec and me with our close friends Verena and Bruno Bischofberger, at our farewell party in Zurich, 1958.
Photograph by René Burri, Magnum photographer, Paris

My best art school friends, Luciana Romang and Marie-Louise Eichhorn.
Photograph by René Burri, Magnum photographer, Paris

With Alec, entertaining in our New York apartment, 1959.

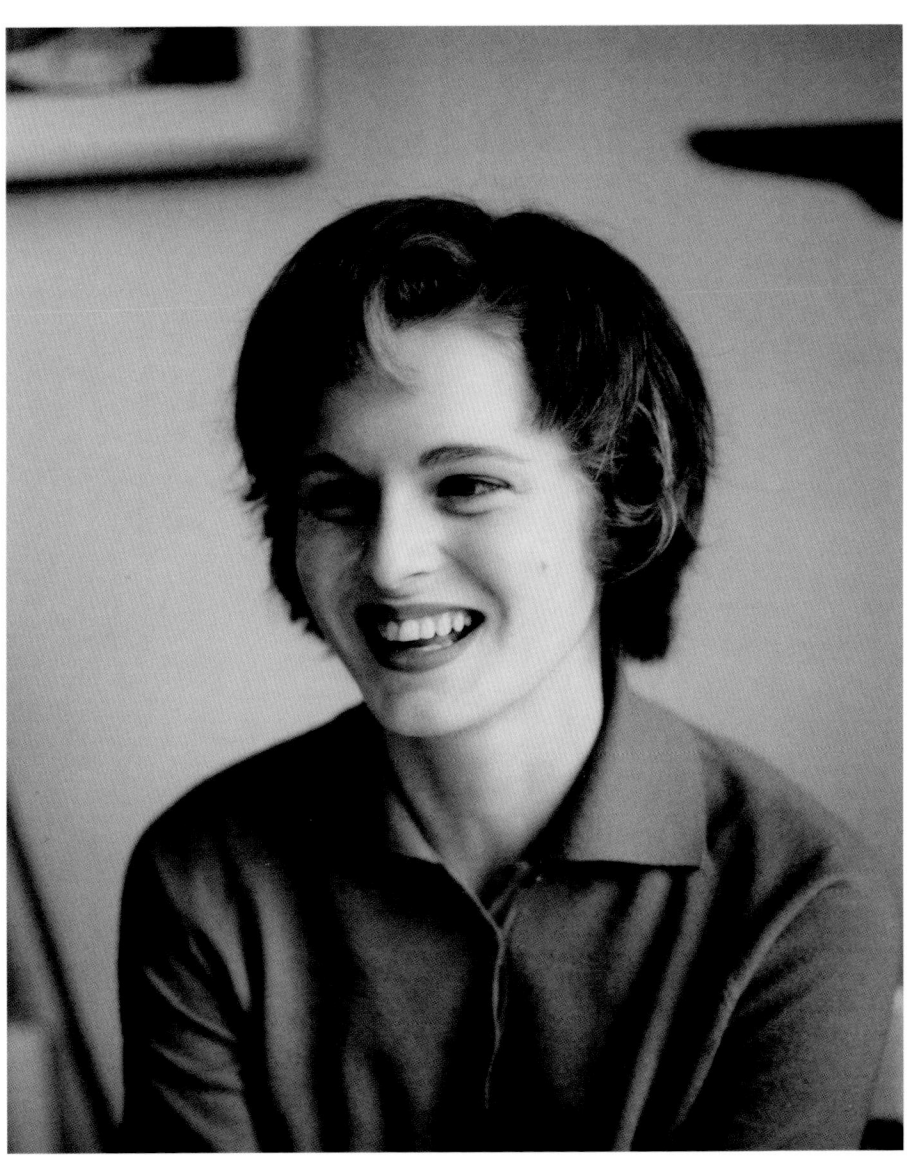

This is the way I looked when Walker and I first met. The picture was taken a couple of weeks after I arrived in New York.
Photograph by Herman Landshoff

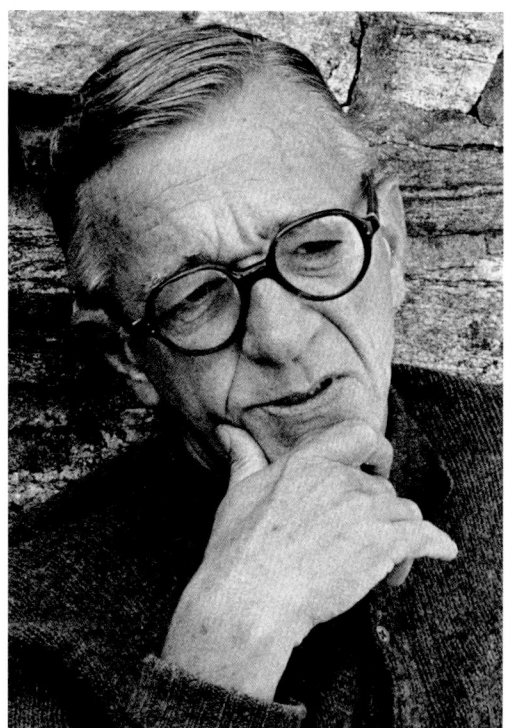
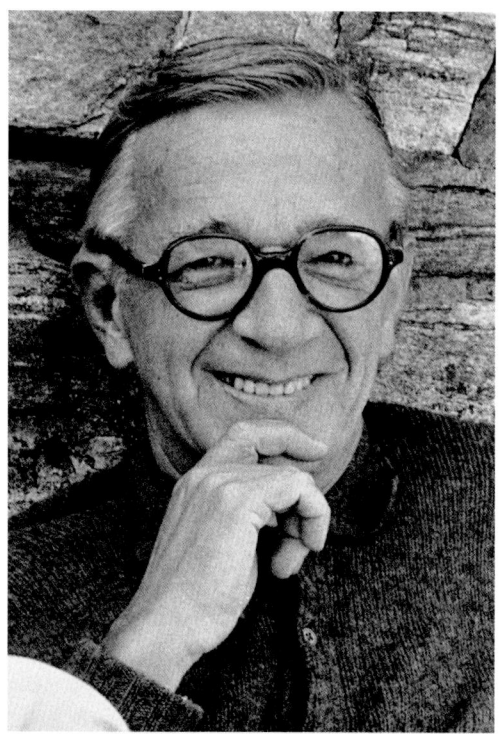

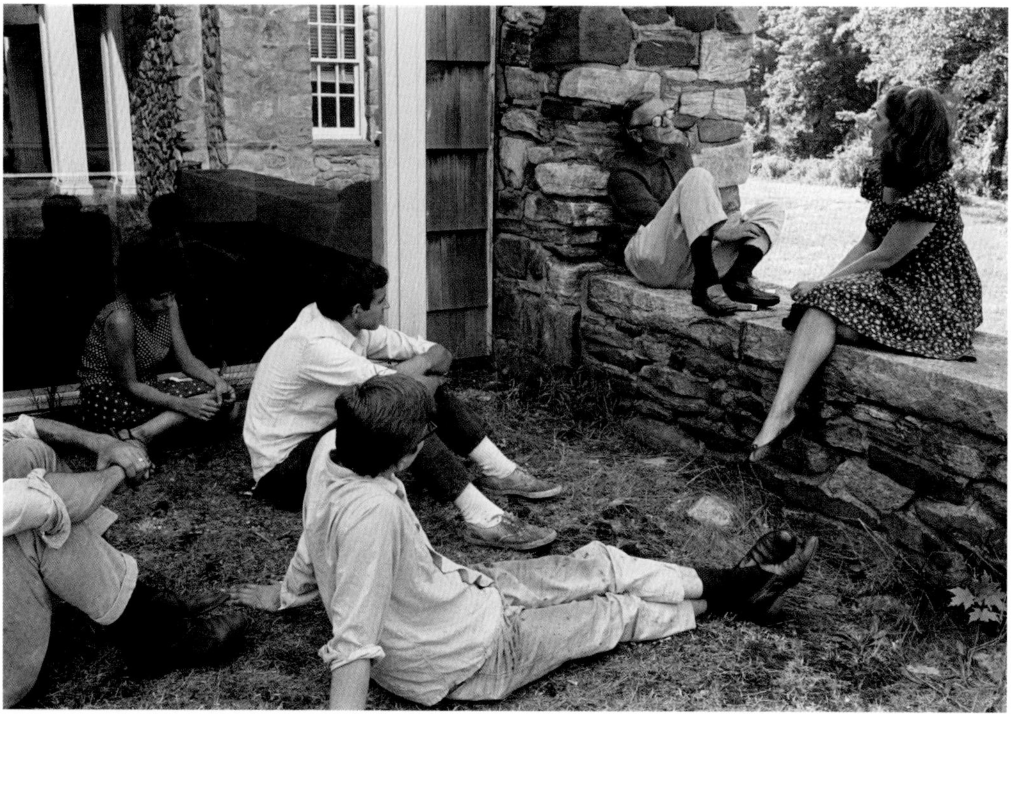

Walker talking to students at the Yale summer school in Norfolk, Connecticut, 1964. Photographs by John T. Hill

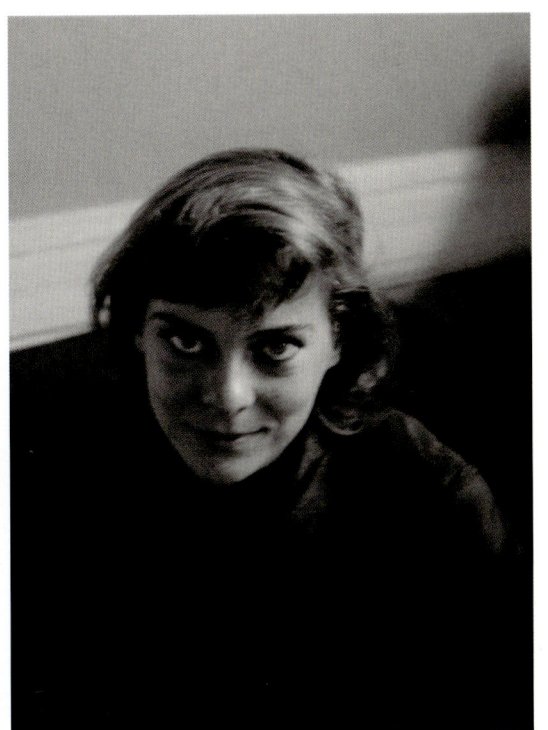
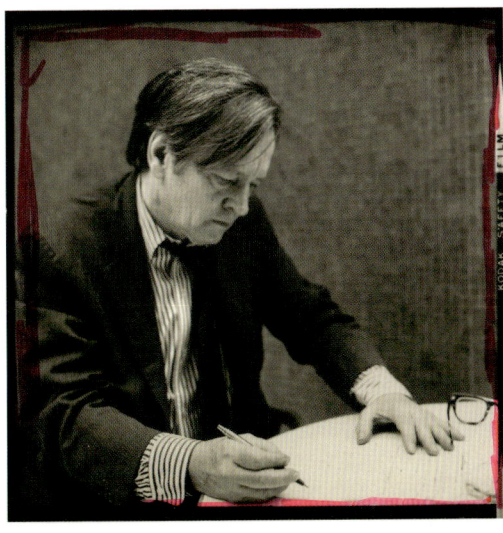

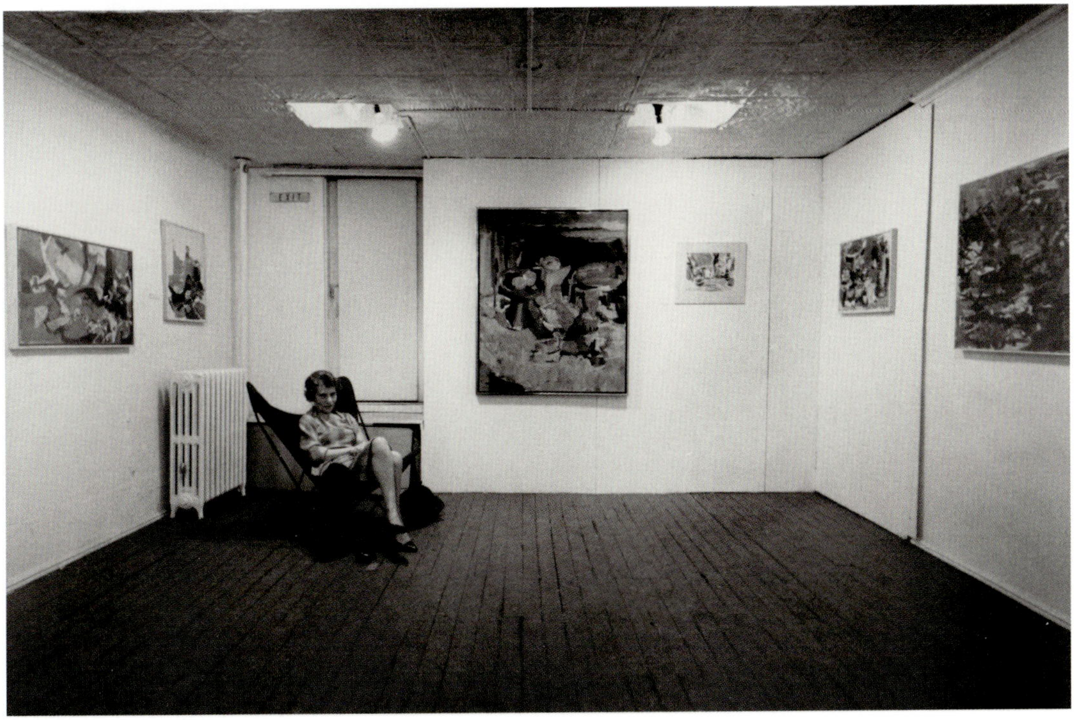

Caroline Blackwood. Photograph by Walker Evans, ca. 1963
John McDonald (Writer for *Fortune* magazine and one of Walker's oldest and best friends). Photograph by Walker Evans, 1961
Dorothy Eisner (John McDonald's wife) sitting down in the gallery of her solo show. Photograph by Walker Evans, 1961

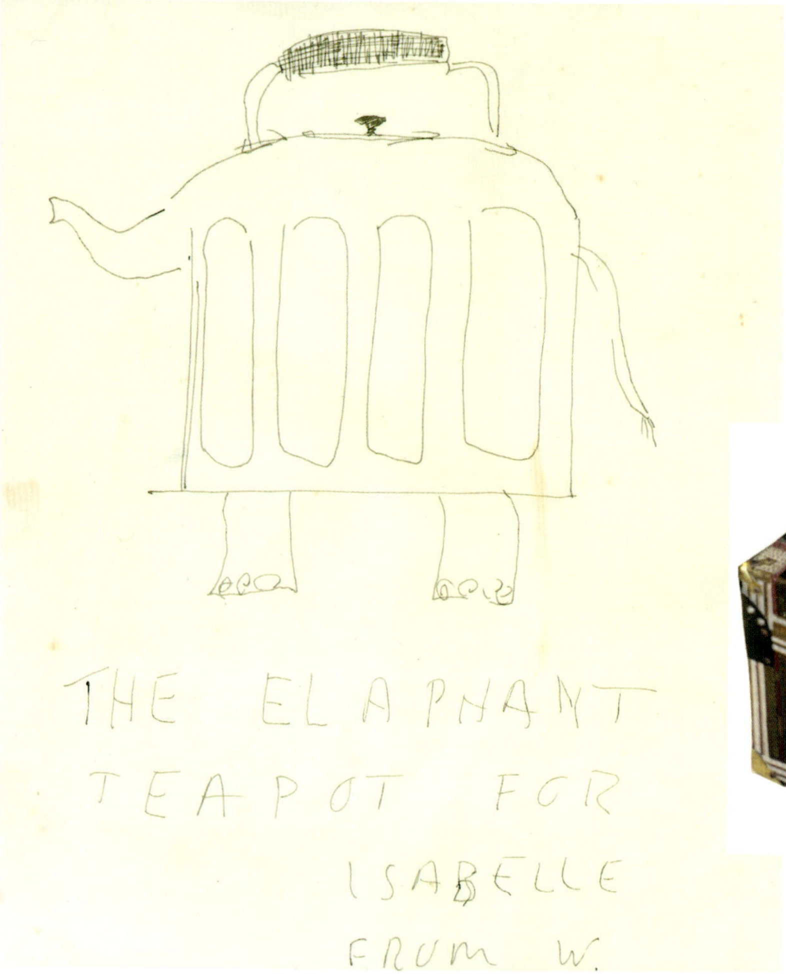

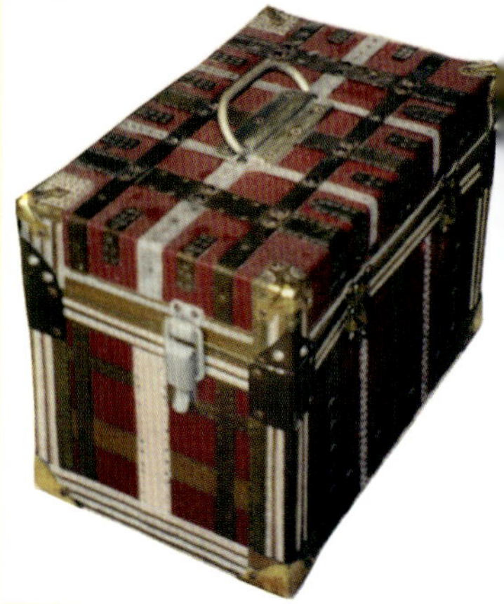

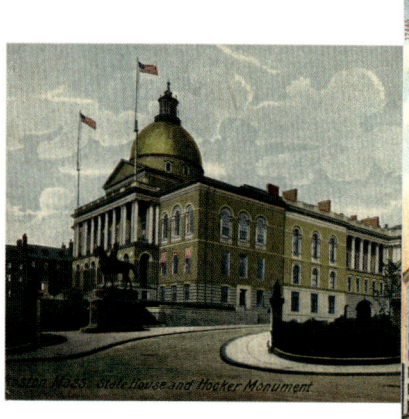
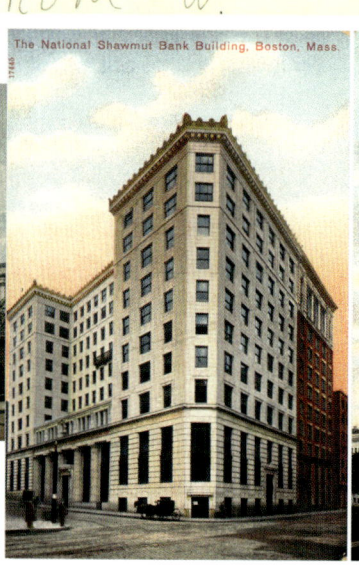
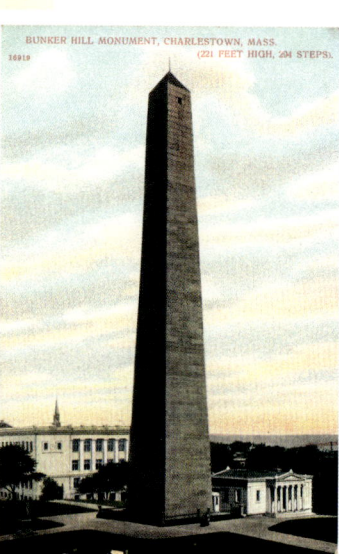

We both loved teapots, especially this one. Drawing by Walker Evans

The mysterious box. Walker kept his pornography in it. After Walker's death it went to our friend the photographer Lee Friedlander, who gave it to me several years later.

The type of postcards Walker collected. (Massachusetts State House and Hooker Monument, Boston; The National Shawmut Bank Building, Boston; Bunker Hill Monument, Charlestown, Massachusetts)

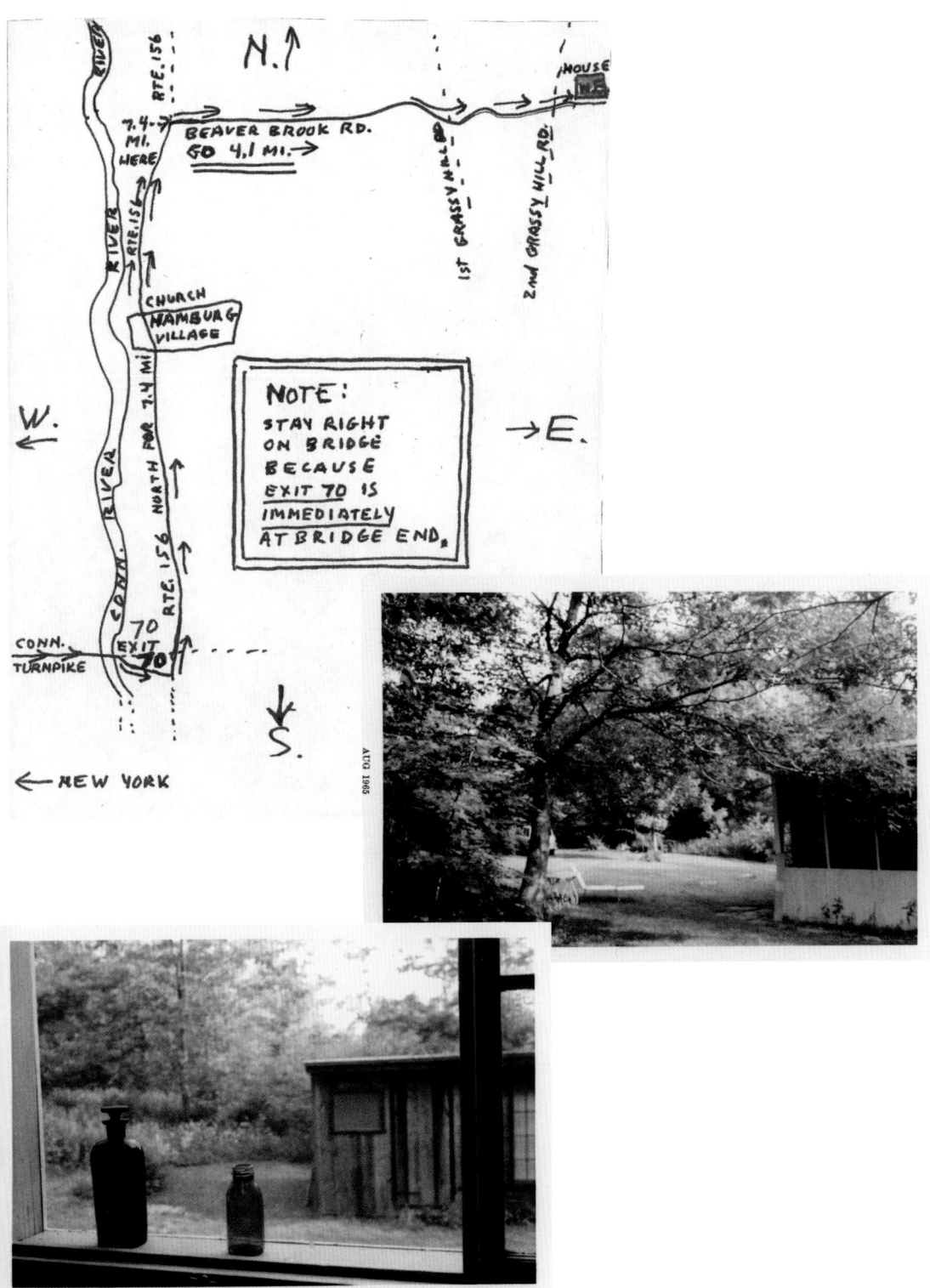

Walker's directions to his cabin in Lyme, Connecticut. Map drawn by Walker Evans
The screened-in porch where we ate our meals.
Walker's cabin in Lyme.

THE CENTURY ASSOCIATION
7 WEST FORTY-THIRD STREET
NEW YORK 36, N.Y.

Nov. 29 1959

Dearest Isabelle

This is your declaration from me, of love, of devotion, respect, admiration and burning excitement. I write because I want to mark the time, I want you to have something from me as a sign. This is your engagement ring, from Cartier. I plight our troth.

Walker

My first letter from Walker. Walker Evans

out explanation into the back room. He was moving things around, rustling papers. When he returned he carried a dusty album of seventy-eight records under one arm. Moments later I heard Fats Waller singing "Ain't She Sweet." He asked me to dance. With the slightest touch he led me into jazz steps and encouraged me to improvise to the music. He had perfect rhythm. When I moved out of his orbit he pulled me back and changed directions. He was so light on his elegant feet. It wasn't until the record stopped that I looked down and noticed the patent leather opera pumps from London gleaming beneath his old corduroys.

He was out of breath—still dancing with his arms and hands when he walked to the bedroom, lay down and kicked off his pumps.

I followed closely behind and discovered a mound of rainbow-colored tissue paper on his bureau. The reflection in the mirror made it look twice as big. This had to be my present, I was sure—only in Florida would a shop use this kind of paper in the middle of winter.

"Ah, I almost forgot—this is for you", he said, waving his hand in the direction of the package. "Go ahead, open it."

From where I stood, in front of the large chest, I could see no more than his head and open neck in the oval mirror. We smiled at each other through a cloud of cigarette smoke as I unwrapped the many layers of tissue. At last I held the white, frilly shirt against my body, spread out the sleeves with the ruffled cuffs and clowned in front of the mirror, pretending to be a toreador. I had never owned such a shirt, made in Mexico, all ruffles and lace.

"Put it on," he said. "I see you like it."

For a moment I hesitated. Should I go back to the kitchen and surprise him wearing the shirt all perfectly buttoned? No, I thought, be brave. Quickly I took off my sweater and watched his expression in the mirror. He looked surprised and delighted.

"Charming—why don't you unhook your brassière."

"My breasts are small…"

"Good. Large-breasted women make me think of cows." He laughed, then his voice changed to a near whisper. "You know what I like—Lolita."

I could never pretend to be his Lolita, not now. Was he repelled by grown women with soft round bodies, I wondered? There was no love in what he had just said about large-breasted women. Maybe he didn't really love me, but only his idea of me as the child woman, the pupil, the caregiver.

Bare-breasted, I stared in the mirror, as if I could find clues to Walker's mysterious behavior in the looking-glass.

He too had his eyes fixed on the mirror, but what he saw was in his mind. He wasn't even looking at me any longer. The change in him offended me. His mouth was coarser, and there was a trace of lewdness in his face. I was reminded of men watching strippers in cheap Paris joints where I had gone as a student years ago.

Without turning around I knew what he was doing. The mattress was moving up and down and making squeaky noises. My first thought was to leave the room, leave all together. Unable to act, I froze, still facing the mirror. I did not want to make him angry, or worse, give him the impression of being a prude and hopelessly bourgeois. It was crucial to make the right move, to show him that I loved him with all his eccentricities and faults.

I tiptoed to the edge of the bed, bent over him and covered his mouth with kisses, waiting for him to move his hands away from his crotch and touch my breasts.

Harshly he pushed me away. "You can't spend the night here. Get dressed and go home in a taxi." He sounded annoyed. I had interrupted him in his pleasures.

The pretty shirt left behind on the bureau, I threw on my clothes, grabbed my purse and ran down the flights of stairs.

It was after ten. There were few taxis cruising around East End Avenue. Too numb to feel anything, I got home like a sleepwalker. The apartment was dark when I opened the door. I went straight to the bedroom, turned on both lamps, and sat down on the bed.

If Alec had walked in and hugged me I would have been able to cry. He'd take me back without asking questions. There was still time to call the whole thing off. Walker didn't need a woman. This idea of marriage was mostly in his head. I guessed that wherever he went, women would line up for him. He could always win the one he desired. Why should he give this up?

As I undressed I felt unloved and unwanted. It was too late to call a friend, and I was in no mood for advice right now. A bath would help me feel clean and warm; then hot tea with a spoonful of rum.

Sleep was all I craved, hours and hours of it. Tomorrow was Sunday, and I had the whole day to myself.

The phone tore me out of dreamless sleep. Walker was on the line. His voice was warm and loving. He said he felt terrible; would I forgive him. He had been overcome with desire—the mirror, my pretty breasts—but he had previously thought about it and decided not to make love to me until we were married. Maybe I thought him old-fashioned. He loved me more and more, and he begged me to forget what happened.

Half asleep, I let him talk. Why didn't he tell me in his letters? This was no time to talk. I promised to have tea with him tomorrow and go to a French movie.

Walker's Way My Years with Walker Evans

Chapter 7

In March, at Walker's suggestion, I moved into the Barbizon Hotel for Women. He thought it was the proper place for me at this time, mostly because my mother had announced her plans to visit and would arrive towards the end of the month, and also because Alec was packing up the apartment.

Walker's concern with propriety on my behalf was a mystery to me. In his letters he made fun of his conventional sister. I wanted to believe that he had cast aside these leftover shreds of Victorian rules and customs that I knew so well and abhorred. When I questioned him on the subject, he said I couldn't possibly know the subtle practices of the American upper classes, and he was soon going to introduce me to his social friends. "All top drawer," he said with a touch of irony, "you can be sure of that. And I want them to recognize that you are a lady."

I took a while to get used to the Barbizon and my solitary nights in the narrow bed. It was disturbing—like living in a giant dovecote with all these identical pale green cubicles inhabited by single women. Most of them emerged between eight and nine in the morning: the elevators were packed. They smiled at each other and said good morning in cheerful voices. Pretty and svelte with shiny hair, they were perfectly made up. Many wore pearls and fitted suits and walked briskly out the door to their offices in high heels. But I never knew anybody's name.

On my days off, after a late breakfast in the coffee shop, I occasionally might notice a middle-aged couple sitting in the lobby with their daughter, patiently waiting. I imagined it was her first job after college. They had driven into the city from their hometown, bringing large suitcases and shopping bags filled with a favorite stuffed animal, a clock radio, a tennis racket. When the room key was finally handed over to the future inhabitant, mother and daughter went up with all the hand luggage, and the old, tired porter would follow with the heavy baggage in the back elevator. The father was left alone reading his newspaper.

I kept overhearing conversations about girls who had nervous breakdowns, anorexia, and illegal abortions in New Jersey. But inside the Barbizon, the rules had to be observed: no men beyond the lobby, no cooking in the rooms, and prompt weekly payments; it was all very clear.

Now that I was alone and Alec and I had signed the separation agreement, Walker included me in his daily life. Most evenings we had dinner together, except on club nights, when I watched him dress for the Century, a ritual I enjoyed because it put him in such a good mood.

Slowly we settled into a domestic routine: I went directly to his apartment after work, and he always gave me taxi money to go back to the Barbizon. It was as though we were already married, and we both felt a beneficial calm returning to our lives. Walker was the one who first mentioned how stressful the past six months had been and how relieved he was for us both to have gotten through the first phase of my impending divorce.

He cleared a few shelves for my books and stationery and urged me to bring a pair of old slacks and a sweater for our suppers at home. Often when I arrived late, delayed by the ride on the slow crosstown bus, he had already shopped and filled the icebox with his favorite foods and a variety of lettuces for me. His ulcer kept him from eating raw vegetables and most fresh fruits. Double lamb chops and thick porterhouse steaks or well-pounded veal cutlets were the important part of our meals, and potatoes were a close second. From an old Fannie Farmer cookbook left over from Walker's first marriage, I learned to make a decent rice pudding and various custards flavored with cinnamon, lemon juice, or vanilla and topped with whipped cream. We usually shared a half bottle of claret. After dinner he lit a cigarette and lay down; eating tired him out. Later we read our books, wrote letters, and talked a little, until the phone rang. At times I felt quite upset when he talked for hours to old girlfriends, but I pretended not to mind at all. It was different when it was a friend I had met, like John McDonald. After he and Walker were through exchanging inside information about *Fortune* business, Walker usually handed me the phone. John and I began then to communicate regularly on the telephone, and kept up our habit until his death a few years ago.

Chapter 7

One rainy Saturday I was still in bed when Walker called around ten, all enthusiasm about a new little French restaurant he had discovered in his neighborhood. Would I meet him at noon and he'd take me there for lunch? "Come as you are," he said, "and don't expect chandeliers and gold mirrors."

As I approached Walker's front door, he was standing outside, his Burberry trench coat buttoned up. A plaid scarf loosely wrapped around his neck and a well-worn Irish tweed hat gave him the air of a country gentlemen. This was my favorite look. All that was needed to complete the perfect picture of Lord Walker Evans of Lyme in *Country Life* were a couple of terriers. I kissed him, and the familiar smell of cigarettes and his lemony English cologne made me shiver a little—yes, I had reasons to be happy.

He had just stopped at the newsstand to buy *The New York Times*. We walked arm in arm against the strong March wind to Eighty-sixth Street and crossed over to the south side, hurrying along to keep warm until we reached a narrow storefront between First and Second Avenues. I would have passed right by Un Coin de Paris, its entrance was so plain and unobtrusive. Walker couldn't remember what had been there before; maybe a dry cleaner or a locksmith.

Madame Blois greeted us with outstretched arms and exclaimed, "*Voilà la petite, enfin!*" She winked at Walker and lowered her voice to congratulate him. "*Mes compliments, cher monsieur.*" Quickly she showed us to our table and sat us down. She was middle-aged, short and stocky, but she moved around at great speed. Her cheeks were flushed from going back and forth to what must have been a small, hot kitchen.

The room was barely long enough for eight tables, four against each wall. The clean linoleum floor, white oilcloth on the tables, and chrome dispensers for paper napkins made me think of my school cafeteria in Switzerland.

Madame Blois brought us two cloth napkins. Since it was early and we were the only guests in the restaurant nobody could be envious of the special attention we received, nor would Madame Blois have cared. She wanted to please us.

"Don't look at the menu," said Walker, "it's always the same." He added that if I asked nicely, Monsieur Blois could make anything I wanted—delicious omelets, creamed mushrooms on toast…. The watercress soup was especially good, and the salads were either endive or Bibb lettuce, not that awful iceberg stuff and tasteless tomatoes that Schrafft's served up.

My *omelette fines herbes* was creamy and light, and the salad dressing tasted piquant but not vinegary. I hadn't expected such perfectly cooked, simple French food in a nondescript place like this. Leave it to Walker, I thought, he has the nose to find the real McCoy, another expression I had learned from him.

Over a *café filtre* and tea (Walker pulled his own Earl Grey teabags out of his pocket), we chatted with Monsieur Blois. Pale-skinned with straight, dark hair and thick lenses in his heavy eyeglasses, he looked more like a professor than a chef. I asked if he came from Paris. He smiled and said it had always been his dream to leave his village in Brittany and open a small restaurant in Paris. "But now I'm 'ere, *pas si mal*, New York." He made a grand gesture with both hands. "*Et voici* Un Coin de Paris."

We both applauded and praised the food. Walker whispered to me: "You made a great hit, *succès fou*."

Preparations for my mother's visit put an end to my contented state of mind. She sounded so gloomy in her letters, unconsolable about my having left Alec, and she made it quite clear that she wanted to spend an evening with him alone, take him to a nice restaurant. She also, of course, planned to meet Walker. This, she suggested, would best be done over tea.

Once again I felt like the bad daughter and I turned to Walker for advice on how to make my mother's stay more pleasurable for all of us. Even though he had a lifelong prejudice against mothers, he wasted no time in assuring me that everything was going to be all right. With the help of his friend (and now my lawyer) Grenny Emmet, whose law firm subscribed to a box at the Metropolitan Opera, Walker got tickets for *Madame Butterfly*. He wouldn't hear of a small hotel in my neighborhood for my mother and enlisted Eileen Maynard to put her up at the Cosmopolitan Club.

I got the week off from Saks. My boss, who called me "honey," insisted that I spend time with my "mom." The store wasn't busy "anyhow," most of Saks' better customers had gone south.

The night before my mother's arrival I felt hot and clammy and had very little sleep. These two years away from home seemed much longer. My whole life had changed and my family had nothing to do with it. Would she be able to understand my love for Walker and appreciate his intelligence and wit? She'll ask questions, I worried, but how could I begin to explain? Often explanations sounded like excuses, which in my case I felt were unnecessary. Also I desperately wanted her to like New York. This was her first trip to America. I tried to imagine her in my new city. Since her time in London in 1953, when my father wrote for an illustrated Swiss magazine, she dressed even more like a British lady. Her suits were made by my father's tailor in shades of gray and beige; she disliked strong colors, finding them vulgar. Pearls and feminine blouses in pastel batistes or cream silks softened her classic, conservative look. She seldom left the house without a hat. I wondered what color rinse she would have on her hair. It used to change from month to month long before I left home, and Christmas pictures were hardly reliable.

"You're very thin," my mother said when we embraced in the international terminal at Idlewild. She held my chin between her forefinger and thumb, turned my head until I faced her, an old habit of hers from my rebellious teenage years, when she tried to make me tell the truth. "Look at me." Then she lightly brushed my mouth with the back of her hand. "Too much lipstick, it makes you look even paler."

She was the same; nothing had changed. Now it was up to me to be grown up and not get mad. Luckily I had Walker on my side. He would know how to make her smile.

Maman felt very much at home in the Cosmopolitan Club. She said it was just like London. The help was polite and the tea on the pretty breakfast tray tasted strong, the way she liked it. On her vacations with Papa in Swiss hotels and on cruise ships he always made her come down for breakfast. He couldn't stand having his favorite meal in a room with unmade beds and underwear on chairs.

On the first morning of her visit I walked over to the club, introduced myself at the desk and inspected the comfortable, airy sitting room overlooking the trellised garden. Later, I thought, we might have tea there. I smiled at the elevator man who brought me up to Maman's room and pointed to her door.

She looked rested and much happier. Her brownish hair was not yet done up in her current style, a French twist, but she was dressed, and her pink cheeks were powdered. I even noticed a faint smile. "Here," she said and handed me a bag from the tax-free shop. "I brought you some perfume and chocolate truffles, of course." She turned to me and shook her head. "What a stubborn child you are, just like Papa. Come, give me a kiss and let's try to have a nice time together."

I gladly accepted her peace offering. Anyone observing us walking down Fifth Avenue to Saks would have bet we were best friends. We spoke "gibberish" (Walker's name for Swiss German), French and English, switching back and forth at random, the same way we communicated as a family around the dinner table.

At Saks, upstairs in my department, Maman received many compliments. "Now we know," said Mrs. Grossman, my boss, "where the little one gets her good looks."

I took Maman through the store. She had never seen such a selection of luxurious lingerie before, and when I pointed out that most of it needed no ironing because it was made of synthetics, she was truly surprised. "But it feels like pure silk," she said and looked at me in disbelief. I held up some flowered satin peignoirs, and she let the shiny, slippery fabric run through her hands. "So this is where Tante Marguerite—wasn't it last year?" she recalled, "spent one hundred dollars for a nightgown. Even I could be tempted here." Maman had thought it wildly extravagant when her close friend Marguerite had proudly shown it to her in Bern.

It was a sunny, clear March day and we ended up in the bar of the Rainbow Room just before sundown. Maman was in heaven. Her enthusiasm was so catching as she walked around with her Virgin Mary that people stood up from their seats to give her a better view of the city in the pink twilight. Mesmerized, she looked down on the moving streamers of lights flaring out in all directions from each window. She even spoke to strangers, tourists, who, like herself, felt overwhelmed by the lighted towers, the bridges, and the vastness of it all. For a moment of intense pleasure she lost her inhibitions and acted like a young girl.

"Maman, Maman," I wanted to say to her, "do you see why I love it here, why I want to stay? This is the world, the whole world—I don't have to go anywhere else."

Walker called me every night to find out how things were going. First I told him about our moments of triumph: Maman's ecstatic delight over panoramic views, the Circle Line boat ride around Manhattan, the Frick Collection and dinner at the Russian Tea Room.

She had a passion for Russian aristocrats, as they appeared in *Anna Karenina*, Russian music, and blinis.

"And the Met?" Walker asked. "Was she impressed?"

Well, I said, I couldn't really tell. She had been to many of the grand European opera houses. Yes, she thought the women were beautifully dressed, but their diamonds seemed too showy to be real. "It was hard going—she cried through most of *Butterfly*."

"Can't blame her. It's a tear-jerker all right."

I wasn't sure, I said, if her tears were for my future with him or for Alec, whom she saw last night, or for herself. She wouldn't discuss it.

"Courage, my child, it'll soon be over." Walker's deep voice was comforting, but I longed for our quiet evenings in his apartment.

"She's ready to meet you," I said. "What about tomorrow? Tea in the Palm Court? We haven't been there yet."

"I hate the place. It's full of out-of-towners. Let me think. I'll call you tomorrow morning. Good night, my darling."

Maman insisted on seeing some of Walker's photographs before meeting him. Reluctantly I suggested lunch at the Museum of Modern Art, one of my favorite places in New York. I knew in advance that she would make philistine remarks about the art and upset me. The Museum was my club, where I could go anytime and watch a film or eat my lunch in the garden opposite Aristide Maillol's voluptuous bather by the reflecting pool.

There were no photographs of Walker's on view in the basement gallery, and *American Photographs* was out of print. Walker kept a few first editions hidden in a closet but he seldom gave one away.

Two hours before tea I called Walker in his *Fortune* office and asked him how to find his pictures to show Maman. As usual he solved the problem with great aplomb. My mother and I were to wait by the Museum entrance, where an assistant from the photography department would come down and meet us.

This was my first glimpse behind the closed doors of these astonishing galleries. Inside the department I lowered my voice to a near whisper. No explanations were necessary: we were expected. Monroe Wheeler, the director of exhibitions and publications, greeted us in a slightly formal manner, arranged two seats at a long table and brought out *American Photographs* and *Let Us Now Praise Famous Men*, both first editions, since neither book was in print at the time.

Maman looked at Walker's photographs with great interest, as though the pictures would give her clues about him. She asked me why he had chosen to photograph these dilapidated buildings, torn posters, and the poor. Had he, as a young man, wanted to help these poor country people? The title, she said, was from the holy Scripture—she knew the words.

I was boiling inside. How could she be so ignorant and think of Walker as a "do-gooder" who tried to save the world like some photojournalists? "And please, Maman, don't mention religion to him. He doesn't believe in God."

We walked in silence to the New Weston on Madison in the Fifties, Walker's choice, an older hotel I had not noticed before.

The room where afternoon tea was served seemed joyless and dark. A few candles in silver sticks and dimly lit sconces made little difference; the dull brown oak paneling swallowed all the light.

Standing in the doorway with Maman, I tried to find Walker among the seated guests. There was no sign of him until, way in a corner, across the room I saw a hand waving in the air. As we approached his table, he got up and welcomed Maman in his most charming way, took her arm, and pulled back a chair for her. He called her *"chère madame"* and mumbled a few French words like *"enchanté"* and *"connaissance."* All I got in the way of greeting was an amicable tap on my back, a wink and a nod.

Maman responded with a smile, and he was quick to compliment her. She thanked him for all his kindness, the comfortable club, the opera and the splendid reception at the Museum of Modern Art. "I saw your books," she said in a serious voice, "and I learned something."

"Très bien," he said, smiling to himself. "Tell me, what did you see?"

She mentioned the rural poverty, how she had not expected such poverty among American white people. In big cities, of course, like London and Paris, she was aware of the slums, and surely in New York, but these unfortunate families in the south, with children who were not cared for, no, she was astonished and shocked. "We think of America as such a rich country."

I wondered how he was going to answer Maman. She couldn't possibly know when he was ironic and when he really meant what he said.

He took his time and waited until the waitress passed the tea sandwiches and poured more tea. I noticed that he refrained from smoking. He cleared his throat and explained that the pictures in the book were taken over twenty years ago, "during what we call the Depression." Then he asked Maman if there was no poverty in remote Swiss mountain villages?

Yes, she thought in some Catholic regions of Switzerland, where people had more children, it happened that during a cold winter a few families did not have enough warm clothes. "But nobody goes hungry in Switzerland," she said in a most definite tone of voice.

Tea was nearly over. Walker never mentioned our plans for the future, and Maman chose not to bring up the subject. She was fading; her face seemed less animated. Already once before she had warned me that it tired her out to speak English for any length of time, because she felt out of practice. She meant with educated people, of course, not with shop girls or waiters.

Walker dropped us off at the club. "Great pleasure, great pleasure," he said as he got out of the cab and held the door. "And don't forget, we have an important date on the twenty-sixth. Meet me at the Century around ten of four." He waved and said he would telephone.

I could hardly wait to hear Maman's reaction to Walker. Her coat still draped around her shoulders, she was turning on the lights in the room. "Don't you think he's handsome? I love his gray hair." I was raving like a teenager.

"He seems very fragile—and he looks a lot older than Papa." She opened some drawers and put her gloves away. "I made a reservation for dinner downstairs. We'll go to bed early."

"He's brilliant—that's all I can tell you."

Still walking around, in her stocking feet now, she said in a flat voice, so unlike her: "Brilliant—maybe, but he can't be trusted. This is a man who has seen everything. There's nothing innocent about him."

I felt my cheeks turn red. How could she dismiss him like that? A great artist, a man of superior intelligence.

March 26 was Maman's second-to-last day in New York. We shopped all morning for presents, went to Dunhill's for Papa, and to Saks, where we got ultrasheer nylons to please Tante Hélène, Maman's sister. At Scribner's we bought modern poetry books for my brother

Bernard. Anne-Marie, my younger sister, whose fifteenth birthday was in March, had asked for something uniquely American. On our way home up Lexington Avenue my eye caught some pink and yellow bathing caps covered with plastic flowers in a crowded shop window. It was just the thing to amuse her and all my art school friends, and Maman assured me that such drugstore items were not yet available in Europe.

The present for my sister Christine took the longest time to find. Her taste was so subtle, and I thought she would be enchanted by Walker's collections of found Americana. After lunch, when Maman went back to the club for a rest, I walked to Third Avenue and poked around in the less pricey antique shops he had taken me to. If only Christine could meet him. I knew they would like the same things. The more I searched for a small, unadorned silver box or a pair of old paste shoe buckles, the more I missed her. In the end I found a single lusterware candlestick. Some of the silver had washed off and it was far from perfect, but I looked at it through Walker's eyes.

In two days Maman would be back in Bern. She would give everyone her impression of Walker, and I would not be there to defend him. It seemed so unfair. I didn't even have a picture to send Christine, so she could see for herself what an attractive man he was.

Already late, I rushed back to the Barbizon to dress for the Century's "Literary Afternoon." Tea with members and their guests was going to be served afterwards upstairs, in rooms I had not seen. On the phone that morning, Walker suggested I wear my black suit and not too much makeup. He liked me in black; it reminded him of the girls in Paris. It made me nervous when he told me what to wear. Why couldn't he trust my judgment? I felt as though I were being presented at the Court of St. James. If his Century friends were mostly writers, artists, and editors as he proudly remarked and not the Social Register types, then what was all this fuss about?

When I met Maman downstairs at the Cosmopolitan, she was flustered, opened her coat to show me her new dress and said this was the best she could do. She looked lovely in navy with a ruby pin and her pearls.

We took a taxi to Forty-third and Fifth and walked the few steps to the front door of the Century. Daniel, the doorman, greeted us in his soft, gentle voice. Our coats were checked, and minutes later

Walker appeared and escorted us up the grand staircase, past the gallery to the second floor. It was packed with a crowd of at least two hundred, and more people were coming in. I tried to look at the paintings, but Walker hurried us along to the seats he had saved earlier. He introduced us to Eileen Maynard and Eliza Parkinson, his other guests. They greeted Maman with sympathetic smiles, and me like one of their own children. I supposed they couldn't help it; I was their children's age.

Louis Auchincloss, Brendan Gill, Malcolm Cowley, and Lionel Trilling were the speakers for the afternoon. Walker knew and admired Lionel Trilling, but he was quick to tell me that Diana, Lionel's wife, was a busybody who tried to compete with her husband. The other speaker he knew personally was Brendan Gill. Like so many of Walker's friends at *The New Yorker*, Gill was witty and exceptionally bright. Walker read the magazine from cover to cover every week. Recently he had acquired the habit of buying an extra copy for me, as part of my education. It took years for me to get some of the jokes.

As I listened to these speakers, I became sadly aware of how little I knew about American and English arts and letters and history. My education was European and so completely one-sided that it barely included the British Isles. This afternoon it did me no good to have studied the Bauhaus, the Italian Renaissance, or seventeenth-century French architecture, gardens and decorative arts. I missed the many literary references, the witticisms and fine points of the speakers. Instead of laughing in the right places, I felt suspended in a giant vacuum with nothing to hold on to. It felt like it would take me a lifetime to catch up.

After the enthusiastic applause died down and people got up from their seats, Walker squeezed my hand and asked me what I thought. I confessed that I did not understand much of it. "Oh, don't worry," he said and lowered his voice. "You're not the only one in this room," he laughed. "This is pretty highbrow stuff. It'll come with time, you'll see. Now let's have some tea."

He led us through the crowded space to a round table in a dark room next to the bar. On the way he greeted many men who responded with jovial banter. It made me happy to see that he was so well liked. Some members waved and made congratulatory remarks and shook my hand in passing. I smiled and felt revived and began to look around at the paintings on the walls. Most of them were large landscapes in gold frames. There was a lovely light in these nineteenth-century paintings, and against the dark walls they appeared even more luminous.

Maman was enjoying herself, too. I could tell it made her feel better that Walker had such well-bred, genuinely nice friends as Eileen and Eliza. These women were familiar to her and made her feel welcome. When the time came to say goodbye they both said that they hoped Walker would bring me around often and wished me good luck.

Walker had made a reservation at Giovanni's, a restaurant he frequented when he was in a celebratory mood and had some cash in his pocket. He wanted Maman to remember her last evening in New York. Right off she was enchanted by the intimate atmosphere of the place. It surprised her that the restaurant was in a row of brownstones. Walker ordered sherry for her, and she became quite talkative, giving high praise to the Century and comparing it to the Garrick in London. Walker was flattered and he complimented her good taste.

All through dinner I paid attention to their courtly conversation, until Walker's vivacious gestures and secretive smile gave away that he was about to do something extraordinary.

After the veal entrées and the mixed green salads dressed at the table, Walker ordered three glasses of champagne with our zabaglione. Was this our engagement party? He reached into his breast pocket and pulled out an envelope of his best stationery. "This is for your husband," he said in a solemn voice, "Isabelle's father. I feel I know him; she talks about him quite often."

Maman took the envelope and looked at him kindly. "Yes, Isabelle likes her father. They both are very strong-willed, not easy to live with." She smiled and tapped my hand.

"I'd like him to have something from me." Walker said. "It's time I declare my intentions. I am a very lucky man."

Maman took his hand. She was fighting back tears, she was so moved. Words were no longer necessary; on the contrary, they would have spoiled the moment. It was all I could have hoped for: a happy end to Maman's first visit in the city of my dreams.

Chapter 8

By mid-April there was an outburst of spring in the city, and everyone went outside. At lunchtime the benches along the edges of Central Park were crowded with office workers sunning themselves. Wide steps leading up to churches and municipal buildings became busy gathering places full of bright colors. This was my third spring in New York, but I could not get used to the sudden change in temperature. The very thought of the impending heat and humidity made me feel anxious and itchy all over. The springs of my childhood had unfolded more slowly and had an almost languid quality. They began small at the end of February, with snowdrops and violets near patches of wet snow, and ended in a profusion of lilacs around Pentecost. It was a time of discovery in the garden: a tiny bird's nest with pale blue eggs hidden in the wisteria above the verandah windows, the green tips of Maman's tulip bulbs sprouting everywhere. In the dark basin of the mossy grotto, Bernard and I would count the goldfish that had survived under the ice. Sometimes we found a dead squirrel near the swings by the old chestnut tree.

Walker thrived in warm weather; like a lizard he basked in the sun. He talked about the light—how he felt the urge to go outside and take pictures. On the first hot Sunday in May he picked me up in his shiny Buick with the top down. He said he was going to teach me to load his Rolleiflex cameras, and then we'd head out to Brooklyn. He wanted to show me Columbia Heights, where he and Hart Crane had lived across the street from each other, near the Brooklyn Bridge and the waterfront. He thought a portfolio on the waterfront was the right idea for this moment—"before it's too late; all this is doomed to vanish."

I had not read any of Hart Crane's poetry until one evening, in preparation for our expedition, Walker presented me with his American first edition of *The Bridge*. "This is my most valuable book," he said in a serious voice as he handed me the slim volume. "My first published work." Walker's photograph on the frontispiece, of the dark underside of the flying Brooklyn Bridge, surprised me. It was reminiscent of the industrial art of the Bauhaus years, so familiar to me, but his was an American version, bolder and bursting with energy. I loved the photograph.

The poem brought to mind Joyce's *Ulysses*, a work I had labored over during my first stay in London, partly because of my childhood infatuation with Joyce's grandson Stevie in Paris.

"Poetry has to be read aloud," said Walker and took the book out of my hands. He read the beginning of the long poem, and his voice changed to a different tone, much lower and quieter than his regular speaking voice. It was the first time he had read poetry to me. In this intimate moment I found him to be vulnerable, realizing that his arrogance was merely an armor to protect himself. He became less and less guarded, and I felt his emotions strongly—a sense of loss, perhaps, which helped me to understand more fully the meaning of *The Bridge* and its importance in Walker's life as a young artist.

I saw the bridge again from the open car. I hoped the towers' high Gothic arches signified a promising beginning: maybe I could become Walker's assistant on some of his working trips. If I did a good job today, he might ask me again.

We crossed the bridge and Walker drove down Fulton Street to the river. He was in a hurry to take full advantage of the brilliant sunlight. Later, he said, he'd take me to see some of the landmarks and Brooklyn Heights. We were under the bridge now, its intricate framework exposed like a giant, black skeleton. The area was seedy, and we did not get out of the car. The vacant Fulton Ferry Pier, now obsolete, reminded me of its counterparts in French and Italian seaside resorts right after the war. The more prosperous times, when the ferry transported hundreds of passengers daily to and from Manhattan, were long gone.

Walker drove along the waterfront, looking for a shady, safe place where he could remove the camera case from the trunk and bring it inside the car. He turned into a deserted side street, stopped, and asked me to stay put. He got out and walked to the back of the car. I heard the trunk shut tight and he came around carrying a most elegant English polished leather case with brass locks. I opened the door and he placed the case next to my feet. All his movements were precise and carried out in slow motion. I knew enough not to talk.

Back in the driver's seat he proceeded to unlock the case and take out one of the Rolleiflexes. Carefully he showed me how to open and close the empty camera and then handed it to me to practice. He seemed pleased that I did not fumble. Then he bent down, peered deep into the padded case, and pulled out some film. Once I got the hang of loading the cameras, I should kneel on the floor and work under the dashboard, so no light would spoil the exposed film. While he gave me a demonstration, I observed his agile hands. They were much stronger than the rest of his body.

He made a U-turn and drove back to the waterfront. Slowly we passed by the run-down brick warehouses, machine shops, and forgotten piers. Sunday was a good day to explore. There were no trucks parked in the wrong places, blocking architectural details and doorways, no moving cars, and only a handful of people.

His concentration was such that I felt completely separated from him: I no longer existed. His eye was so practiced, and this was familiar territory. I could tell that in his mind he knew exactly what he was looking for. He just had to see it, and he was confident that he would. As I looked around, I began to enjoy the straightforward beauty of the warehouses with their unadorned brick walls. As long as they were in direct sunlight they seemed almost weightless.

Walker stopped rather abruptly, backed up to a corner, and parked on the wrong side of the street.

"Camera, please," he commanded as he climbed up and stood on the seat. He worked fast. He used up the film in a matter of minutes. I had no time to watch him work; my job was beneath the dashboard. It gave me great satisfaction to be ready when he asked for a loaded camera, then take the film out of the one he handed back and store it securely in the appropriate metal canister. I treated the film like the most precious gold dust. I lost all sense of time while he photographed in this one place. When he climbed back down he made notes in his date book and lit a cigarette. "I think I've got something. I may have to come back another day," he said more to himself, still completely absorbed in his work.

Walker was not able to skip lunch. His delicate stomach had to be fed every two hours. He had stashed away a thermos of English Breakfast tea with milk and some Carr's Table Water crackers in the camera case. He said he never traveled without a thermos. I held his cup while he searched in his many pockets for his pillbox. His pockets were bulging with a heavy bunch of keys, at least half of which, as he admitted one day, laughing, were to apartments, storerooms, and cars he no longer had; and, of course, his money clip, a pocket knife, all kinds of labels and small pieces of printed papers, even trash that he had found interesting and picked up along the way.

I surprised him with chicken sandwiches, seedless grapes, and cookies. We picnicked in the car, under the warm sun. He changed to his dark glasses. When he was through eating he made a pillow with his cardigan and took a short nap. It was peaceful all around us. Now and then a boat whistle and screeching gulls overhead penetrated the Sunday quiet.

Walker said Brooklyn Heights was best explored on foot, but today we drove through some of the oldest parts and he pointed out a few of his favorite architectural gems.

Revived by his nap, he talked about architecture in New York. In Brooklyn, one could see and study every possible style, from Federal to Shingle, with the exception of Egyptian, he laughed. But to his delight there were still a few Egyptian railroad stations left in this country, and he had postcards of them in his collection. He never lectured me or recited tedious facts—quite the contrary, his remarks and opinions on a particular period were often highly subjective, and it was up to me to sort out what interested me. His eagerness and pleasure in showing me authentic examples of styles he liked, and of details such as a curved doorway, a granite lintel, a lacy gothic window and front stoops, "beauties" he pretended to have found just for me, transformed these "lessons" into intimate and sometimes hilarious initiation rites. Best to leave art history to the academics, he half joked when I asked too many serious questions, and named more reasons why he was painfully bored in college.

In an hour's time in Columbia Heights we had seen a row of perfectly preserved mid-nineteenth-century brownstones, some with Corinthian capitals, mansard roofs, and dormers; on Remsen Street, the Italianate, classical façade of the Brooklyn Union Gas Company headquarters, its entry embellished by sturdy fluted columns; on Hicks Street, a Renaissance Revival brownstone of the 1880s, which stood next to a Shingle style terrace of about ten houses built in corbelled brick and shingles, each different from its neighbor; on Grace

Court, a block-long cul-de-sac formed by Grace Church on one side and the deep backyards of Remsen Street's houses on the other; in Grace Court Alley, a hidden mews, early carriage houses still retained their iron hay cranes; on Joralemon Street, over twenty Greek Revival houses were built as if they stepped down Joralemon's hill to Furman Street. Even the subway ventilator on Joralemon was Greek Revival.

I wanted to linger a while longer in the tree-shaded Willow Place and walk around to have a better look at some of the Federal and Gothic style row houses, particularly at four houses joined by a wood colonnade I had not seen anywhere else in the city. The square wooden columns must have been a carpenter's fantasy to add class to the rather plain façades, but in their dire need of restoration the columns seemed vulnerable.

Walker emphasized that few of these structures were designed by architects. It was all part of the indigenous American architecture to which he had been attracted for decades. The light was still good, and he wanted to get over to lower Broadway and have a look at the warehouses there. He must have noticed my disappointment, because he promised me we'd return soon for a late-afternoon walk followed by dinner at Gage & Tollner's Restaurant, a place he knew I loved.

The deep rose of the sun-lit brick buildings in lower Manhattan suited my nostalgic mood. There would surely be a glorious sunset, a spectacle I will always watch in New York. Once, on my way to the theater, near Times Square, I stopped in the middle of the sidewalk, dazed by the explosion on the horizon. The orange sun had just gone down over the Hudson, leaving behind a liquid glow, when the neon signs lit up one by one—shocking pink and acid green words bouncing in the purple sky. I would never leave this beloved city, I thought. I was overcome by a wave of all-too-familiar emotions from my girlhood: a sense of longing and of not being in charge of anything in my life. Uncontrollable tears had rolled down my cheeks, reminding me of my mother's tears in church on the Easter Sunday after my confirmation. Way up, in the balcony near the organ, a group of young people joined the choir and sang the high notes like angels. I had been embarrassed to sit next to my sniffling mother with many of my newly confirmed friends around me. Later that day I found her alone in our flowering spring garden and it took all my courage to ask her why she had cried. She looked straight ahead and assured me that hers were tears of joy.

Today I had better hold on to myself. Walker disliked all displays of emotions in public, and especially teary women, whom he called "sad sacks" or "tragedy queens."

We were cruising through the streets south of Houston, which were deserted and much darker than the ones in Brooklyn Heights. A few bums lay in entryways, passing their bottles to each other or sleeping, old newspapers, cigarette butts, and torn brown paper bags marking their places for that day. Like nomads they claimed a set of steps or a doorway until the police ordered them off those premises. On Sundays nobody bothered them.

The area between West Broadway and Broadway was familiar to me, but with Walker everything took on a new meaning. I was struck by the concentration of cast-iron-fronted buildings. Some could be called industrial Palladian, while others had black Corinthian columns. More important buildings designed by known architects, like Richard Morris Hunt's Roosevelt Building and Ernest Flagg's twelve-story Singer building, displayed elements and materials that seemed very advanced for their period—filigreed cast iron, composite columns, curlicued steel, recessed glass, and terra cotta. Walker said they were the forerunners of New York's metal-and-glass skyscrapers. Whole long blocks were still intact and had not yet been disfigured by ugly signs and other alterations.

Walker stopped and looked down a row of uniform cast-iron façades, their grid of shiny columns painted a black green. These less fancy examples were of great interest to him, and he wrote down the street name and numbers and the approximate time of day when he thought the light would be right. I could tell he felt a certain kinship with the late nineteenth century, when prosperous urban commerce and the beginning of the Gilded Age produced this new, highly sophisticated architecture. He had a penchant for Victorian lamps, furniture, and decorations, but at the same time he was intolerant of Victorian morals and he detested anything sentimental.

It was close to six; Walker was hungry. "I'll take you to Lüchow's for an early dinner," he said, pleased with himself. I was surprised by his choice. Why Lüchow's, I wondered, when the Village had some of the best Italian restaurants? Lüchow's was the restaurant my Swiss-German friends usually chose for its excellent venison. I felt out of place in those dark, richly ornate German rooms, and there was nothing that tempted me on the menu; the food was very heavy. Often on Saturday nights a brassy oompah band played loudly, so you couldn't even talk. A glance at the musicians' lederhosen and Bavarian hats reminded me of the Nazis and made me feel uneasy. In spite of all this I didn't resist; Walker looked tired and he had given me a wonderful day.

We drove up Sixth Avenue and turned eastbound onto Fourteenth Street. Walker said he should have put the top up, that we were too conspicuous among the hoi polloi. I told him there was nothing to fear. After all, we'd spent most of the day moseying about in empty parts of town looking at things from the past. I almost welcomed the noisy crowds of Sunday shoppers hunting for bargains, the cheap merchandise spilling out onto the wide sidewalks, the people arguing in foreign languages. It put me right back in touch with the tough, ordinary life in the city. I had met some of these people at work: they were good, tough and funny and could laugh at themselves.

The traffic was heavy and we crept along until we passed Union Square. There were fewer cars on the East Side. Walker was very quiet; without a word of warning he pulled up to the curb and stopped behind a waiting taxi. He had seen something or someone across the street. A few seconds later I found the subject of Walker's consuming curiosity: a tall dark man in black clothes coming toward us, moving slowly, almost aimlessly. He could have been an actor who had walked off the stage and into the common world of Fourteenth Street. His broad shoulders and somber head towered above the little people passing him on the sidewalk.

Walker sat motionless, like a hunter, stalking the man with his eyes. I watched for a while, until the man disappeared in the crowd.

"Do you know who that was?" Walker asked and turned to me, still somewhat bewildered.

I shook my head.

"Lincoln Kirstein." Walker seemed distracted.

"Lincoln Kirstein—your old friend," I said. He was a hero of mine. I was addicted to Balanchine's New York City Ballet, and Kirstein was the ballet's founder and spiritual leader. "Why didn't you cross the street and say hello? You could've caught up with him, he was walking so slowly."

"Lincoln and I haven't seen each other for years." Walker's unforgiving attitude convinced me that his was a final statement and further questions would be in vain.

Chapter 9

Soon after that day in Brooklyn, doubts and questions began to keep me awake at night. Walker's unpredictable moods, and his refusal to discuss personal matters and accept the most natural intimacy between us, even when he seemed to invite closeness, began to wear me out. Lately he had given me reason to feel more confident about our life together, but at Lüchow's he withdrew once again, drifted off and became silent. Was he worried I might pry into his past, or worse, invade the secret, dark places of his soul? I wished I knew what to expect of him, or what he expected of me. All I longed for was a simple gesture—his arm around my shoulder, a chance to rest my head on his chest and feel safe.

These thoughts whirled around in my mind while the walls seemed to close in around my narrow bed. I named this new trouble the racing thoughts. Night after night I lay in my airless room at the Barbizon and waited for sleep to come, dreading the racing thoughts and summer in the hot city.

Walker said he was worried about the deep circles under my eyes. I mentioned the lack of sleep, though I was careful not to tell him that his behavior might be the cause.

"Poor child," he said, like a caring father. He was an expert on ill health. The first thing he did was to give me a bottle of his sleeping pills with the assurance that there were plenty more where they came from. His newest supplier was his sister's drugstore in Florida, he joked, "most generous with refills. After all, Florida is a place where people go to die, and if they need Demarol to make them feel better they should goddam well get it." He reached into one of his pockets for his silver pillbox and handed me yet another pill. "Take a Valium, it will calm you down."

The pills produced a sense of numbness all over. I overslept the first morning, and it took hours and strong black coffee to come out of this heavy, dreamless sleep. After the third night my face and eyes were swollen as if stung by bees. I was obviously allergic to his wonder pills.

Walker arranged a visit to Dr. Leland, who examined me in a rather casual manner and gave me a shot of cortisone. His hands smelled of cigarettes and soap. I had only met him once before, very briefly, during Walker's stay at Doctor's Hospital.

I sat down across from him, and he smiled at me and mumbled something about the prescription he was about to write out. He leaned back in his chair, crossed his legs and looked out the window, then slowly turned to me. I detected a touch of irony in his voice when he finally spoke. "Are you sure you want to go through with all this? Walker told me of your plans—he's not very well, you know."

I was angry. I thought it unfair of him to warn me about Walker's health. If anything I needed encouragement from him.

Walker defended Jim Leland and thought I had overreacted. He said he was lucky to be his patient. In time, he was sure, I would learn to appreciate Jim's intelligence and his sense of humor. He was one of few doctors who understood how artists and writers lived. When he told me that John McDonald was Jim's patient too, I felt a little better.

With the warm weather Walker's spirits rose higher and higher, and our life turned into a frenzy of parties. Many of his friends wanted to meet me and do something nice for us before they disappeared to their summer places. Walker, eager to cheer me up and satisfy my hunger for glamour, dotted the pages of my little Leathersmith engagement book with dates. Soon the racing thoughts were drowned out in gaiety and champagne.

I lived at night. The days at Saks flew by with barely enough time left after work to rush home and change for the evening. My first gala was a black tie opening for the trustees and patrons of the Museum of Modern Art. We were the guests of Eliza Parkinson, a much-loved member of the board.

On Walker's arm I glided through the galleries, observing him amidst celebrities, curators, and collectors. I asked him to point out the artists, but he said that few artists he knew felt comfortable wearing a dinner jacket and nobody was really looking at the art tonight. He introduced me to René d'Harnoncourt, the director of the Modern, an urbane, gallant man, who reminded me of my father's ambassador friends in Bern. A while later, Walker's museum friends Henry Allan

Moe and Monroe Wheeler came to chat with us, and Dorothy Miller smiled at me and shook my hand. In the middle of our conversation a gushy woman Walker seemed to know well interrupted us. In a hoarse voice she exchanged some inside gossip with him, moved us closer to the bar, where she ordered another drink, and laughed a lot. I had no idea what they were talking about. "Lucky guy," she said, winked at him and hurried off. He looked amused and told me her name. Elizabeth Shaw, head of publicity at the museum, was worth making a fuss over, he thought. "She'll be helpful with the press, when the time comes."

Every so often Eliza joined us for a brief moment to make sure we were having a good time. With her I met Nelson Rockefeller and Philip Johnson, whose glass house in Connecticut I had visited on a benefit excursion, advertised as Modern House Day, a few weeks after I had arrived in New York.

Walker did all the talking and I studied the crowd. Parading before my eyes were the stars of the worlds of art, finance, and *Vogue*, playing their parts as if on a giant stage. They moved with ease and gave flawless performances. Some women stood out in exotic clothes and black lacquered hair and strutted like spiky bird-of-paradise flowers—too artificial for my taste. I gave the prize to a pale, gauzy patterned silk sari bordered in gold and draped on a Botticelli blonde—until I spotted the sea-green Fortuny, a pleated column-shaped dress that clung to its young wearer like a shimmering second skin. Movements and dress became one. Was she perhaps a Balanchine dancer?

Then, without warning, Walker yanked my arm and pulled me away. I nearly tripped over my hem and bumped into a group of tall men standing near the bar. "Sorry," he said, trembling with anger, while he held my elbow to steady me. "I can't stand the man."

"Who is it?" I looked around but couldn't find anybody who acted strange. It took a while for Walker to calm down. He searched his pockets for a cigarette. Just holding it would make him feel better, I hoped. Still pale and shaky, he explained that Edward Steichen had been coming toward us, obviously to take a look at me and say hello, but Walker wouldn't give him this satisfaction. "Not Steichen with his *Family of Man*, such overrated sentimental rubbish."

I suggested a stroll in the garden, where he would be able to smoke. In single file we made our way toward the open glass doors and stepped outside into the warm June night. I found us two empty wire mesh chairs and we sat down. Walker lit his cigarette and took off his glasses. I looked up into the velvet sky and wished I could help him forget Steichen and enjoy the rest of the evening. Seldom had I seen him so agitated. I sensed that his uncontrollable resentment came out of being underappreciated at *Fortune* and half ignored here at the Museum, because of Steichen, who headed the Museum's photography department and whose 1955 exhibition *The Family of Man* had drawn the largest crowds ever and brought him worldwide fame. None of Walker's books were in print in the spring of 1960, and his photographs had not been exhibited in New York since the late thirties, with the exception of a few pictures here and there.

We sat in silence. The garden's familiar sculptures calmed us. People wandered about, their voices muffled by street noises. At the far end I noticed a handful of men surrounding a woman. I saw Walker look in her direction and put his glasses back on. We were both ready and waiting to have a look at this slender figure in silver-gray chiffon. Slowly the group moved toward us. A slight breeze uncovered one shoulder and filled her wide scarf like a sail. I guessed she was in her forties, a woman of innate style and elegance. The way her long neck curved and grew out of these perfectly formed shoulders was more exciting than all the young Paris models' bodies I had seen on runways. As she walked by us, her head with the dark bouffant slightly tilted, the museum lights near the door lit her narrow face. Just before she went in, she turned, facing the garden once more. I stood up and by chance looked into a pair of large, shiny eyes softened by life's mystery and blows. As soon as she was gone I recognized her from pictures in *Vogue* and *House and Garden*, wearing a Givenchy evening dress or a planter's straw hat, but not in my dreams could I have imagined her as beautiful as I saw her tonight.

"Is this who I think it is, the famous Babe Paley?" I asked Walker.

"Yes," he said, "the youngest of the legendary Cushing sisters. Her husband's a big wheel here, tough guy."

In the taxi on the way home I leaned against Walker, exhausted and content.

"You liked this, didn't you?" He squeezed my arm. "I promise you, there'll be many more parties."

Chapter 9

I kissed him good night in the lobby of the Barbizon and went upstairs to my room. The unexpected appearance of Mrs. Paley wiped out the racing thoughts and brought comforting sleep.

When I was in my teens, Ursula and Landshoff had given us Saul Steinberg's book *The Art of Living*, published in 1949. It had become a family treasure filled with riddles and much puzzled over by us children. The possibility that one day we might discover the real meaning of these fantastic line drawings depicting subways, taxis, saloons, chairs, sidewalks, cats, and women was a challenge that kept our young eyes and minds focused on them for hours, searching for clues. Most of the time we did not know why some of these drawings without captions were supposed to be humorous, but we were wildly attracted to them for their originality and subject matter. Steinberg's dressed-to-kill ladies who sat cross-legged, smiling to themselves, made me laugh out loud, and made me curious about America and everything in New York.

So I eagerly awaited our dinner with Saul Steinberg and his wife, the painter Hedda Sterne, at their townhouse on the Upper East Side. We ate in the kitchen, an uncluttered, well-lit space that filled an entire floor. It had an airy feeling: white walls, pale, spotless bare wood floors and a fire-engine-red enamel cook stove.

Walker and Saul talked about their travels in America during the Depression years and the forties. Unlike Walker, who had traveled south by car and train, Saul had gone to Chicago, Los Angeles, Arizona, and Texas by bus, to many places Walker didn't know at all. But their observations and points of view were similar and they liked the same things. Neither was interested in making pictures of landscapes. Saul said he needed man-made situations, the art in things, their style, artifice, the way people made themselves up, costumes and role playing—all this and cities, hotel lobbies and people. The letters of the alphabet played a part in his early life. His father had been a printer and bookbinder, and his favorite toys as a boy were boxes with letters and numbers in them, and tools.

Walker relaxed and listened to his friend with great interest. He referred to Saul's book *Passport* and called his use of rubber stamps, fingerprints, and mock signatures a veritable stroke of genius. He even offered to lend him some hard-to-find rubber-stamps from his own collection. Saul's rather angular face was delineated by black-rimmed glasses that were like a trademark drawn by him. He behaved rather mischievously towards Hedda and me. She was obviously used to this, but I was intimidated by him, until we talked about Milan, where he had studied architecture as a young man and published his first cartoons. He responded to my enthusiasm for his drawing of the Galleria di Milano, a shopping arcade with vaulted ceilings.

After a perfect pasta dinner Walker talked to Hedda about friends they had in common, but he did not mention her work. He respected her as an artist but he wasn't much interested in recent painting and for the most part he ignored Abstract Expressionism and the New York art world. I was not familiar with her work and would have liked to see it, but there were no paintings on the walls of the pristine kitchen.

Saul said, in his quiet, nondemonstrative way, that he was a writer who drew, and Walker wasted no time responding that he had always thought of himself as a writer with a camera.

Walker was pleased with the evening at the Steinbergs. He thought I had done all right and he was ready to take me along to see Mary and Robert Frank. He asked me if I had some old clothes to wear, because they lived on lower Third Avenue, near the Bowery. I was annoyed. We had a tiff, like married people. Would he please understand that I had moved to a new continent two years ago and couldn't possibly own old clothes? Also, I refused to change my looks according to my hosts. And Robert Frank was my countryman. He became well known overnight at my Zurich art school with his book, *Les Américains*, published in 1958 by Delpire in Paris. It was praised by groups of anti-establishment artists and left-wing intellectuals in Western Europe before it appeared here, as *The Americans*; when they saw Frank's photographs they felt justified in their doubts and scepticism about postwar America. Alec and I were sent a copy by Swiss friends. At first we were careful whom we showed it to, for fear we might be labeled anti-American. Frank's bold photographs showed me a side of ordinary life in America I knew little about. There is a quiet humor and sadness in some of the pictures. People are alone, unconnected to their surroundings. The television is on in an empty roadside restaurant; in this orderly, clean place the only moving thing is a picture of a man talking on the bright screen. Juke boxes the size of refrigerators light up dark bars; outside huge parked cars, polished chrome, and gas stations obliterate the natural landscape. This was a world that could no longer be ignored. It was going to become part of everybody's life.

I was nervous about meeting Robert Frank, and Walker was no help. Distracted, he put on his work clothes, threw a stained raincoat over his shoulders, and decided to leave his cameras at home. He paid no attention to me. To be ignored was much worse than having an argument. By now I knew that it was impossible to reason with Walker when he was angry.

He hailed a taxi and we rode down Second Avenue without saying a word. He asked the driver to let us out a couple of blocks short of the Franks' low building. We walked down Third Avenue, looking for a small basement window where a recluse was living, a man who made boxes out of junk, stuff he found in the street. Nobody knew where he had come from and he seemed to be nameless. The Franks had discovered the man and brought Walker to see him. Walker described the box the man made for him, covered in wine-red oilcloth used for steamer trunks. The box had handles, locks, brass corners, and strips, a piece of superior craftsmanship, highly original.

The avenue was littered with broken bottles and trash. It was warm and damp. A dirty yellow haze covered the whole city. The smell of garbage and gasoline hung in the air. I welcomed Walker's cigarette smoke and inhaled it deeply.

We slowed down, and Walker made sure he had the right number. The front door was open. The hallway was dingy. It was a typical Third Avenue building, with pressed tin ceilings and a single large window facing the street on the second floor. On some of these windows a name or a painted shop sign was still left on the glass. Before the war, Walker said, the second floor might have been the workshop of a tailor or cabinet maker, and the family would have lived in crowded rooms on the floor above, with tenants and boarders on the top. The toilets were in the hallway. Walker had one friend who grew up in such a place on the Lower East Side—Harvey Breit, a poet and writer.

We were halfway up a short flight of stairs when Mary came down and took us through her dark studio, where she was working on pieces of wood. She gave us no chance to look, partly because the light was bad. She led us up another narrow stairway to their living quarters. A little out of breath, she greeted us, kissed Walker, and gave me a shy smile. I thought she was beautiful, with her fair skin and mane of light brown wavy hair, much like a pre-Raphaelite's vision of a young woman. She appeared to be vulnerable and strong at the same time and spoke in a tentative manner and fragmented sentences. Walker and she liked each other and had their own private pleasantries, but she soon included me and asked if I wanted to see the children.

We moved through the loft-like space into two improvised cubicles where the children had drawn and painted on the white walls. Pablo, about nine, leapt from his narrow bed when he saw Walker. They had become friends during a summer visit in Truro, on Cape Cod. Andrea, younger and shy, wanted to show me her treasures: sea glass in a bottle and some tiny shells. She gave me a drawing on a piece of colored paper.

There were many still lifes made with small pictures and objects, old pieces of embroidered silk, crushed velvet, and bunches of dried, faded flowers, all assembled by Mary, mostly with things found in junk shops. I complimented her and told her of my love for textiles. She brought out beaded dresses and lace bodices from thrift shops around town. My favorite was a small, beaded jacket, turn of the century, trimmed in black satin. Pleased and animated, she urged me to try it on in front of an old mirror. I slipped it over my cotton shirt, and if I sucked in my stomach I was able to close the tiny jet buttons. "It's yours," she said, "I'm taller than you, it would never fit me."

I hesitated and felt myself blushing, but Mary put the jacket over my arm and led me across the room to the big windowsill covered with healthy plants. Kitchen herbs, avocado trees, wild geraniums, and field flowers grew in jungly profusion. She said she loved plants and grew them mostly from seed.

We joined Walker and Robert and some of his friends who sat around the table talking and drinking wine. The cheese was almost gone and the ashtrays were full. Walker introduced me, and Mary pulled up a chair for me next to Robert. We talked about Magnum photographers like Robert Capa, Henri Cartier-Bresson, and the late Werner Bischof, whose work he had known in Zurich. We spoke English. Both of us had accents. At times he slowed down and searched for the right word. I listened to his low voice and waited for a smile, but his face remained somber. When I mentioned his book, he waved his hand and said he was more interested in making films.

It was getting late, and Walker worried aloud about finding a taxi in this neighborhood. He was fading. We had eaten every morsel of Mary's delicious food when more friends, many of them painters, dropped by for a cold beer or a glass of wine. They were hungry and nobody had money to eat out. No matter how late, Mary would have fed them all night long.

To everyone's surprise Walker decided to stay a while longer. He felt comfortable with these people and was curious to hear what they had to say. He also recognized that he was with the best of the Beat Generation and their followers, who had rediscovered him and understood his work. Some of Robert's friends revered him and brought books for him to sign. Where on earth did they find these, he asked, in some Vermont book barn or obscure second-hand bookshop?

This was the moment I had been waiting for: to see Walker surrounded by younger, articulate men and women who talked to him about their ideas and projects. Discussions ranged from Wittgenstein to Kerouac, Picasso to de Kooning, and were interrupted by in-jokes and laughter. Little was said about photography, which pleased Walker. He listened and eventually spoke of his growing interest in the "visual power of the aesthetically rejected object." Stuff people threw out had been a lifelong obsession. He looked at debris on the pavement; candy wrappers and tin beer caps in the gutter and in garbage cans. The positive response he received from this honest and outspoken audience reassured him that his reputation was growing among today's artists and writers, a talented, dedicated, and hardworking group with energy to spare. He needed their companionship and physical help on his working trips. My hope was that with them he would experience some kind of renaissance and be stimulated to pursue new ideas in his work.

Later, in bed, as I relived the evening before falling asleep, I wrote down some questions to ask Walker the next day. Could he live with the lack of decorum and style the Beat Generation espoused? He hesitated. I didn't get a clear answer. I told him I had enjoyed myself very much last night, but that I needed more order in my life and physical comforts and nicer surroundings. He teased me and said I was hopelessly Swiss.

Chapter 10

Casually, on the phone one morning, Walker asked me to quit my job at the end of June. Would I spend the summer with him in Lyme?

My answer was "yes" without a moment's hesitation. I packed up my belongings at the Barbizon and stored them at his place on York Avenue. Just before we left, we were invited for a weekend with Tappy and Mott Schmidt in their house in Katonah. Walker called it a house party. I wasn't sure what he meant, except that he asked me to pack a long skirt for dinner on Saturday night. His friend and my lawyer Grenny Emmet would be one of the guests. Grenny was Tappy's cousin and neighbor. He had scheduled my divorce in Mexico for the very end of August and would talk to me and explain the procedure step by step. There was nothing to it; a flight to El Paso, a short limousine ride to Juárez the following day, and then back to New York. Two days was all it would take.

Walker and I arrived Saturday after lunch, and I was welcomed warmly by Tappy and Mott, as if I had grown up with their children. Even though we were seeing each other for the first time, they could have been my favorite aunt and uncle; everything about them, their pleasant manner, soft voices, and natural grace, was familiar to me.

Mott, who was an architect, had designed their comfortable, light-filled house many years ago. It was lived-in, and the walls and floors had acquired an old-world patina. The colors were soft, the cushioned sofas inviting to curl up on and read, and some of the paintings were recent works by friends and artists who showed at the Katonah art gallery that Tappy was involved with. The furnishings were an eclectic mixture of old and new.

Tappy took us through her garden, which was filled with perennials, and we followed her along a stone path to a guest house. She pointed to a round pool edged with the same gray stone. "Have a swim later on, I might join you." She said Mott designed the pool and it had just been finished. Now she was looking forward to planting some shrubs and a ground cover.

The door to the guest house was unlocked, and we stepped into a cozy set of English cottage rooms. Tappy checked the bathroom and pulled down a shade to keep the afternoon sun out. "You'll make your own sleeping arrangements, there's a single bed in the smaller room." She smiled and was already out the door when she called from the garden. "Take your time. See you for tea."

How nice of Tappy to give us this little house, I thought, she wasn't the least bit stuffy. I lay down on top of the double bed while Walker unpacked. After all these parties and countless people, we were alone at last in this lovely calm place. This was the moment to break all his ridiculous rules and stop pretending. I longed to be touched. There was no better time to make love than a summer afternoon—and then cool off with a swim. It was my turn to be daring. I had nothing to lose, in a few months we'd be married.

I unbuttoned my shirt—he had watched my breasts before in the mirror. Maybe he'd run his tongue over my nipples and kiss me like a lover, if I knew how to excite him. I closed my eyes and waited. Every part of my body was open and ready for him.

I heard the water running in the bathroom—what was taking him so long? Was he undressing? He returned with the newspaper, lit a cigarette, and sat down near the window. "I'll sleep in the other room, you'll have more privacy," he said without looking at me. "You know I like narrow beds."

Why was he punishing me? Was I less desirable than the women of his past? Words would only make things worse now, and I was fighting tears. Where was the Kleenex box? Everything was coming apart: my hairdo, the new makeup, and my whole life. He had such power over me. Something was wrong. I deserved to be happy in this perfect place. But the day was spoiled.

I took a couple of aspirins and fell asleep. When I woke up, Walker was standing next to my bed in his bathing suit. He kissed the top of my head. "You all right?" He touched my forehead. "Poor child, your eyes are red, have you been crying?"

I nodded and looked at him. "Why can't we sleep together?" I was wiping new tears with my sleeve. "Even Tappy must think it's okay. She wouldn't have put us in here."

He kissed my hand and said he loved me and asked me to be patient, to give him more time. He would think about us. He hated to see me so upset. In Lyme things would be easier and we'd relax and both feel better.

Two days before the Fourth of July we settled into Walker's dwelling in Lyme (he didn't like me to call it a cabin). I had brought my summer clothes and books and not much else. Walker unpacked for days. I was surprised by what he pulled out of the trunk and backseat of the old Buick. Aside from books, cameras, and tripods, his summer paraphernalia included golf clubs, folding canvas deck chairs, jazz records, an electric tea kettle, a pocket transistor radio, boxes of Twinings tea and English biscuits, beach accoutrements, tweed caps, and a bush jacket with deep pockets. The screened porch looked like a thrift shop in a Westchester suburb. It was his domestic side that amused and touched me most. The first thing he did was set up the rusty barbeque on the uneven grass. Then with a tangle of extension cords and three-way plugs, he tested all his appliances and instructed me how to use them, and which to unplug before others could be plugged in. He had not counted on my hairdryer, which, much to his annoyance, blew all the fuses the first time I used it. All the while he was puttering around, fixing a screen, hammering a few nails to support a sagging shelf. He was fully absorbed and in a happy mood.

The big surprise, my pre-wedding present, was the little bedroom and bathroom he had had a local carpenter tack on to the kitchen early in the spring. He generously gave me carte blanche to decorate, but there was little space for me to play with. The bed and a painted country bureau filled up most of the bedroom, and the claw-foot bathtub and corner wash basin were already in place. Proud of his finds, he promised to take me to the junk shops off Route 1.

Walker's friend Clark Voorhees, who had granted him squatters' rights to build the original studio on a small piece of his land, lived across the road in an old farmhouse. The two men had met through their wives, Jane and Billie, who were classmates at Sophie Newcomb College. Jane, Walker's first wife, was a painter.

One morning after breakfast, Clark brought a bushel basket of kitchen herbs from his garden and helped me plant them near the porch, where the afternoon sun was warmest. I liked him right away. Unhurried, with a quiet sense of humor, he waited for others to talk, like the dairy farmers in the villages near Bern. He was observant and knew what was going on. Walker always said that Clark should have been a gentleman farmer, but his acreage was mostly swamp land. Sadly, around Lyme, the smaller farms were already disappearing.

Early in the morning, when Walker was on his porch bunk taking his nap, I often got up and crossed the road to watch Clark work outdoors. He was so skillful that shovels and saws seemed like extensions of his arms and hands. Sometimes he asked me to steady a ladder or hold up a branch so he could get underneath a tree. We exchanged few words. Passing tools to each other and occasional smiles was enough.

On warm evenings, Walker would get the charcoal going at cocktail time and Clark would sometimes come over and join us for dinner. No one asked about Billie. He kept Walker company outside with a drink in his hand, and the two men discussed the neighbors, parcels of land for sale, and the changes in Lyme. I was usually in the kitchen preparing a salad and vegetables, and then I would set the table on the porch and listen to them talk. Clark was quieter than Walker, who was capable of laughing at his own jokes with childlike abandon, much to the amusement of others.

Walker's lack of friends dated from his early youth. At Andover, Joseph Verner Reed was his only friend, and he had envied the boys whose fathers drove up from New York in expensive cars to watch their sons' games. Walker's parents were separated, and the tuition bills were not always paid on time. Already then his taste for good clothes, luggage, and cars was overdeveloped, and now, after all these years, he still craved luxuries like Abercrombie's picnic baskets and long raccoon coats. Clark came closest to the favorite roommate Walker never had during his one year at Williams College, before he left, disappointed and bored by his English and French courses, with the wish to continue his education in Paris.

Our porch meals were civilized, as Walker liked to point out, partly because of his perfectly grilled double lamb chops or steaks (from the Hamburg Cove butcher, the best in town), a decent Bordeaux, linen napkins, and candles. What gave us a tranquil mind was the warmth and simplicity of Clark's friendship, and the stillness of the place. When the sound of the katydids became fainter and darkness enclosed the porch, we stopped talking and listened as the moon rays shone around us through the leaves. A bird cry near the swamp, the flapping of wings—tree trunks and stones awash in bluish light—the night's creatures and changing shadows kept us together at the table until the fireflies appeared and large moths stuck to the screen.

As I got to know Clark better, I understood that his unencumbered lifestyle was not a matter of choice. He came from old money and it was running out. Some of his relatives, the Stuyvesant Fish family and others, were well off compared to him. At times his small income was barely enough to support Billie and the two children, Christopher and his sister, Michael.

Billie was always in the house. Walker called her an "artist girl" and said she had been pretty and lots of fun when he first knew her but now the alcohol had gotten to her and she was a mess. I knew little about alcoholism. At home, at a New Year's Eve party or a wedding, we all occasionally drank too much, and once in a while my father would come home tipsy after one of the evenings with his artist friends at the Harmonie restaurant. We three older children found him hilarious, especially when he turned the radio way up and lifted one of us out of bed to dance with him.

With Billie it was different. She could be funny, like a wise child, and appealing when she asked me in for a cup of coffee, and we would talk about making things. We had something in common: our love for colors, fabrics, and crafts, and we were both good with our hands. In the evenings she turned into someone sad and pathetic and alone. Huddled in the corner of a stained, rumpled couch, a glass of bourbon or cheap sherry in her unsteady hand—it could have been mouthwash—she slurred her words and looked at me out of half-closed, dark brown eyes, like a sick little dog, begging to be held.

I talked to Walker about Billie, and he said Clark had tried to help but she was too far gone now, a hopeless case. He urged me not to get involved. "Poor Clark," he said, "he has to get his own dinner, and the children eat out of the icebox."

These lazy sun-filled days and their uneventful sameness were a new experience for me. I had spent recent summer vacations touring and sightseeing in new places. My family went to hotels on the seashore, and during the war my mother, who loved the water and found the mountains gloomy, was clever at discovering small pensions that served good country food and were surrounded by gardens and old orchards along the lakes of French-speaking Switzerland. Daily excursions to medieval castles, churches, and historic sites with my father were thinly disguised history lessons. After long, hot walks around Roman ruins, syrupy refreshments in outdoor cafes often failed to cheer us up.

I began to like the rhythm of this quiet life in the back country: birdsong on my solitary early morning walks before the humid heat closed in on us like a wet curtain, and later, the drives home from the farm stand before noon, canvas bags full of summer vegetables on the backseat—shiny zucchinis, corn on the cob, ripe tomatoes. Lunch. The heat rising; dappled sunshine on the porch table; glasses of strong mint-flavored iced tea; cheese and a loaf of newly discovered home-made bread. Walker drove far for good bread.

After lunch he usually napped. Eating made him sleepy, and digesting his food seemed like hard work. I thought he looked much older when he was asleep. As I read my beloved Colette in a comfortable deck chair I became aware of his breathing. He was a quiet sleeper and seldom changed position. He slept during the day, like a cat, and often was awake for long spells at night, he told me. I slept alone in my new room and had no way of keeping him company in these late night hours, but I had the feeling he was not troubled by that. All I knew was that he smoked and read, made tea, and ate a few crackers.

The heat sapped his energy. It would be almost four before he woke up, and soon we would drive to the beach for a swim. A couple of glasses cases lay on top of a pile of books next to his bunk. He read several books at the same time. Earlier I had studied their spines: Graham Greene, Norman Mailer, back issues of *Esquire*. A heavy French novel with the title *The Horrors of Love*, highly recommended by Wilder Hobson, he told me he saved for night-time reading. John Updike was his new discovery. He praised his short stories and now his first novel, *The Poorhouse Fair*. A born writer, Walker thought, someone to watch and pay attention to. Lovell Thompson, senior editor at Houghton Mifflin—Walker called him Lovable—was a neighbor of Updike's in Ipswich and promised to invite him and his wife Mary to dinner with us.

These small daily pleasures were heightened by the exciting prospect of John F. Kennedy's nomination at the Democratic Convention in Chicago. A new decade with an intelligent and glamorous first family in the White House turned Walker into a news addict glued to his pocket-size transistor radio. Trips to the post office and the drugstore to buy *The New York Times* and *The New Yorker* could no longer be postponed, and I had *Paris-Match* forwarded from the city. Jackie's pictures in *Paris-Match* showed her as the worldly cosmopolitan she was, a woman of taste, an art lover who read books and spoke French. The *Match* photographs of her were more daring and the accompanying stories didn't try to fit her into the American mold. I followed the news with Walker, and he explained American politics to me. Though he generally regarded television as lowbrow, we often watched the six o'clock news at the Voorhees. I cut out articles and pictures of the Kennedys in Hyannisport, playing on the beach with Caroline, entertaining friends on the Honey Fitz. My mirror was full of Jackie pictures. I studied her clothes, her hair and what she liked to eat on her boat picnics—*oeuf en gelée* and grapes. Every day I learned something new about her. For me she was a modern princess, who would change people's attitudes towards culture and style and insist on good manners in the rough world of politics.

Walker's Way My Years with Walker Evans

Chapter 11

August brought jellyfish to Niantic beach, a signal for Walker to prepare for our trip to Maine. The excitement of the convention was over, and the race between our fair and smiling knight Kennedy and the somber Nixon had begun. We could do without television for a while.

Dorothy and John McDonald had rented a house on Cranberry Island in Maine for the summer and urged us to come and stay a few days. They told Walker to bring his cameras. Their painter friends on Cranberry could get him into some native houses that were mostly untouched by modern civilization. Dorothy said she painted in a shed near the water and on sunny days the light was strong and clear, changing all the time. She described the fog and how it suddenly lifted, hung in white ribbons across the mountains.

John was working on a book. He had no desire to leave the island; there was enough going on, games like tennis and croquet and hearts when the weather was bad. Christie, their teenage daughter, helped deliver the groceries with a friend in a jeep and was having a great summer. As a family they liked the people, a good mix of islanders and summer folk.

I had visited Mount Desert Island with Alec and stayed at the Kimball House, a turreted shingled summer hotel with a good dining room and entertaining guests. I enthusiastically mentioned it to Walker and he booked a suite with our own little porch. He had heard of the fifteen-hole golf course in Northeast Harbor and planned to play a few rounds. This would be our vacation, exploring the big island, shopping, and eating as many lobsters as we pleased. On Cranberry he would work.

It was hot when we left Lyme. We drove right through Boston and took the Maine Turnpike and Route 1 to Wiscasset. Our first visit was to the Calvert Coggeshalls on the River Road in Newcastle, midway between Boston and Mount Desert. Some of the town's many grand sea captains' houses were in the early stages of careful restoration, others were sadly neglected, surrounded by weeds and broken fences where gardens once grew. For such a small town, there was an unusually rich collection of coastal Maine architecture dating from the mid-eighteenth century to late Victorian. Even the stark commercial nineteenth-century brick buildings on Main Street had generous granite lintels and steps. Walker liked their uncluttered façades and good proportions. We stopped for tea and blueberry pie in the village restaurant. He used a pay phone outside the post office to call Calvert, who drove up in an old car and led the way across the bridge to his mother-in-law's brick house.

I had met Calvert, his wife Susanna, and their young son, Tomlin, in New York. On most days Calvert entertained in their old apartment on Eighty-ninth Street and Madison Avenue for drinks and good talk. It was a constant flow of old friends of all ages. At times Calvert's grown children from his first marriage showed up and stayed for supper. He made the drinks, organized the house, and cooked the meals. At one of these gatherings one might run into Marcel Duchamp and his American wife; Betty Parsons, who showed Calvert's paintings; Arthur Young, an inventor from Philadelphia; or the painter Jack Tworkov and his wife, Wally. Calvert, who was a trained architect and also an abstract painter, designed rooms for the very rich and knew where to find antiques and oriental rugs for them. For himself he liked things sparse, almost monastic: bare floors, a couple of sofas and comfortable chairs covered in off-white linen, fresh flowers, and a large abstract painting on the big wall opposite the fireplace. Often known artists lent him a painting; sometimes he hung one of his own, usually in shades of blues and black.

Around eight, Calvert counted heads and disappeared into the kitchen while Susanna had another gin and bitters. Her discussions about English writers and poets of the past had begun to bore Walker. She liked him very much, but in her eyes I was a young thing not worthy of him, so I chose to keep Calvert company while he prepared a supper of lean hamburgers with fresh mushrooms, young greens, and endives tossed in the best olive oil and crusty bread. Ripe pears and crumbly Stilton cheese were set aside for dessert. He had a talent for finding good inexpensive wines, which he opened just before he went into the living room to gather up the small group. Walker was barely awake, and I knew from looking at him that he was anxious to leave the smoky, used-up atmosphere after an intense and long cocktail hour. He'd revive around the dining table, however.

Walker had not seen the establishment in Maine. Calvert hinted that he was not free to redo the interior of the house as long as Frances Perkins, Susanna's mother, was still in charge. He was fond of the property, the early brick house, the land, a King's grant, sloping down to the river, and the barn and sheds. The bones were good, but Ma Perkins, as she was called in Roosevelt's cabinet, was attached to her furnishings and disliked any changes.

As we turned into the driveway we saw Susanna sitting in a lawn chair, a crownless hat on her head, her long, wet hair spread out on the wide brim to dry. She laughed and embraced Walker and greeted me rather formally. Her slender arms and legs and narrow feet were bare. She was tan all over, a light cotton shift covering her slim shape. In her silly hat she seemed girlish and moved about in a gawky manner. Tomlin ran up to Walker, who lifted him high in the air. He was a blond, sensitive boy, and now that his color had changed to a warm honey tone, he looked less delicate than in the city.

I was always surprised to see Walker with the children of his friends. He attracted them like a magician and he knew instinctively what would interest them. Was it his lonely, unhappy childhood that gave him insight into children's minds? Or are artists closer to children, their sense of play, discovery, and dreams still intact?

We had tea with Ma Perkins in the front parlor, a dark room with mustard-colored curtains. Presiding over the tea table in her linen suit and panama hat, she listened to Walker's comments about his work for the Farm Security Administration and responded knowledgeably, remembering facts and dates as though they were recent history. Her undemonstrative, controlled demeanor and lack of small talk gave me the impression that she might have preferred to be a man. Calvert, who took care of her house and the grounds and knew how to humor her seemed to be on her good side, but when Susanna arrived late, barefoot, her light hair tied in a ponytail, Ma Perkins sent her back to put on shoes. I felt more sympathetic towards Susanna than before. Here she was in her forties and still being disapproved of by her mother. No wonder she posed as a femme de lettres and talked too much.

Calvert put us in the same room. Twin beds, country furniture, and a faded wallpaper pleased Walker, but he didn't like sharing a bath down the hall. Ma Perkins had the best suite of rooms and her own bath.

The next morning, Tomlin knocked on our door and brought in his pet rabbit. He let him loose on Walker's bed, where he jumped around, sniffing.

"Oh-oh—he's pooping," said Tomlin and buried his head in my pillow. Walker scolded him in a loud voice. Tomlin, close to tears and confused, didn't know what to do. I cleaned up the mess and promised we wouldn't tell anyone. Tomlin gently picked the rabbit up and held him close to his chest.

At breakfast there was no milk for Walker's tea. Susanna had stopped buying milk after reading Rachel Carson's speech on pesticides. Tomlin was given only condensed or powdered milk. Walker, who liked quiet breakfasts with the paper, was in no mood to discuss the effects of DDT on the environment. When the articles had first come out in *The New Yorker*, he said to me that these problems did not concern him. "Let the rich worry about it, it'll give them something worthwhile to do for years to come." Remarks like these confused me, since he envied people with money. He changed his allegiance, even in the same conversation; it all depended who he was talking to and whether he liked the person.

Calvert came in from the garden, his arms heavy with corn, lettuce, and purple basil. He had been working for a couple of hours, restaking some tomato plants and moving pots into the shade and weeding. His blue work shirt was open to the waist. Lean and sunburned, he moved twice as fast as Walker, though he was only a few years younger. A two-inch crewcut made his narrow face appear longer. In the garden, absorbed and serious, he looked like an American icon, but the moment he smiled, his easy, unaffected manner gave me reason to believe that he liked the company of women.

Calvert and Walker made plans to drive off for the day and take a look at a specific interior Calvert knew would interest him. I was not asked to join them, but Calvert promised to show me the little one-room schoolhouse down the road where he painted later.

Susanna asked me if I would like to go canoeing in the afternoon. She said the tide would be just right after lunch, and Tomlin would be at a friend's house. Calvert had launched the canoe and tied it securely to the bank. It was an old, heavy, beautifully crafted boat, and I felt a sense of adventure when I stepped in and took my seat. Susanna was limber and quick, and in minutes we were paddling along the water's edge, passing woods and open meadows. The current helped us along. Susanna said there were swans and cygnets in the next cove, a mile down; she would try to find them.

The first mosquito bite made me reach for my bug spray. Susanna yelled: "For God's sake, don't spray! It kills everything around it. We need all the bugs in our poor universe." She stopped paddling and handed me a bunch of citronella leaves to rub on my arms and legs. Half an hour later I was covered with bites. Stiff upper lip WASP department, I thought, and we paddled on.

Walker was exhilarated when he returned with Calvert. "Wait 'til you see the pictures," he said with a conspiratorial air. "Calvert has an eye—he knows what I like." He described the house at the mouth of a tidal inlet. Men who built boats a hundred years ago, he thought, knew what a house should look like. The proportions were good and the windows faced the right way. He liked the fluted moldings and the simple lines of the mantelpieces. Everything from the newel post to the wide floorboards were solid and without useless ornament. The cast iron stove in the kitchen was worthy of the time he spent on it today, and the brand name Home Clarion written in shiny chrome letters across the oven door gave it just the right touch of humor.

When he was stimulated and working well I was confident that as soon as *Let Us Now Praise Famous Men* was reissued (there was talk about a new edition), he would once again be in great demand and asked to do jobs that interested him and paid enough. His work was important to him, and he needed to be alone to think. On his photographic expeditions he preferred having a friend like Calvert or a young artist around to assist him. Eventually I found out that this person couldn't be me; he said I distracted him. "I work when I'm thinking," he often remarked when he left the room and lay down with a book. I understood what he meant and was less resentful.

Since I had left New York I had not given any thought to my own future. Right now I lived for each day, trying as best I could to cope with my new life. Some days were light with laughter, others seemed gloomy and worrisome. It was like being in a gigantic house with many doors. As I opened them one by one I found myself in rooms I had not seen before, with people I did not know. The rooms were symbols of Walker's different worlds, and in time I learned to move more easily in and out of them on my own.

After four days with the Coggeshalls, Walker thought it was time to move on. The hot and humid weather had followed us up the coast, and we longed for the open ocean. It was an easy drive to Boothbay Harbor, where we were met by Verna Hobson, who was looking years younger in a short pleated tennis skirt, her dark hair pulled back under a smart captain's hat. In a grand gesture, Walker took off his straw hat, waved it around, and kissed her hand. Verna saluted like a naval officer, and the kidding began. I watched enviously. What pleasure to be so quick with words and humor and never let the ball drop! Verna tried to include me in the game, but all I could do was to express myself with gestures in the manner of Marcel Marceau.

As we waited for the ferry to Squirrel Island, children and friends called hello and waved. Everybody adored her. She was a party girl with a good mind and gutsy too, Walker said, a rare combination. "An English beauty," as he was fond of saying, because of her rosy skin and some years she had spent in England during her youth. When the boat arrived, she welcomed us aboard the ferry as though it were her private yacht. On the way over she told us that all our friends were involved in a tennis tournament. "I've already lost my singles match, so I can play with you."

It felt good to be on the water, despite all the tourist places around us. The Boothbay region was the opposite of Newcastle and the River Road. Painted summer cottages and gift shops, outdoor lobster eateries, floats and docks and pleasure boats cluttered the coast and the surrounding islands. Walker contemplated the familiar summer vacation scene and quickly decided that he would not unpack his cameras. "It'll be a social visit," he said to me. "We'll have some fun."

Squirrel Island was one of the region's oldest summer colonies, founded in 1871. The island was small, and the earliest shingled cottages lacked architectural distinction. The largest structure was the stark Squirrel Inn, which had a wrap-around porch and many dormers. Walker's friends came here for the love of tennis, recreational reading, and jazz. Boating was rather looked down upon.

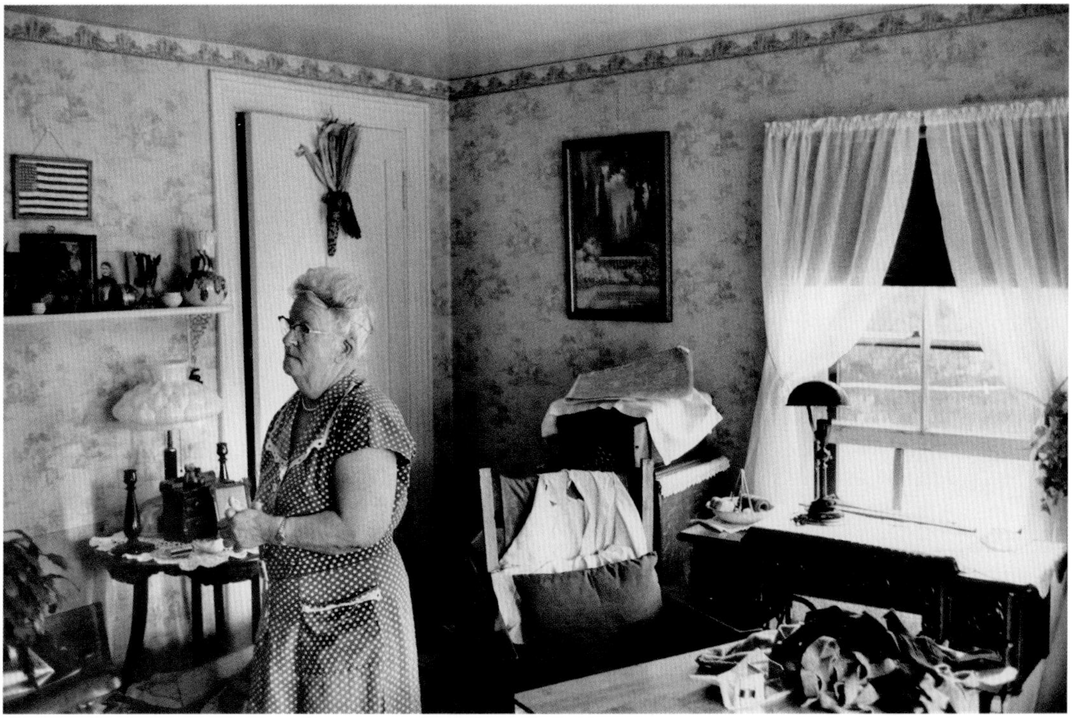

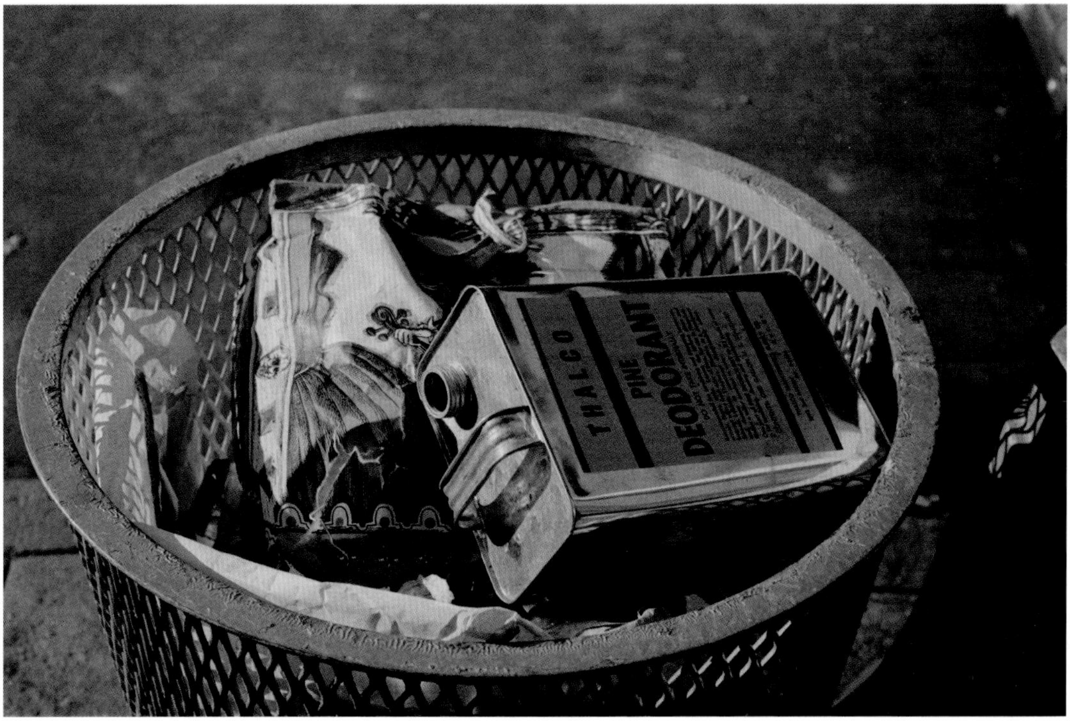

Addie Duren in her living room, Cranberry Island, Maine, 1962. Photograph by Walker Evans (courtesy of the Heliker-LaHotan Foundation)

Trash Can, New York City. Photograph by Walker Evans, 1962

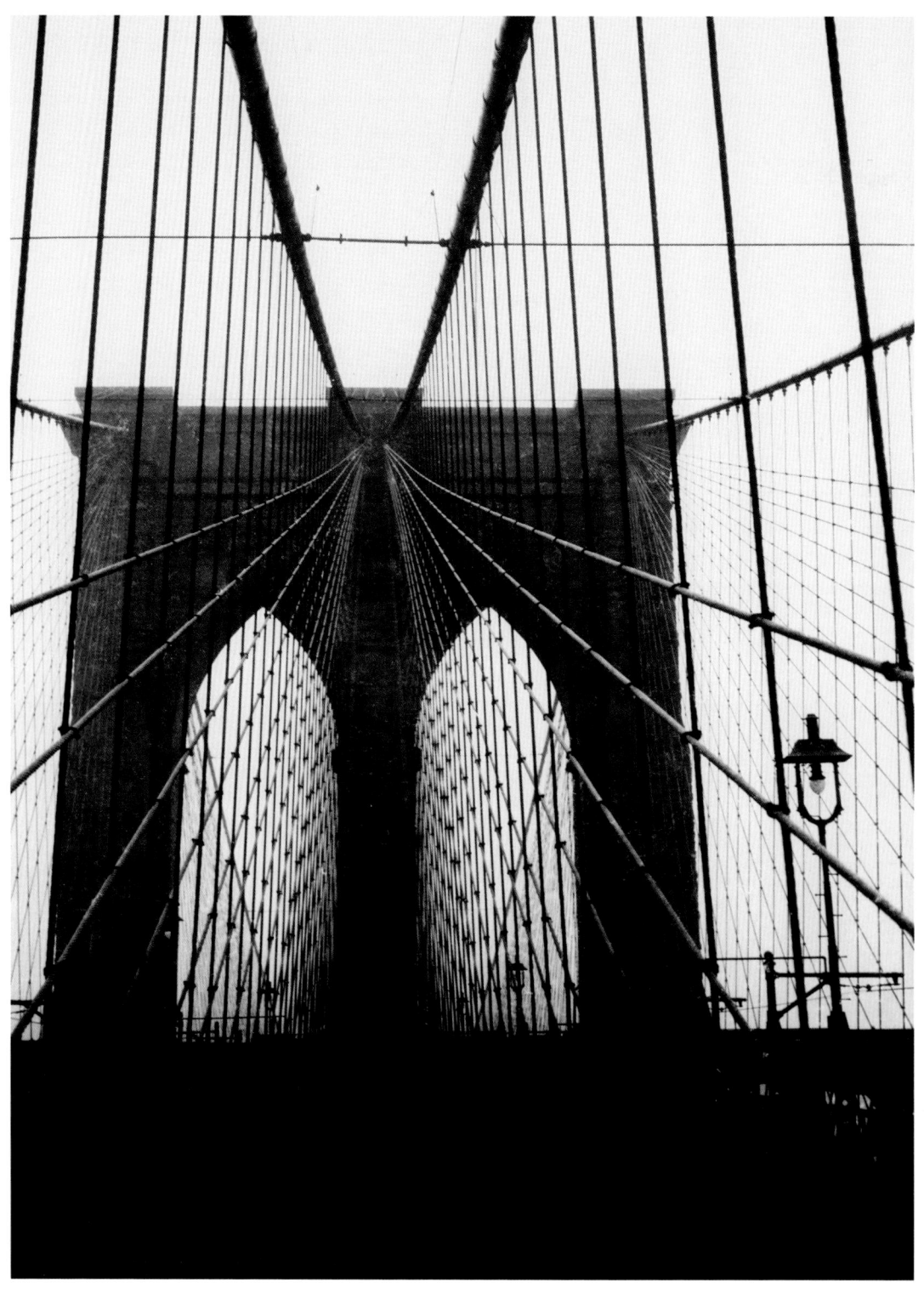

Brooklyn Bridge, New York. Photograph by Walker Evans, 1929

Underneath the Brooklyn Bridge, New York. Photograph by Walker Evans, 1928–1929

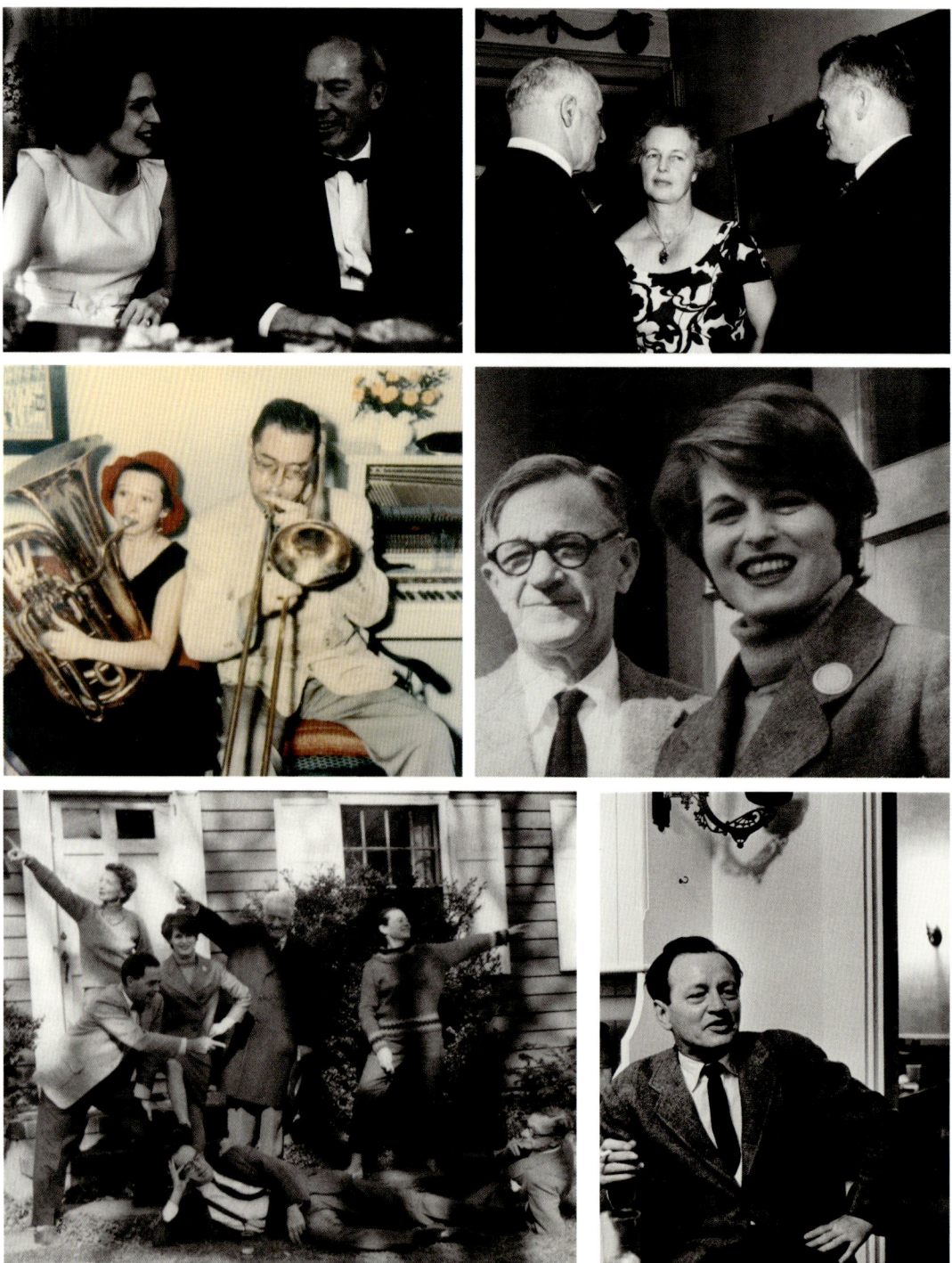

With Grenville Emmet, Walker's friend and my lawyer, at a New York party in 1963.
Maman at my brother Bernard's wedding reception in Bern, 1963.
Jazz: Verna and Wilder
With Walker at a party at the Wilder Hobsons' in Princeton before the Princeton-Yale game, 1961. Photograph by Sylvia Salmi
Wilder and Walker lying down on the lawn; Verna, Herbert Solow, and me in high spirits before the game.
Photograph by Sylvia Salmi
John McDonald on Cranberry Island, Maine, early 1960s.

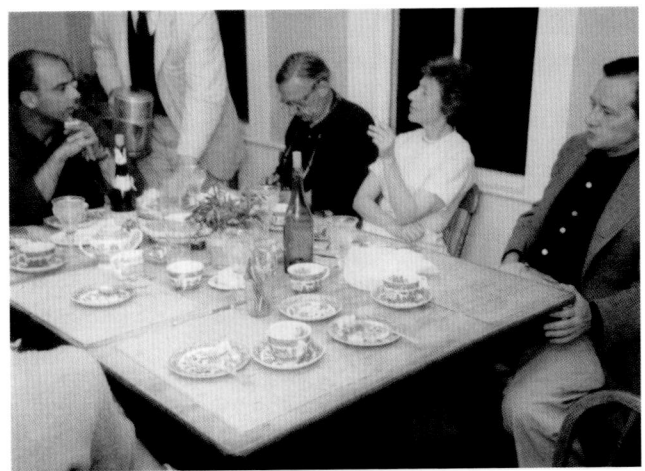

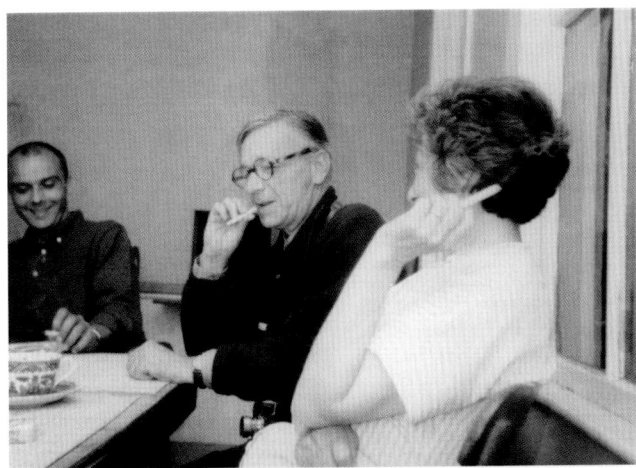

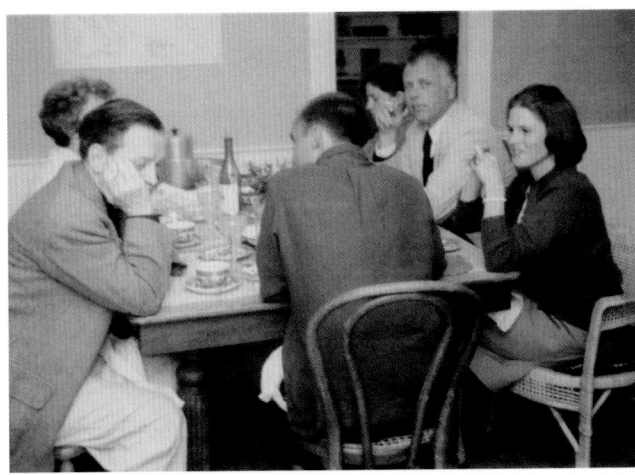

Jack Heliker took these pictures with his Polaroid camera after a dinner at his house during the summer of 1962 on Cranberry Island. (All three courtesy of the Heliker-LaHotan Foundation)

The McDonalds, Bob LaHotan, and Walker enjoying good talk. Photograph by Jack Heliker

Walker, Dorothy McDonald, and Bob LaHotan. Photograph by Jack Heliker

The painter Bill Kienbusch, Walker, John McDonald, Bob LaHotan, and me. Photograph by Jack Heliker

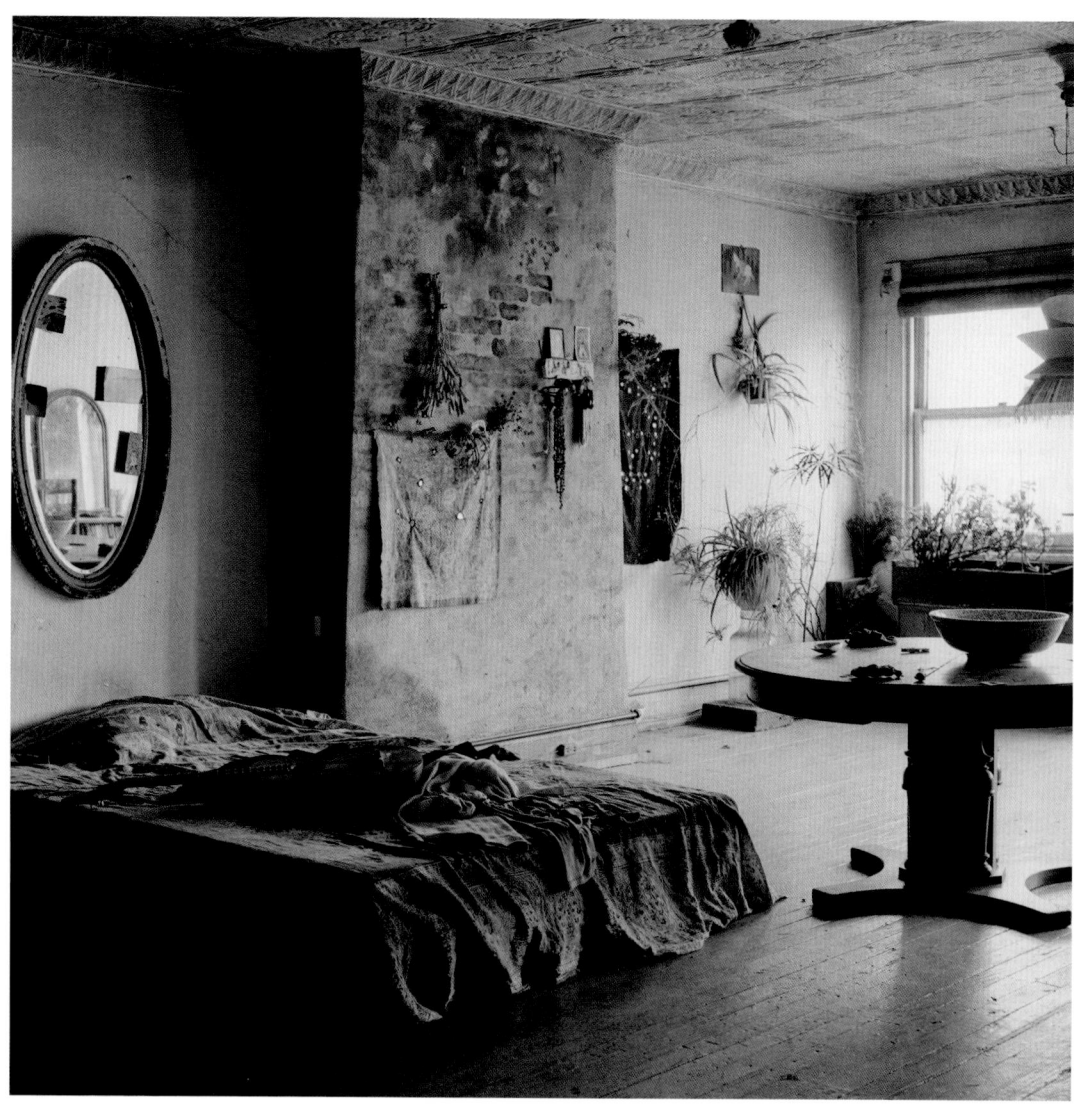

Interior view of Mary Frank's bedroom, New York City. Photograph by Walker Evans, 1959

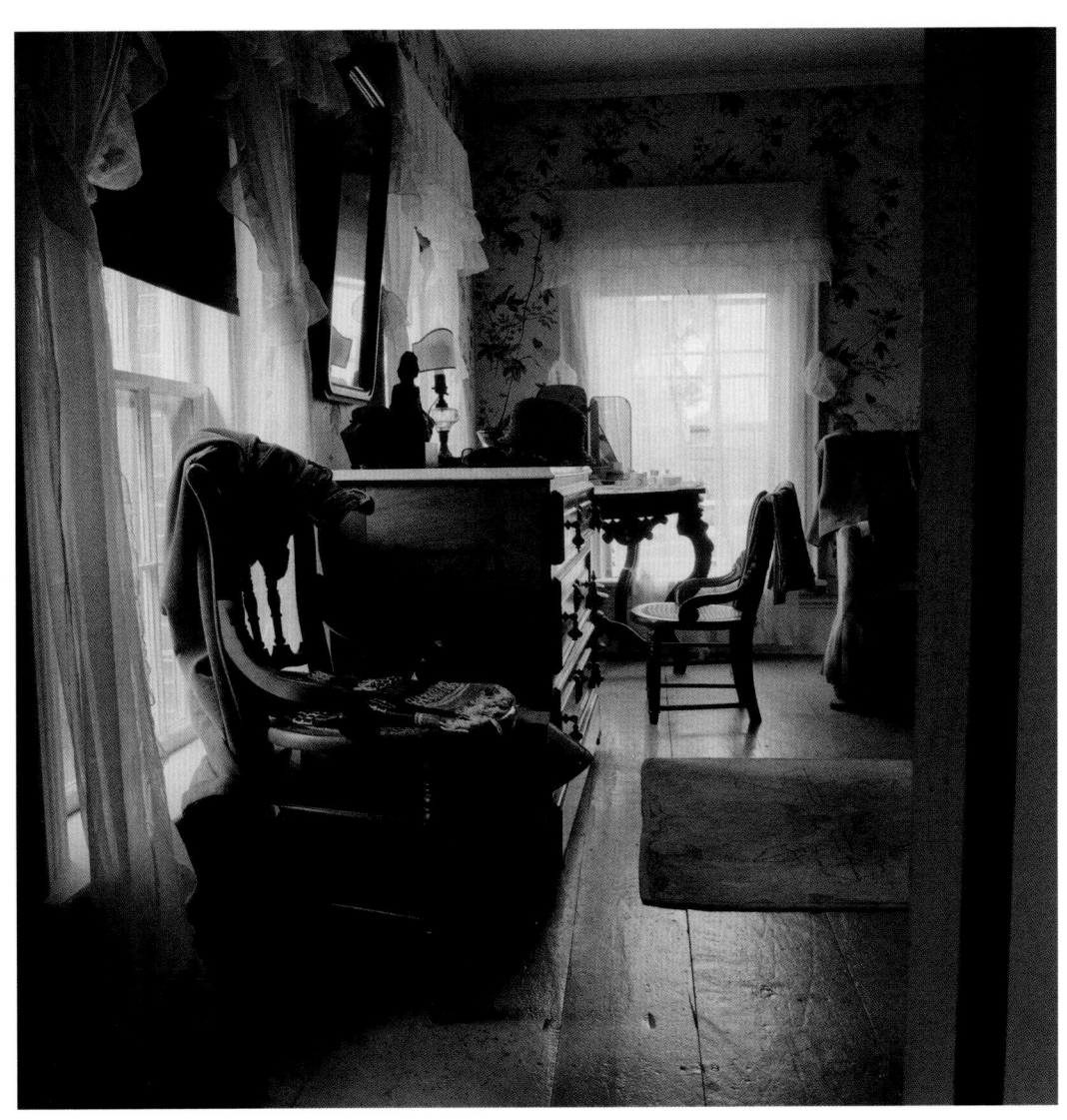
Interior view of the Coggeshall house, Newcastle, Maine. Photograph by Walker Evans, ca. 1967

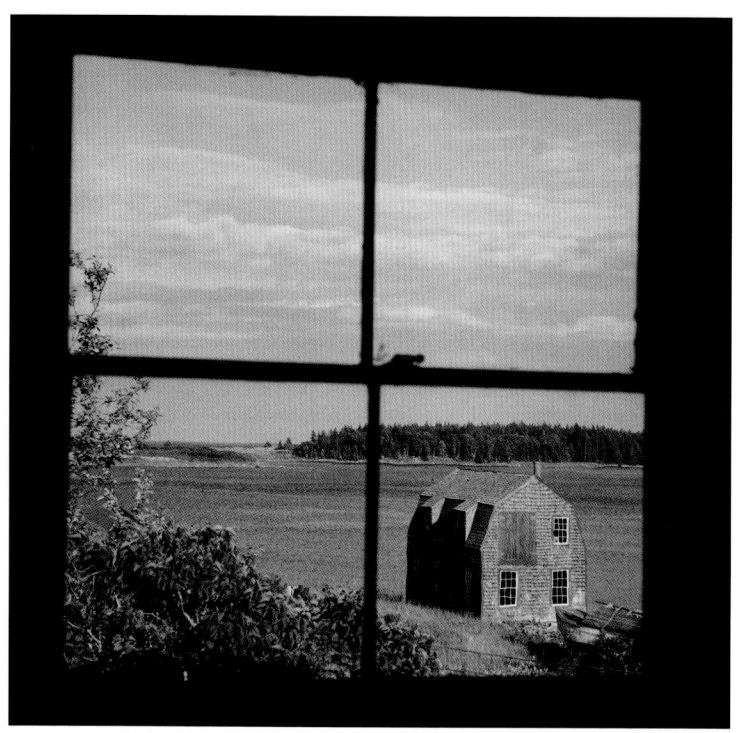

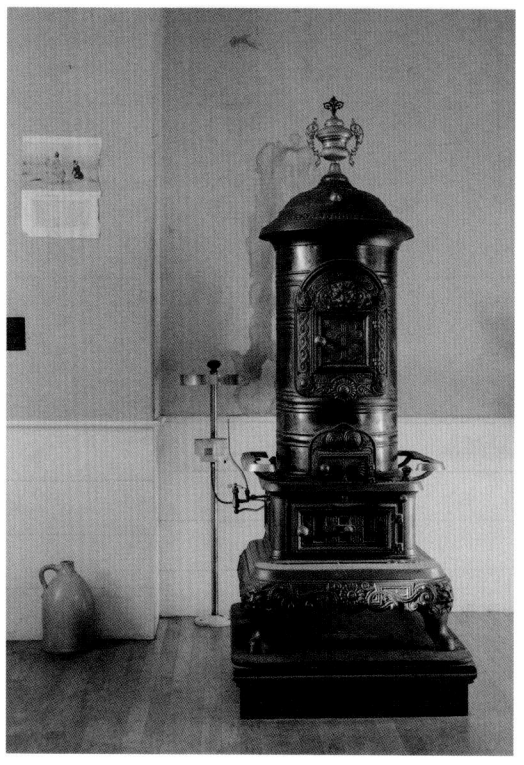
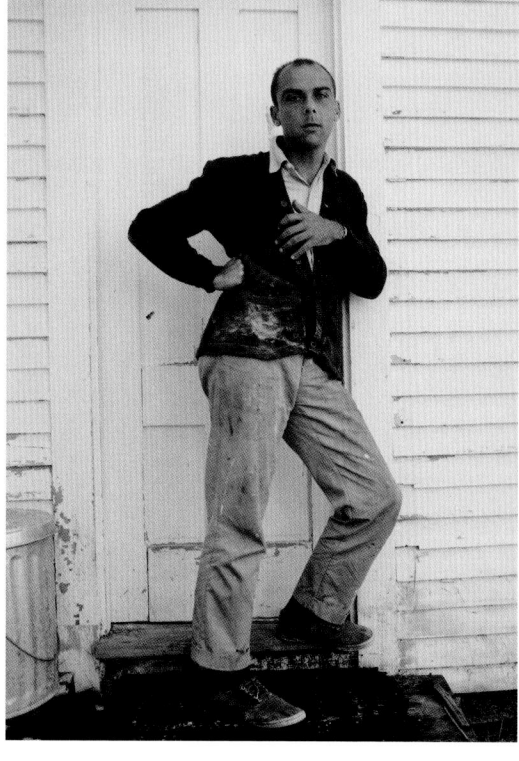

View from the Heliker House (Peter Richardson's boathouse), Cranberry Island, Maine. Photograph by Walker Evans, 1962
Stove, Heliker house, Cranberry Island, Maine. Photograph by Walker Evans, 1967–1968
Robert LaHotan, Cranberry Island, Maine. Photograph by Walker Evans, 1962

As we disembarked, young men grabbed our suitcases. Most people knew each other and helped with luggage and groceries. We seemed to be the only strangers here.

As soon as we stepped on the porch of the house, Verna showed us to our room, which was brown and hot and had twin beds covered with chenille bedspreads. No attempt had been made to bring a touch of color or charm to any of the rooms in the house. The dark wooden walls were just one board thick, and one could hear everything inside. Voices drifted in from the neighbors' porches through open windows and screen doors. This was a camp for grownups, rustic summer living among friends and families who had been coming here for generations and who didn't need privacy. Verna mentioned the evening's entertainment at the Jessups' place: drinks and pot-luck supper followed by a reading of *A Midsummer Night's Dream* with all the children, and jazz later on.

Walker asked for a glass of iced tea and decided to take a nap. Pot-luck suppers always worried him; casseroles and salads seldom agreed with his stomach.

I took my book to the porch and watched some good-looking blond teenagers returning from tennis, swinging their rackets. The way they talked and joked, secure in their place from childhood on, made me feel inadequate and a little jealous. Our family had moved so many times and lived in so many different cities. As summer hotel children we did not belong to the same clique year after year.

Walker reappeared when he heard Wilder's exuberant voice. The three of us greeted each other on the porch, and Wilder put his arms around us, delighted to see us together on the island. Like so many friends he had worried about Walker living alone. Walker dropped all his guises and became sympathetic and thoughtful. I watched this transformation with great relief. He was capable of showing his emotions after all.

Verna brought out the ice and poured us some white wine, and the party was on its way, moving us along, as though we were on an adventurous journey. Drinking and talking, we welcomed the evening breeze coming off the water until it was time to gather our sweaters and casserole dish and walk over to the Jessups'.

The Jessups' porch was as crowded as a tour boat on the Fourth of July headed for the fireworks. Children outnumbered adults. The porch rocked and shook with the young ones' excitement over the play. Eunice Jessup, surrounded by her five children and all the others, handed out copies of *A Midsummer Night's Dream* with each assigned role underlined in a different color. She knew every child's name. "Oh, can Mary and I be fairies?" begged a little light-haired girl, holding the hand of a five-year-old. "We could share." Eunice nodded and carefully chose the readers for the major parts. When everyone finally sat down, a few notes of Purcell's trumpets played on the gramophone called the group to attention, and Jack Jessup began the play as Theseus. Verna was Hippolyta and read in her lovely BBC English, which didn't sound at all affected. She enunciated every word, every consonant, as clearly as the actors in the Royal Shakespeare Company. Boys whose voices had just changed and sounded like cracked cellos hammed it up as Quince, Snug, Bottom, Flute, Snout, and Starveling; their younger siblings held their hands over their mouths to keep from laughing out loud.

Walker made a hilarious Puck, having wrapped a tangle of a creeping vine around his head. The children listened, their eyes filled with curiosity and wonder: Who was this funny man who seemed to know their moms and dads? By the time Oberon and Titania made their entrance, the little girls, who were waiting for Eunice to give them their cue for the fairies' lullaby, could hardly sit still.

Before long, children and parents began tiptoeing into the house to get a bite to eat and refill their glasses while others read. They had to pass Eunice, who stood by the record player and put on parts of the Mendelssohn whenever she thought it appropriate.

The familiar clinking of ice cubes and an occasional roar from the tennis party hosted by the college set near the courts were the only other Saturday night noises on the island. Dusk had softened the color of the water, and the first stars appeared in an indigo sky. Would the moon rise over the ocean at the end of the Dream? I hoped so.

Loud clapping and cheers followed the last lines of the play, and the children jumped up from their perches on the steps and the railing and ran around outside in the dark. Mothers tried to catch them and urged them to go home. More neighbors arrived and joined the men, who stood in a corner discussing what instruments they would play later that night. The Hennessy Five Star Jazz Band, founded on the island in 1921, was going to close the evening after the children were put to bed.

I went to look for Walker and found him in the living room with Jack and Wilder. He looked pleased, though tired and cold, and said he would listen to the music right here in this comfortable chair. Friends came in to chat and compliment him on his Puck and brought their older sons and daughters to meet him. Would I make him a cup of tea and bring some crackers?

Later, out on the porch, I discovered the first moonlight on the rocky shore. It was silvery pale. I remembered from last year in Maine that the late August moon was a warm yellow, or was it the harvest moon that hung like an orange paper lantern in the sky?

Chairs were being re-arranged to make room for the musicians, and the old upright was pushed close to the screen door. Verna came back with her tuba and poured herself another drink. The moon was over the water now, nearly full.

"Muskrat Ramble" jolted me out of my seat, it was played with such vigor in a racy tempo. Jack was at the drums. All eyes were on Verna, who squeezed out the deepest notes on her tuba. Her face was red and contorted, and when she was through playing she received a round of applause and her triumphant smile lit up the whole porch.

This was the music Walker and I loved. I wanted to dance but knew that Walker wouldn't be up to it. "St. Louis Blues" was next, and some couples got up, held each other close, and moved slowly in place. Wilder's trombone solo made me homesick for my friends in Zurich, who used to hold jam sessions just like tonight, their girls and wives swinging with the beat, ready to dance. We'd dance all night barefoot on the grass, our eyes closed, until we nearly dropped, hungry, in love, and exhausted.

Walker slept poorly that night. Before the sun was up, I heard him move about in Verna's kitchen. He turned the water on to make tea and left it running for a while. When he came back to the room he fumbled and switched the lights on.

Half awake I turned to him, "You all right?"

"I'm worried about Wilder." He sat down on the edge of my bed near me. Wilder hadn't been well for some time, he said. There was something the matter with his innards. All these martinis and late nights couldn't be good for his health, but his friends were most important to him.

"And his family?" I had met Eliza and Archie, his children.

Of course he loved Verna and the children—he had them late, and they needed to be educated. The *Newsweek* job was not worthy of him, just a hack job. And Verna worked all the time too. Did I know she was Oppenheimer's secretary?

"You mean the Oppenheimer who invented the atom bomb?"

"Yes, yes. He's very reclusive, but he trusts Verna. She's extremely discreet." Walker said she was much more than an ordinary secretary. Oppenheimer depended on her; even Saturdays she would go over to his house when he called.

Walker shifted position and lit a cigarette. He went on to describe Wilder's music library in his Princeton house. It took up one whole wall. The records were filed meticulously in special holders. He could put his hand on the record he intended to play for friends and point out all the subtleties. The talk and the music held everyone's attention and nobody went to bed. He would pour another round of nightcaps and then make them listen to different versions of the same piece performed by his favorite soloists and conductors. He had written a book on jazz and knew its history. Often he went to a black church because of the music and the beautiful voices. "Such talent," said Walker. "A perfect ear. And he writes very well. We like the same books."

Sunlight came through a crack above the window shade. I could have listened to Walker talk for hours. He had treated me like a friend and confidante. I felt equal and important. Once we were married, I hoped, these moments might occur more often.

Chapter 12

Just before we crosssed the small bridge to Mount Desert Island the late afternoon light on the purple mountains became intense and made them glow. They seemed to float above the dark blue water as if lit from within. Uninhabited islands appeared in the distance, some shaped like lozenges, bare and low, others wooded and round, resembling furry hats. When I first discovered this landscape and its surreal light I would go back to the same places every day and wait for this hypnotic moment before sunset; it was an addiction. Now, a year later, I was back with Walker. I wanted him to like it as much as I did, though I knew he wouldn't photograph in such a place. The low sun on the pink granite along Somes Sound, and opposite, in the shade, the high black cliff rising from the water like a giant wall were too much drama for him.

He stopped the car at a lookout and smiled while we watched a schooner sailing up the sound. "Boats always move me," he said, watching the vessel in silence until it was nearly out of sight.

I mentioned my parents' love of boats and the ocean, and that many of us had some of Robinson Crusoe's spirit in us. Sailing gave us the illusion of total freedom and adventure.

Yes, he agreed there was a romantic quality about boats. Their names alone—but in order to sail well they had to be built right. He liked everything about boats, especially the brass hardware, the fine woodwork…. The same could be found in certain cars and trains, but he hated flying. "I won't fly if I can help it." Again he mourned the disappearance of the grand ocean liners.

We drove up to the Kimball House. Tea was over and blue-haired ladies in pastel knits were gathering their needlepoint bags and novels and leaving the porch to retreat to their rooms before dinner.

"I hope the clientele is more interesting," Walker said. He made a face and nudged me.

His dislike of old ladies, unless he knew them, was so strong that when we walked down Lexington Avenue near Bloomingdale's and found ourselves behind a group of them on their way to a matinée, he would grab my arm and we would cross the street at the next light.

An eager young man in a green apron came out to help with our bags. "Nice Buick, sir. What's the year?"

Walker looked pleased. "1949 touring car." He rubbed his hand over the back of the driver's seat. "Good quality leather. Now it's mostly synthetic."

Our rooms on the second floor suited Walker just fine. Both were airy and summery white, and the small porch had comfortable wicker furniture. Without asking he gave me the larger room and threw his raincoat on the narrow bed in the other. Between the rooms was a large bathroom. I wasn't surprised by Walker's remarks on the two-legged oval wash-basin.

"These curved porcelain legs always remind me of farm girls with their sturdy, rounded calves," he said. "Maybe I'll photograph it."

The cheery busboy carried up our suitcases and Walker's camera bag and asked if there was anything else we might need, like ice or water. Walker pulled out some bills to tip him. The boy's cheeks turned red; he wasn't used to five-dollar tips just for the luggage. On his way out he reminded us that dinner was a tad earlier tonight because of the Thursday evening dances. "The band starts playing around nine. I hope you'll join us, it's fun."

We went down in time to look into the dining room. Every table was reserved. Parents and their teenage and college-age children greeted each other in the front hall and waved to their friends. Girls in bright sleeveless dresses darted back and forth, their gold bangles jingling. The boys stood around in small groups and kept their voices down, until one of them must have told a hilarious story or a favorite joke and their outburst of laughter drowned out all conversations. The dinner gong got everyone moving. I watched the young men walk by us to their seats and wait until it was polite to sit down. Tall and sunburned like their fathers, they wore blazers, light linen pants and Madras ties.

Amused, Walker took in the whole scene as we were shown to our small table near the door. "Ah—*la jeunesse dorée* at play," he said. "How charming." He kept looking around.

The lobster bisque was creamy and laced with good sherry, just the way Walker liked it. He spread butter on his small soft rolls and ate slowly. I felt relieved. The evening had begun well, and with luck he might feel like dancing later on.

While the band was assembling we explored the place and stepped into the dimly lit library. Nobody else was in there. I turned on a table lamp for Walker to have a better look at the books.

"Not a lot worth reading here," he murmured. Suddenly he reached way up for a particular volume. "Can you get it down? I don't want it to fall on the floor."

I moved a side chair, took off my sandals and climbed up on it. Once I handed him the book it received his full attention. His half-glasses were way down on his nose. I waited for him to talk. He raised his eyebrows and whispered something about a real treasure, a first edition of Lytton Strachey's *Eminent Victorians*. He sat down on the tufted sofa and began to read. I leafed through a yachting magazine and *Country Life*. The ads for grooms and butlers and villas in Spain always intrigued me.

The music started, and I was anxious to leave this dreary library, but Walker was in no hurry to join the dancers. Finally he put out his cigarette and brought along the Strachey book. Arm in arm we strolled in the direction of the music and sat down as far away from the band as possible. A few grandmothers sipped their crème de menthe in a corner near us, watching the young.

There were no older couples on the dance floor. It was a swingy band with good rhythm. The floor seemed to undulate with the fast-moving crowd. How I wished I were among them. My feet were tapping under the table. I asked Walker to dance with me, but he didn't feel like butting in on the prep-school set. A while later the waiter arrived with my Cointreau and some hot tea for Walker. It was too noisy to have a real conversation.

The band took a break and the room quickly emptied out. The porch was the place to cool off. Walker got up and I followed him out through the double screen door. A large convertible full of older boys had just arrived. Their friends ran down the porch steps and brought them bottles of beer. Shouts and bear hugs were part of their welcoming ritual. Other cars backed out of their spaces and turned into the road.

Walker complained of being tired. All that driving, the sea air—would I mind if we went upstairs? I could do some reading before going to bed. Lytton Strachey, he half joked, would keep him busy for a while.

I begged to stay longer, secretly hoping that someone might ask me to dance. Just half an hour—please, please—it was still early. Tomorrow I'd do anything for him.

"That's a deal," he said and winked. Slowly we walked past the bar and settled into our corner.

Everyone hurried back to the dance floor when the band played a bang-up "Mack the Knife." The beat was fast, and I couldn't help swinging with the music in my chair. I was startled when a tall blond young man appeared at our table, nodded to Walker and asked me to dance. I turned to Walker to get his approval. He simply waved his hand for me to go ahead, laughing.

The moment I felt the young man's arm around my waist I knew he was a strong leader. He smiled and twirled me around, and pretty soon we were in the center of the floor, doing all the fancy jazz steps without ever bumping into others, our bodies in tune, as though we had always danced together. I let him take me all over the place, following him as he turned and bent, moving faster and faster, no longer looking at him, just knowing instinctively what he intended to do next.

Without a pause the beat slowed way down and a schmaltzy Frank Sinatra song changed the whole mood. Some couples moved closer and danced cheek to cheek, now that their parents had gone home.

The young man introduced himself as we danced. "Thad Warner," he said. "We have a place on the sound. Are you visiting with your father?"

Is that how Walker and I looked to the outside world—like father and daughter? With Walker's friends I no longer had to worry about our age difference, but tonight most mothers would have been shocked if they knew the truth. And fathers? Some might be jealous, others would probably call Walker a dirty old man. It wasn't worth bothering to explain.

I told him my name, and he asked where I came from. New York, I said and didn't mention Switzerland.

Would I like to go with him to watch the races on Saturday? He would arrange for me to go on his father's boat.

I said we were on our way to Cranberry Island to visit friends.

"There's a great beach on Cranberry," he said, drawing me closer. "We might sail over after the race and have a picnic. The Western Way is the best place to watch the sunset."

The song weighed me down. Walker might be jealous if he saw me now, so close to this handsome stranger. I no longer felt like dancing. Thad and his friends lived in a safe and proper world so different from Walker's. I was sure nobody here had ever heard of him or seen his work. But was I ready for Walker's world? It overwhelmed me. At times I wished I could just be myself and rest for a while—be my age and not worry. I was only a few years older than Thad and yet I was living the life of a person twice my age. How would I meet new young friends? I needed them now.

The music stopped and Thad brought me back to our table. Walker was gone. I thanked Thad and said good night. The lady at the desk came over and told me that my dad had gone upstairs about twenty minutes ago. "He looked a little tired," she said, "but he'll get a good rest tonight." She smiled sweetly and went back to her desk.

Chapter 13

John McDonald was waiting for us at the Southwest Harbor town dock. He was sitting in the hot afternoon sun, his face half hidden by *The New York Times*. His pale legs and arms were just like Wilder's, I thought—two intellectuals with white legs who looked funny in Bermuda shorts. During my first summer in Manhattan, when I saw professional men in gray pleated Bermuda shorts with dark knee socks and city shoes on their way to work carrying their attaché cases, I burst out laughing.

John did not see me until I put my arms around him and kissed him on the cheek. "Nice surprise," he said in his quiet voice and returned the kiss. "You found it all right—where's Walk?"

I said he was parking in the place John had mentioned in his note. We went and helped him with the bags.

"I ordered a special boat for us, there's no hurry." John pointed to what looked like a very clean lobster boat tied to the side of the float. Her name was the Malesca. Who was she named after, a special island girl?

We found Walker poking around various large boat sheds across from Beal's lobster pier. "Say," he said, greeting John with outstretched arms, "this is a damn good place. I'd like to come back in the fall and paint." He had already picked up a piece of rusty fishing gear for his collection.

John introduced us to Clarence Beal, our captain. The moment he looked at us and smiled we felt accepted. He piled our luggage onto the engine box. Any moment now, I felt sure, he might tell us a joke, and with luck I'd catch a new funny saying, like "the cat's meow," a favorite expression of mine that Walker had banned forever. Just looking at Clarence was a pleasure. His blue eyes were so much lighter than the water in the distance; Nordic eyes, possibly Viking? And he had a beautiful tan, which made his creased face resemble the Marlboro man's.

We all sat down, and Clarence started the boat and untied the bowline. Every movement made sense: the way he took the lines off the cleats and quickly coiled them and walked back to the stern.

Several fishermen waved to Clarence and yelled their good-humored greetings over the noise of engines and clatter as he steered the Malesca out of the busy harbor. Before long he pointed to an island on the port side. "Greenings Island, they don't have electricity," he said, lowering his voice as though he felt sorry for the place. "Just a bunch of summer folk, no year-rounders. Never been over there." He laughed.

"Do you know who he looks like?" Walker said to John.

"We all know he's good-looking. Who do you have in mind?" A gust of wind came up, and John almost lost his panama hat.

"Leverett Saltonstall," said Walker in a loud voice. "That long horse face, and the gap between the two front teeth—a perfect likeness."

"You're not so far off," said John. "There are some Saltonstalls on the island. You'll meet them."

As long as we were out on the water, my island fantasies and illusions remained intact. Deep in the woods, I imagined, I would discover the narrow paths to abandoned graveyards and walk to the end where the waves crashed into pink rocks, sending sprays of foamy white surf high above the shore. There, alone with the wind and water raging around me, I would dispel my doubts. Walker loved me, I knew that. Why was it so hard for me to believe it? You need to have faith, Maman used to say long ago, but I didn't want to listen.

We docked at Spurling Cove among a clutter of lobster boats, skiffs, and small outboards. On the shore, large boat sheds took up much of the available space, and trucks outnumbered people.

We piled our luggage on a wheelbarrow that John and I pushed. I worried that life on the island was too primitive. What if the well ran dry or the power went out? Walker liked his bath water hot, and I needed to wash my hair. Before I had time to think of more troubles a truck rumbled past us. We jumped out of the way and waited in the tall grass near a tennis court until the smoking, doorless vehicle veered around the curve. Clearly mufflers were not required on Cranberry.

Walker asked John if he still played tennis. John said he had a good time playing doubles with a couple of neighbors and that Christie beat him regularly, but he didn't mind. "I taught her strategy when she was very young; it paid off."

"Wilder plays every day," Walker said. "I've given it up. Golf is a better game for my old bones."

We were higher up now, surrounded by a small cluster of old clapboard houses. A wavy meadow with patches of fireweed sloped down to the water's edge. Dorothy loved to paint in her rickety shed in the meadow, John told us, pointing to the water. All the big schooners sailed through the Western Way, and the color of the water was always changing. On race days the spinnakers flew like balloons above the water—red, yellow, bright blue—as many as thirty.

I asked why the porches of the houses faced the road and not the lovely view. Walker cleared his throat and remarked that the houses dated from the early nineteenth century, when most people whose work was on the water wanted to get away from it. Views and cottages built on the rocks were the summer visitors' preference, the rusticators. He looked amused when he said they imitated the Indians with their camps. "All through New England the oldest houses are always on the road, it was the people's lifeline." Aware that he had just lectured me he squeezed my arm and tried to whisper something in my ear, but he was laughing so hard I couldn't understand it. I loved his childlike laughing fits; my siblings and I called them *"fou rire,"* and they were very contagious.

"This was lesson number one," he said. "Tomorrow we'll talk about the local flora and fauna." I hugged him, and he didn't pull back. John watched us quietly, smiling. Strange, how quickly all my anxieties seemed to vanish, and feelings of pure pleasure filled my mind.

Children's voices and dogs barking were the only sounds around us. The wind had died down, and there were pink clouds in the west.

"Let's go in and find Dot," said John. "We'll get a drink and watch the sunset." He lifted the first bag off the wheelbarrow and we followed him through a narrow, wallpapered hallway to the back of the house.

Even before I got to the kitchen I heard Dorothy's warm crackling voice and her high laughter as she greeted Walker and John. It always surprised me that such a petite woman could fill a whole room and draw everyone in. She kissed me like a favorite daughter and called me honey. Walker, who normally couldn't stand the word used as endearment, smiled at Dorothy and put his hands on her narrow shoulders. "We're both getting smaller," he joked.

So many years of time spent together, of praise for each other's work, loving, and worrying when illness struck had made these three tolerant and accepting of one another's peculiarities and faults. At times, feelings of strong dislike for certain people or political disagreements would flare up between them, but they never lasted long enough to spoil an evening.

We had our first drink in the kitchen. Scotch for Dorothy, half-sweet, half-dry vermouth with a twist for Walker and me. Walker watched in envy as John make his straight-up martini. "Let me smell it," Walker said when John dropped the lemon peel into the frozen glass.

Dorothy cooked and we sat around the kitchen. Walker investigated everything and seemed delighted. The house was one of the oldest on the island. It looked as if the owners who rented it to the McDonalds had left the place with all the things they used every day clean and in good order. Nothing was new. The soapstone sink and the black cast-iron stove must have been a hundred years old. Gray and blue-and-white spatterware enamel pots and baking dishes were neatly stacked on open shelves beside nests of tan mixing bowls. Through the half-opened doors of a painted cupboard Walker spied a set of Depression glass. "Isn't it hideous?" he remarked. "But they already sell it in antique shops around Lyme; twenty-five years is all it takes."

Dorothy had a natural feel for preparing food and seldom used cookbooks. No two dishes were ever the same. I asked if I could help and she let me make the salad. She said she felt at home in this kitchen. In June, the fog had rolled in and didn't lift for a week, so she moved her paints into the kitchen. "I started several paintings of the stove—they'll have to wait until I get back to New York." But the August weather was too good to paint interiors. Walker agreed that the kitchen was the right subject for her paintings. He, too, might give it a try. Cranberry, from the little he had seen, was the place for him.

John said he was writing between games of tennis and hearts with Christie. He hadn't found a poker game yet. After all, it was their first summer here. One couldn't rush things.

Walker genuinely liked Dorothy, I felt, and he considered her a gifted painter, an intelligent reader. He wanted to hear her impressions, though at times she was very outspoken. Women who said what they thought usually got on his nerves. He found them tactless and avoided them—but Dorothy was an exception. He trusted her instincts.

Walker had already told me that logic was not part of Dorothy's being, nor were organizational and practical skills. She couldn't drive a car, read maps, or balance a checkbook, but she often made fun of her own shortcomings. With him, he said, she was apt to laugh over remarks they had heard in passing and silly little things people did. At times they made the same observations, though I thought their interpretations must be very different. Dorothy was unselfconscious and had no trace of snobbery in her.

John moved us to the living room, where he had his second martini. There was a picture window above a table set for dinner. We had just missed the sunset, but the orange and pink sky, reflected in the calm water, made up for it. We stood and watched for a while. Walker commented on how the burnt ochre of the late-summer meadow was unlike the green hills of southern Vermont, where his sister and her boring husband spent their summers. No wonder painters liked Maine, Marsden Hartley and John Marin and—oh, and Calvert mentioned Grace Hartigan, who had rented an old house near him.

"She's a good painter," Dorothy said as she came through the door with a pot of delicious smelling stew. John went to get the roasted potatoes. There was no dinner without potatoes for John and Walker. Rice was a poor substitute, and macaroni was cheating.

Christie raced into the room, her wavy hair tangled from the salt air. "I'm starved," she said, catching her breath. "What's for dinner?"

"Sit here, honey, next to Walker." Dorothy said, and went to get another plate. Christie kissed each of us three times on the cheeks: right, left, and right again. "French style," she said and gave us a flirtatious smile. Walker addressed her in French, but Dorothy interrupted him and told her to speak French with me. We launched into a three-way conversation about Paris, Marcel Proust, and André Gide. Walker led our merry performance in his impeccable Parisian accent. We chattered on, knowing full well that neither John nor Dorothy knew the language, though John read Sartre and Jean Genet, and Dorothy was rereading Proust.

Christie's charm and eagerness to communicate with her parents' friends provoked all kinds of thoughts in my mind. Given more time she might become my friend, a younger American sister. At seventeen, she had an impressive knowledge of French civilization, and in her humor and feminine gestures I detected a broader curiosity for all things life had to offer. Her future was ahead, and she would not bury herself under books. John, who loved music and played the piano, had praised her clear singing voice and said many times that nobody danced the Charleston like Christie.

John asked about the Kimball House, how the food was and the people. Would it be a nice place to take his ladies out for an evening? They had not been to Northeast Harbor. I described the dance, the beautiful girls in their flowered dresses, the tall handsome boys, and their chaperoning parents who arrived in shiny convertibles. Dorothy wanted to know who these elegant people were and where they came from.

"Mostly Philadelphia blueblood," said Walker. "I didn't know a soul. Darling, do tell them about the library." Yes, the gloomy stuffy library and Walker's find: Lytton Strachey's *Eminent Victorians*, a first edition. "I shall produce it after dinner," Walker said. "I took it. They'll never miss it." His voice sounded triumphant.

Christie didn't laugh. Like me, she waited, unsure of what to make of this. Dorothy and John didn't act surprised. They asked to see the book, and nothing more was said about the Kimball House.

My small room was to the right of the front door, and Walker was across the hall. Dorothy apologized for not putting us together, but these were the only extra rooms in the house. She had left the window open and there were no screens; I should undress in the dark so as not to attract mosquitoes. The room was just for sleeping. She handed me a flashlight. The bathroom was on the second floor. I thanked her and we kissed good night.

Walker had retired earlier and his door was closed. I was still upset over his theft of the book and felt no desire to see him. What was I to do if I couldn't read in bed? I would have to think myself to sleep, and I wanted to put the book incident behind me, forget it. It showed me once again how little I knew him.

It had been a flawless summer day—the boat trip to the island, the view of the meadow in the evening light, a long evening with the McDonalds—but Walker's arrogance had broken the flow of my happiness.

And yet I wanted to be fair to Walker. The McDonalds were a gift from him. I had not realized how much I missed being with a family. Here I was with a mother who painted, a father who wrote, like my father, and their gifted daughter. They welcomed me for who I was. I finally calmed down as I lay in my narrow bed, so different from my bed at the Barbizon. The cool night air blew on my face. I looked out at the stars.

A thump and a crash woke me from the deepest sleep. A heavy lump had landed at the foot of my bed and scared me half to death. I heard a long cry, then short moans, like a creature in pain. Slowly the creature moved toward me. I touched the furry ball and recognized Tippet, the McDonalds' pure white angora cat. I got out of bed and turned on the hallway light. There was blood behind Tippet's ear, and drops of blood on the floor. From a room above John called Tippet, who flew up the stairs.

John appeared at the landing, holding Tippet. "Probably a wild mink," he said. "He's quite a fighter." Tippet loved to stay out at night and roam, a dangerous habit for a New York apartment cat. "I'll clean the wound and he'll be all right. Sorry he scared you."

Wild mink—I had never seen a wild mink. The island had many animals. I opened the window, which had come crashing down after Tippet jumped through it, and looked at the night sky. The Milky Way stretched as far as I could see. There was light on the water. A falling star—then another—quick, make a wish, and don't tell or it won't come true!

The next day John took us on a tour of the island. Walker was particularly interested in the life of the natives. The fishermen's houses, where piles of stacked wood and lobster traps crowded the messy yards, and further up the road the homely white church and modest school convinced us that little had changed here since the turn of the century. Some families still used outhouses and hand-pumped water from dug wells.

"What money they have goes into their boats," said John. "The summer people's taxes help pay for the school, and the Ladies' Aid is in charge of the church."

"Yes, but they all seem well fed, not like the Depression," said Walker. He aimed his camera at a sign for fresh crab meat on the side of the road. The uneven lettering and a small red hand pointing to a shed door reminded me of his earlier sign pictures. If he saw something he wanted to photograph, he would sometimes just take a quick picture and return at a better time. He touched the sign to test its stability, gave it a little shake, and laughed, but didn't photograph it. After Labor Day, John might be able to buy the sign, he suggested, and bring it home to him.

John paid no attention to Walker's request. He looked at his watch and said we should go to the post office. The mail boat must have come in by now, and we would see everybody there. He loved going for the mail. It was the social time of the day. The talk alone made it worthwhile—and now that the summer was almost over, he understood the jokes.

Every island vehicle passed us as we made our way to the little post office on the dock. Walker commented that these patched and hand-built cars were a form of folk art, highly original, especially when they had some kind of writing on them. He was interested in how young people expressed themselves with things they found in junk shops. And he was interested in looking at trash. Half joking, he asked John if he thought *Fortune* might accept one of his portfolios on the cars of Cranberry Island.

John was doubtful but understood what Walker meant. "Not bad—a sixties kind of folk art," John said, mostly to himself. He was allergic to the sun and always kept his head covered, but his hat didn't cover his amusement.

Walker pressed his face against the lace-curtained windows of an uninhabited house near the road. The horsehair-covered parlor furniture and a framed oval photograph of a young child, the only picture in the murky room, stimulated his imagination, and he developed a burning wish to get inside some of these island houses.

Quite a crowd had gathered outside the post office. People greeted one another and chatted, their newspapers and bundles of mail wedged under one arm. Some men looked as if they had just gotten up, unshaven and rumpled. Nobody wore resort or yachting clothes.

Clarence waved at us, and John introduced us to Wilfred Bunker and his older brother Tud. Wilfred and Clarence owned the Beal & Bunker ferry business and had the U.S. Mail contract. Tud was the Saltonstalls' boatman. It was easy to distinguish the boatmen from the fishermen. The boatmen had short haircuts under their tan duck caps with the black visors. Belted khaki pants and white shirts gave them a neat appearance, almost like a uniform. The fishermen were a more

Chapter 13

independent lot. John pointed out a couple who had been hauling traps early that morning. Their knee-high rubber boots and gloves seemed clumsy in the noonday heat.

We hung around and listened to the men talk. Grunts and laughs were interspersed with one-syllable words, until Walker heard the word diff-view-culty. He roared with laughter. "Yup, we all know about diff-view-culties, ha, ha, ha." From time to time the voices grew louder, drawing our rapt attention. We caught a sentence about a "fella" who had been "rode hard and put away wet." Walker promised to explain it to me later.

Lunch was a crab roll from the Porthole, the local take-out at the end of the dock. When Walker smelled the ocean he developed an insatiable appetite for lobster and crabmeat. Directly ahead was Sutton Island, which was sparsely populated. There was a path going around it, but according to John it was rumored that Sutton Island people didn't welcome day trippers, so nobody on Cranberry went.

Mount Desert Island was visible across the water. The mountains rose high above the ocean. I imagined how surprised the early settlers must have been when they first spotted it. I borrowed Walker's binoculars for a better look at the inlets and headlands along the coast. Boats of all sizes moved in and out of my focus. I longed to sail and anchor in some of these deep and silent coves.

Dorothy was scrubbing the paint off her hands in the old sink when we returned. We were in for a treat tonight, she said. Dorothy's friends, the painters John Heliker and Robert LaHotan, had invited us all for dinner. I had met them briefly in New York, in Dorothy's studio on Cornelia Street where I sat for her during one of her drawing sessions. They lived in the same walk-up. Walker didn't know them, though Dorothy often talked about them. Bob and Jack knew that Dorothy would be inspired to paint here, and had introduced the McDonalds to Cranberry a few years earlier. For less than ten thousand dollars, Bob and Jack bought a large property on the Pool, the island's only tidal estuary.

"Jack just called," Dorothy announced. "He suggested we get there early, so we could catch the best light." Snooks, who drove the island taxi, would come for us at six.

When we stepped out of the house that evening, Snooks was leaning against her car, smoking. Slim and long-legged, with a short bob, she had an air of worldliness in contrast to the stout, heavy-ankled ladies I had seen during the day. Walker winked at her and held up his cigarette. "You won't mind if I smoke in the car?" he asked playfully. "That'll make two of us, go right ahead," she said. Her voice was deep and gravelly, and she treated us more like chums than customers. She asked me where I was from. She couldn't place my accent. Swedish? I told her I was Swiss. "I was in Germany during the war," she told us, "driving army vehicles, but I never made it to your country. I hear it's beautiful."

"I like the ocean," I said. "Cranberry is beautiful."

"You should be here in the winter—the storms we have," she said, coughing and clearing her throat. "Waves as high as the dome in Cologne. And some lonely!"

I loved to hear her talk, the broad a's and the extended o's. She said Bob was "a goood cook" and he was "flying around the kitchen like a faaart in a skillet," and all four of us roared with laughter.

"Just call when you need to ride back, don't worry if it's late...and have one on me," she said with a wave and drove off.

Bob and Jack's place was at the end of an unpaved road on the shore of the Pool, with views of Fish Point and far beyond. The tide was going out, and round rocks of every color were emerging from the shallows. The soft light on the shimmering water, the rocks and seaweed, and the green orchard dissolved into an impressionist landscape. We were surprised at the different shores in the sheltered cove. Gone were the dramatic coast, jagged rocks, and mountains. This was an intimate, hidden place, a "real discovery," as Walker was fond of saying.

"This is the best time of day to be here," said Dorothy, "or early in the morning."

Jack came out to greet us, and John introduced Walker. The two men shook hands and Walker thanked him for his kind invitation. "Don't mention it," said Jack. His voice sounded like a lovely tenor. "It's my pleasure." Dorothy was already inside, avoiding the mosquitoes and talking to Bob. We took a short walk to the wharf through the lush grass; in other parts of the island the grass had already turned brown. We climbed onto an old dock with a huge boat shed where Bob had jerry-rigged his studio. A smaller structure, which Jack called the fish house, stood at the end of the dock, like an ornament. To the right, farther along the beach, stood a small boat house owned by a native. Both buildings were perfectly proportioned, strong and beautifully detailed, rare examples of indigenous maritime architecture. Walker was enchanted. He wanted to come back another year when he had more time and do some work. Jack was delighted and invited Walker and me to stay with them anytime. "You haven't seen the house yet," said Jack on the way back. "It belonged to Captain Lew Stanley. Nobody lived in it for years after he died." He and Bob were still finding old parts of boats in the barn, fence posts with acorn tops, the same ones that went around graveyards, some books and tintypes, all kinds of stuff. Much history and endless stories went with the house.

Jack led the way through the kitchen and spoke lovingly to a cat sitting against the door. Dorothy, her drink in one hand and a cigarette in the other, continued her conversation with Bob. Delicious smells escaped from several pots on the stove, and the dark chocolate cake on the counter looked as perfect as if it had come from the best patisserie in New York.

I stayed in the kitchen with Dorothy and Bob. She laughed at his gossipy tales about the islanders. He talked fast, in a low voice, with great intensity, moving back and forth between the stove and his drink on the table. I thought him exotic and curious. He was interested in everything I liked and was easy to talk to. Dark and foreign-looking with huge green eyes, he had the charm of a performer.

Bob and Dorothy urged me to explore the whole house. Bob and Jack worked on the place for the first three weeks of each summer, painting floors and walls, putting up shelves, and planting the garden.

On my solitary ramble through the house I began to appreciate their taste more and more. It was unfussy, even on the sparse side, but the colors were lovely and every object was chosen for its unusual history, shape, patina, or color. There were pale sea-green bottles, stoneware jugs, compotes and bowls. Some cutaway models of boats built in their wharf evoked the times when Cranberry was a thriving community. Several odd pieces of furniture had come with the house: a rare Masonic bed, an ingenious nineteenth-century folding bed specially made for use on boats, and other artifacts like fans, boxes, and old photographs. Finely stitched quilts bought at the annual Cranberry Fair covered the beds. The house was a maze of rooms:

bedrooms upstairs, a guest apartment with its own staircase above the kitchen, a dining room, and a small yellow library where Jack kept a low fire burning. Nothing was overdone. Thriving plants, field flowers, and flowers from the garden were on every table. I looked in on John, Walker, and Jack as they sat in the library, talking and looking at books through a cloud of smoke.

In the dining room, I came upon a tall, fancy, cylindrical black parlor stove with a helmet-shaped top. A curlicued urn decorated the very top like a plume. It dominated one wall with its Victorian presence. Wait 'til Walker sees this, I thought.

Soon we all sat down to dinner. Walker was animated and hungry. He complimented Bob on the tasty food. The two had barely exchanged a few words when he discovered the stove. "I can't believe my luck," he said. "This alone is worth a trip—a rare beauty, what a find." He lifted his wine glass and toasted Bob and Jack. "Here's to both of you, and to John and Dot for bringing us here."

Jack agreed to take us to a native's house a couple of days later. He and Bob picked us up after lunch. Walker was napping on a daybed in the living room. I was reading *God's Pocket* by Rachel Field, an out-of-print book about the adventures of a Cranberry Islander who had kept a diary in the nineteenth century. His ingenuity and practical skills astounded me: he not only built his own house, the biggest on the island, but also a ship that was seaworthy enough to sail to Europe.

Bob and Jack waved from their car, and I smiled back. They were pleased to see my reaction to their car, one of the earliest models of Volkswagen Beetles sold after the war, a convertible model with the top down.

Walker emerged with a Leica around his neck, and a cigarette cupped in his hand. We squeezed into the Beetle. Bob drove and Jack pointed to various houses and told us about the best and most handsome fisherman who lived in the tiniest house with many children, and how he delivered fresh fish several days a week and always told them a new joke. But right now Addie Duren was expecting us. Jack said she wanted to show her photographs to Walker. Addie, an older spinster, had been born in her house and had never lived anywhere else.

The small clapboard house was set back from the road. With its steep roof, bay window, and good-sized detached barn, it resembled countless rural dwellings in Maine. We walked up over the rough grass, past the pump, and knocked on the kitchen door.

"Come in, come in," Addie said in her high, friendly voice. The spry little woman opened the screen door and welcomed us in. She directed us to the living room and fetched us iced tea and cookies. Such a hot day, but wasn't it nice to have sunny weather.

The windows were closed and the only light, cool touches in the stuffy room were the starched ruffled curtains and numerous white crocheted antimacassars that lay like fresh patches of snow on the arms and backs of the overstuffed chairs and the couch. Every possible piece of bric-a-brac crowded the tables and windowsills. I prayed for a breath of air from the kitchen.

Addie, cheerful in her clean apron, looked sternly at Walker and said, "You can take pictures of anything you like, but you can't take my picture." She rummaged around in a cabinet and returned with an armful of albums.

Jack had told us in the car that Addie had documented with a little box camera every major event on Cranberry over many years. He opened the first album: page after page of black-and-white and sepia photographs of waves and crashing surf after hurricanes, the winter when the water froze over all the way to the mainland, children skating, weddings, christenings and funerals, firemen's suppers, boat launchings.

Walker skipped the big waves and extraordinary natural occurrences, but examined every photograph with people in it, determined to find out more about their lives. Groups of darkly clothed men and women stood in the bright sunlight staring at the camera, their hats pushed down on their heads. There was hardly a smile, and nobody struck a pose. Young women held up infants in long christening dresses. A bride peered out between her groom and her father, middle-aged couples, husbands stiffly standing behind their seated wives—all their faces were serious and their expressions impassive. Having one's picture taken at a wedding was an event; one stood at attention.

Addie had carefully written descriptions under each picture. The early ones often showed activities in the Pool. Jack mentioned that until the war it was the major place of industry on the island. "Large sailing vessels were built in my big shed," he said, "it was protected from strong winds and surf." Barges loaded with coal and provisions sailed in before the winter months so the islanders could fill their bins. In the summer boatmen from Northeast Harbor and Seal Harbor motored over in polished mahogany launches full of family members and guests who enjoyed tea and popovers at the Hamors' teahouse. The Pool was a place where children could safely play in the water and sail pond boats made by their fathers.

"Jolly good, jolly good," said Walker. "Now I know a lot more about Cranberry." He turned to Jack and mumbled how grateful he was for this visit. Did he think it was rude to leave now? He wanted a cigarette. Jack thought we could go soon. Bob followed Addie into the kitchen and told her what a good baker she was.

On the way out Walker stopped in the doorway and peered through his Leica. Addie beamed when he took several shots of her stove—and then, like lightning, he snapped a picture of her without her noticing.

Our last island days passed too quickly. It was time to go back to Lyme. We were packing our bags, and though there was no outward sign it felt like the end of summer.

I was apprehensive about the coming weeks: my divorce in Mexico, traveling alone since Walker was afraid of flying; finding an affordable apartment in the city and moving Walker out of York Avenue. The soot-covered piles of paper, boxes filled with his collections, and a whole basement full of stuff I had not seen were enough to make anyone anxious. He often spoke of his mother's charming rosewood sofa in the basement, but every time I asked to go down there and have a look he'd say, "Oh, not today, I'm too tired."

Often, when I was alone, I wondered what my new life as Walker's wife would be like, how it might develop. Was there going to be love, sex, and give-and-take? All summer I felt like something between a daughter and a companion, and yet the new friends and what I thought of as the champagne moments far outweighed the occasional loneliness and disappointment. Most of Walker's close friends must have viewed our marriage as a risky adventure, but I did not see it in that light. I didn't know myself very well.

At night, just before sleep took over, the same image kept recurring: I was balancing on a high wire between two skyscrapers, smiling, doing well, approaching the halfway point. And then I got the jitters. A crowd was watching from below. There was only one way to go and that was forward, as fast as possible. I couldn't possibly turn back in front of all these people. They'd think I was a failure. My father and the whole world looked down on failures, and I wanted desperately to succeed. Here was my chance—I could shine with Walker and help him become more famous. I must ignore my desire to crawl into a warm place, far away from people, and shut out the world.

Chapter 14

How quickly everything changed.

We were married at the end of October and moved a couple of weeks later. Our new apartment was in a row of brownstones on East Ninety-fourth Street, between Lexington and Third. I had good reasons to feel optimistic. *Let Us Now Praise Famous Men* was in bookstores again at last and was receiving the attention it deserved. Some stores designed a whole window for the book. Younger writers and photographers became interested in Walker's work and wanted to meet him. Houghton Mifflin gave a book party in a private room of the New Weston Hotel, where I was introduced to John Dos Passos. The telephone kept ringing, and Walker went to celebratory lunches at the Century with publishers, important editors, and *New Yorker* writers. He was riding high, to use his own words.

The Kennedys were in the White House, and this too pointed to a cultural renaissance. At parties all our friends talked about who among their acquaintances would be nominated for the top jobs in Kennedy's administration, and who was lucky enough to have been invited to the Inaugural Ball. There was much speculation and gossip and, once again, I read every word in German, French, and British magazines, hoping to find yet another piece of news about Jackie. Her wardrobe was of great interest to me. Who would she choose among the best American designers, now that she could no longer wear French and Italian clothes to official dinners?

When I wasn't out with Walker in his many worlds, I was fixing up the apartment and decorating. Our top floor apartment had high ceilings, tall windows, and in the living room a black marble fireplace. Walker arranged his library in the bookcases on either side of it and hung the paintings. A portrait of him by Ben Shahn, painted in 1930 when they shared a house in Truro, was given the place of honor. Walker's tiny study and our bedroom overlooked the gardens of Ninety-fourth and Ninety-fifth Streets, a large open space lovingly planted by each house owner with a variety of trees and shrubs. Vita and Peter Petersen, Walker's friends and our landlords, were particularly proud of their Ginkgo biloba, a Chinese tree with fan-shaped leaves.

Walker seldom left the house before eleven o'clock. Slowly, endless cups of tea and buttered English muffins gave him enough strength to get up and plan his day. He'd read the papers, telephone, lie down again with a book, snooze and take his pills. I was on call, but asked not to disturb him since he was thinking. For me these mornings were long and wasted. I could hardly wait to turn the radio on and do some work. It was the first time in my adult life that I did not have a job.

Once he was gone I got out my sewing machine and set it up on the dropleaf table in a corner of the living room, where we ate. I would listen to jazz and cut out pieces of fabric on the floor for sofa pillows and tablecloths. My bureau drawers were filled with fabric from outdoor markets on Orchard Street and Delancey Street. As I basted and sewed, the past few weeks unwound in my mind like a film reel played at high speed.

The flight to El Paso, over vast stretches of land I had not seen before, arrived at night; a warm air blew in my face as I got off the plane. Where was the land? A narrow strip at the end of the runway. I seemed to be floating in the big sky, silky dark blue and sprinkled with stars. A taxi pulled up. I was annoyed at the driver, who asked me if I was down there for a "quickie."

In the morning, before breakfast, I made sure to remember the five hundred dollars and my Swiss passport. The sun was already hot when I stepped outside in my silk linen Chanel suit. An oversized black limo was waiting for me in front of the hotel. Gangster car, I thought, out on a creepy errand. So far everything was on schedule, as Grenny Emmet had assured me it would be. In Juarèz, the courthouse was the largest edifice in the town square, aside from the church. Stray dogs lay in the shade, and chickens scurried aimlessly under the burning sun. Everyone stared as I got out of the limo. People took one look at my Jackie Kennedy sunglasses and thought: here comes a movie star. Inside the courthouse it was cooler. I heard my steps echo on the tile floor through the vaulted hall. Nobody was around to help me find the right place. Finally, in a wide open, square room I saw a uniformed official sitting in an armchair behind a huge desk. He wore a toothbrush mustache and a revolver in his belt. The only English word he knew was OK. *Si, si, señora,* OK? He pretended to read Grenny's legal document and then looked up and asked the inevitable question: "Dollars?" He smiled and his mustache doubled in size when I handed over the cash. With gestures fit for an orchestra conductor he stamped the document in several places and put a red government seal under a fancy signature, until it resembled a Steinberg drawing. Producing a second sugary smile, he gave it back to me—and my divorce was official. Nothing but a farce, I thought, a scene from an operetta: the gay divorcée, a flirtatious soprano, and the suave captain in a white, full-dress uniform, singing their hearts out in a passionate duet.

It was unbearably hot when I came out of the courthouse. The noon bells rang: first the courthouse bell, then the higher-sounding ones in the church. The silent limo driver was ready, and I rode out to the airport in cool comfort, clutching my divorce paper.

It shouldn't be so easy, I said to myself, thinking of Alec and wondering how he was doing. But Grenny was a good lawyer, and he wanted to help Walker and me. He wouldn't do anything to jeopardize my future.

Using my hands to stitch all these thoughts into a tablecloth was better for my nerves than one of Walker's Valiums. The tablecloth could be finished by late afternoon. I'd have time to walk down Lexington Avenue to the good fish market and buy Dover sole for dinner.

Walker called to tell me that he'd pick up the prints from our honeymoon on his way home and had ordered a full set for my family. I had left our wedding plans entirely to Walker and asked him to surprise me. He thought of everything and put himself in the background. No church—Grenny said the necessary words, and Tappy and Mott stood by. Their living room was full of flowers, the last roses from the garden. A pale sun lit up the whole room. Walker and I stood in front of the fireplace, he in his soft gray Shetland suit and pink shirt, so fine and quiet. I could tell he was moved—he let me hold his hand. We all embraced, drank the Moët, and ate Tappy's creamy quiche. The drive to New London was easy, and Walker had reserved a roomette on the train to Boston.

I folded the tablecloth to see if all sides were even. The hems were done. The four mitered corners were all I had left to sew, by hand, but they needed to be pressed first. The ironing board and my professional steam iron transformed the living room into an atelier.

(There was no space in the bedroom, with the armoire and the new double bed.)

In Boston, Walker had hired a car and driver for two days and showed me around the city, including Cambridge and Harvard. Every time we got out of the car to look at a house on Louisburg Square or on Brattle Street, the soft-spoken driver stepped out too, brushed the ashes off Walker's navy overcoat, and stood by the car until we returned. He treated Walker like an English lord. "Thank God he isn't telling all the familiar Boston jokes about Mayor Curley and the lady who was found dead in the elevator of her Beacon Hill house," he said, as the driver let us out in front of our hotel before it got dark. Walker tipped him well.

Walker was disappointed that the Ritz had been fully booked and we were forced to make do with the Copley Plaza. After one drink in the Merry-Go-Round Bar he took a dislike to the hotel, though we spent the greater part of our mornings in the room. With the exception of breakfast we ate most of our meals at the Ritz.

He documented our honeymoon well. He photographed me at the breakfast table with a dozen roses. One of my presents from him was a white nightgown and matching peignoir. In the New London train station he took a picture of me in hat and coat, teased me and said I was in my going-away clothes. Sorry, he couldn't resurrect the Liberté for me. We laughed. He showed me how to take a picture of him. I sat in the designated chair, and he made sure the light was right, and I was in focus. He handed me his camera and we quickly switched places.

We did not make love on our honeymoon. Walker had a cold. Towards the end of the long weekend I was in a melancholy mood, and nothing we did dispelled my sadness. It was as if a black shadow had covered the sun. I asked myself if I should tell him how I felt, but he had been so thoughtful and ordered flowers and champagne for me in the room. The books and Spode teacups he gave me were generous presents. It would only upset him if I brought it up. I had waited so long that a few more days, even weeks, didn't matter. Besides, how many times had I heard stories about awkward sex on honeymoons? But he sensed something was wrong, and on the last day, before our lunch at the Ritz, he took my arm, walked me around the Public Garden, and spent time telling me about each statue—the Ether Monument and the fountains. The leaves were on the ground, and he said how much he loved city parks in the late fall and winter. Paris was in his blood. Maybe next year we could travel to Europe.

Christmas was approaching and I had no money left. Walker and I had not yet discussed our household budget and my allowance. After dinner, I thought, when he lit the fire and we talked, would be the best moment to tackle this delicate subject. One evening I came prepared with a sheet of paper and what I thought were reasonable figures. Since he took care of the wine and liquor bills, and Irmgard, our German cleaning lady, as well as his shirts and dry cleaning and the drugstore, my job was to estimate how much money we needed for food and paper goods, and lightbulbs and such from the hardware store on Third Avenue.

My personal list was quite long. One of the few things I had in common with my mother was frequent visits to the hairdresser, at least once a week. Walker looked at my list with amusement. The fourth largest item, after shoes, stockings, and underwear, all pieces of clothing I wasn't able to make myself, was presents. "Presents for whom?" he asked. "I hope they're for me." I promised they would be mostly for him, but my family and friends in Switzerland loved American books, fashions, and toys, and they too deserved presents. Christmas was full of rituals and traditions in our family; and some day we would travel to Bern and celebrate with them.

As I had guessed, there was no hope of getting any information out of Walker about how much money we could spend a month and what we should save. He dismissed my attempt to make some kind of budget for us, and by the tone of his voice I realized that if I expected any allowance at all I'd better stop this conversation right now. I hadn't previously seen this side of him. He seemed threatened, almost hostile. The money was his, he had worked hard all these years, he said, underpaid and unappreciated. Unless he had a windfall, I should not count on very much. My answer was that I'd be pleased to get a part-time job, nothing could be easier, and earn all the money I might spend on myself. In future months I would want to visit my family, and these trips were an added but necessary expense.

No, he wanted to try it without my taking a job this winter, and in the summer we'd be in Lyme, where life was cheaper and nobody needed clothes. He would give me two hundred dollars a month for the house and put fifty in the Oxford dictionary, under *Money*, for my allowance, and that was that.

Well, at least I knew where I stood, and this winter I could count on my father to send me a Christmas check. I channeled my unexpressed frustrations into new sewing and craft projects, making presents like silk scarves, lingerie travel bags, and Christmas tree ornaments. The only presents I would need to buy were for Walker, my father, and my brother.

I got used to Walker getting up at night, smoking, making tea and taking it back to his study. Calvert had built him a sturdy bunk with a cushioned cover. It was as well built as if it were on a luxury liner. He kept his camera equipment in it, and every time he lifted the cover, the brass piano hinge sparkled. He often spent the rest of the night on this bunk. After the money episode, for a few nights I slept alone in our double bed, but he always kissed me good night and tucked me in like a child.

I was homesick for the first time since I had left Switzerland. Old and new feelings about Christmas, being alone in the apartment for hours, not working, not seeing my friends, drained my energy. I was not used to living like a sleepwalker.

At night I read until late. Sometimes I cried: it felt comforting. Early one dark, chilly morning, when I was half awake, Walker came back into my bed and seemed agitated. He rubbed against me, spread my legs and came inside me, letting out a few little moans. I hardly moved, and it was over in seconds. Before I could look at him he turned away from me and fell asleep. I lay next to him for what seemed like hours, feeling empty, and worse, my love and tenderness towards him badly shaken. For all his talk of desire and excitement, was this all I could hope for? I had imagined waves of pleasure: discovering each other's bodies and touching our hidden, moist places, kisses and long orgasms. I thought we would never make love in the dark.

What if he couldn't change? Sex was important, and I needed more. How would I tell him? He was so touchy. No man wants to be told he isn't a good lover. My whole future life was to be close to him, to make him well—but not without love.

Only two weeks 'til Christmas, and little airmail packages and cards arrived daily from home. I put them up on our mantelpiece. Friends sent pictures of their new babies. I had long ago convinced myself that having children of my own wasn't going to be part of my life, and Alec had felt the same way. Walker and I discussed this issue early on and he was relieved when I agreed not to have children. Though we were both interested in our friends' children and spent time with them, I understood the reasons he couldn't afford a family. As for me, I was charmed by the role of being the aunt from America who would send my little nieces copies of *Eloïse at the Plaza* and later, in their teenage years, be a sympathetic listener. If allowed, I would borrow children from friends and let them entertain me. Their imagination and humor was often more inspiring than adult chatter.

The pre-Christmas season brought out Walker's childlike qualities. He acted like the most playful Santa Claus who turned stones into gold with his charm. The urge to forget his selfish attitude and live again in his fantasies was so strong that I willingly ignored the recent disagreements and hurts. Give in, give in, I said to myself, and all will be well.

Most evenings he would come up the stairs loaded with prettily wrapped packages and disappear into his walk-in closet and hide there for the longest time. The sound of rustling paper indicated that he had found yet another surprise for me in an antique shop.

How was he going to pay for all this? The basket in the hall was already full of unopened bills. Since I was short on money, I decided to make a faded blue shirt for him, a custom work shirt for Lyme. He had no idea that I had taken the pattern from one of his favorite shirts.

After a couple of crowded holiday cocktail parties Walker thought we should give a dinner party for close friends to show them our apartment. He telephoned around, hired a butler he vaguely knew, and ordered the wine to go with my veal blanquette. We'd be ten, he said, if they all accepted, which meant eating on our laps.

I was pleased when he told me he had invited the Petersens. They were an urbane, attractive couple, both Germans (Vita was brought up in Berlin, Peter was from an old Hamburg shipping family), and they had a wide circle of friends. She was always ready to exchange a few words in German with me in the morning when I came down for the mail. "*Ach, du Kleine*, tell me the news," she'd say and offer me a cup of tea.

Vita, who surrounded herself with artists, was very interested in meeting some of our friends, especially well-known writers. As a painter she had studied with Hans Hofmann in Provincetown and claimed the Abstract Expressionists as her favorite group. She seldom missed an art opening. A small painting by Jackson Pollock hung on the wall of her studio. Clever in her double role as Peter's aristocratic wife and an ambitious artist, she seemed to generate a competitive relationship with Walker regarding their friends. Even though they were only kidding each other, it irked her that he so openly found his writer friends more interesting and articulate than her painters. With the exception of Calvert, Robert Motherwell and his wife, Helen Frankenthaler, and Jack Tworkov, he had little interest in abstract artists of the moment.

When the butler showed up, Walker was surprised to see a total stranger. He introduced himself and said his friend Danny was called away at the last minute, so he came instead, if that was all right. Walker offered him the study to change his clothes. Something about the butler made me nervous. He paid attention only to Walker and used up too much counter space in my small kitchen.

Dorothy and John were the first to arrive. They hugged me and complimented the apartment and the paintings in the living room. None of Walker's old friends had seen his York Avenue digs. Trini and Courtie Barnes, Vita and Peter, and the Alfred Kazins all complimented us as they looked around at the art and the books. Everybody had a drink, and the voices and laughter grew louder. A small group formed around Vita and Peter, who shared a house with the Arthur Schlesingers in Wellfleet. The talk switched from politics to art, plays, and book reviews in *The New Yorker*. Walker delighted our friends by taking pictures, and my job was to smile and keep an eye on the kitchen. I told the butler to please serve the food hot and the bread warm and not to dress the salad until after the meat was served. I would have preferred Irmgard in the kitchen, but Walker thought she wasn't classy enough. People ate with gusto and praised the food. Just as I was passing around the pear tart, Walker waved to the butler, who came in with a tray of crystal champagne flutes, a wedding present from John and Dot. Cheers all around—the party ran itself, an evening of spontaneous rapport among friends. I felt embraced by all, especially Walker. He showed great skill at being a host and talked to each guest in turn.

Vita and Peter finished the champagne with us. We laughed and chatted on the landing and watched them go downstairs. Then Walker went back to the living room to make sure the fire was out. I checked the kitchen. Everything was cleaned up. "You gave a wonderful party, darling, come back," he called. He was glowing but looked tired and small on the sofa, like a birthday boy surrounded by new toys after his party. We kissed and sat quietly, watching the last log burn down.

Walker usually undressed in his study and hung up his clothes. He was careful and slow. I was already in bed, waiting for him. The door between the bedroom and the study was ajar, but I didn't hear him moving about. Not a sound—was he unwell all of a sudden? He had drunk very little tonight and eaten his food. I got up and tapped on the door. His voice sounded weak when he answered to come in. What could possibly have gone wrong? He was still fully dressed, sitting at the desk, his head buried in his hands. "Are you feeling sick? Do you want some tea?" I asked and put my arm around his narrow shoulders. "No, I'll be all right." He lifted his head and looked at me. I could hardly believe the change. There was no color left in his cheeks, and the lines in his face seemed much deeper. "The butler has stolen all our Christmas money, three hundred dollars. It was in this envelope, here," he held up the empty envelope, "in the middle drawer."

"I didn't like him when he walked through the door," I said and sat down on the bunk. "Shifty guy—too smooth." I had not known about the cash, our Christmas money. He had saved all this money for us. Such a villainous act, to take advantage of an older man! This hateful butler, couldn't he tell we weren't well off? It was worse than Gogol's story of "The Overcoat." I had to get the money back by Christmas; it was my responsibility. Walker had done his part, poor darling. I hated to see him so crushed.

In the morning his stomach felt queasy. I warmed the milk for his tea and brought it to him on a tray. Crackers and my Swiss honey might help, I thought, and was easy to digest. The heating pad was already on his stomach. He asked for his transistor radio. Would I get him the paper? Sure, I'd be back in a minute. More time to think, to work out the details. Last night, before going to sleep, I had an idea how to recover the money.

The newsstand was on Third Avenue, a block away. It was cold and I ran down the street. The Motherwells' blue Bentley was parked on the corner. They lived a few doors down. The princely car looked out of place on Third Avenue, but Walker found it humorous to see it there among the poor storefronts. "Well, Picasso has a vintage Rolls," he said when he first saw the Bentley. "I'd have one too if I could afford it."

He was up in his study when I returned with the paper and a bunch of small yellow roses. Vita stopped me in the hall and said what a good time she and Peter had last night. How was Walker? She hadn't heard him come down. I said fine and didn't mention the theft.

By one o'clock he wanted to go out. A short walk, he said, would do him good. No rich food, maybe the creamed chicken at Longchamps, nothing more. He might poke around in the bookstore—Kazin had mentioned the new Styron novel.

Perfect timing, I thought. I had hatched this plan. In my art folder I had a Franz Marc woodcut, dated 1912 and posthumously signed by his widow. It was given to me by my brother's godfather, an old friend of my parents who was an art historian at Bern University. The small woodcut, *Tiger*, mostly black and white with just a touch of drab yellow and green, seemed to foreshadow Marc's death in combat during World War I. Walker of course knew Marc's work and the Blue Rider group, but he thought this particular print depressing and did not want to frame and display it in the apartment.

I wrapped it in tissue between two shirt boards from Walker's drawer and set out on this daunting errand. Every time I had passed a certain gallery on Madison Avenue near the Parke-Bernet Building, I would stop and look in the window. Small paintings, works on paper by Paul Klee, the German Expressionists and Austrian painters like Gustav Klimt, reminded me of certain teachers in art school and museum visits with my family. I grew up with this art, intellectual and angst-ridden because of politics and war.

The gallery was open and I walked in. Right away a small man came forward and greeted me in a jovial manner. He drew up a chair and I sat down at a table. I couldn't quite place his accent, possibly middle-European. The place was crowded with prints and books and made a scholarly impression. I felt confident that I would not be cheated if he decided to buy my print.

Once seated, the rotund little man asked if I wanted some coffee. "Lovely," I said and thanked him. "Let's see what you have in your folder," he said and smiled like an uncle. I removed the tissue and he turned on a special table lamp. He glanced at the image as I placed it under the light. "Ah, very nice, I know the print well. His widow's signature—very good." My heartbeat was almost audible. He pulled out a magnifying glass from his coat pocket and went over the print very carefully. I sipped the strong coffee. "Excellent condition. And how do you happen to have this Marc?" he asked. I explained the provenance. "Bern? I correspond with a collector in Bern—wait a minute, I'll get his name." He got up and quickly disappeared behind a door, presumably his office. Waving a letter when he returned and genuinely pleased to have found it, he pointed to the name Rolf Bürgi on the letterhead. "Do you know him?" I nodded and smiled. "I've met him. His cousin is my uncle by marriage." "Not possibly, what a coincidence!" he said, playing nervously with the magnifying glass. "You know he has set up the Klee Foundation. Soon all the paintings will be in your museum in Bern." He scribbled a few words on a piece of paper. "I've always said there are very few anonymous collectors, if any. We dealers know most of them. And why do you want to sell it?" I told him about the theft. He commiserated with me. "It's unwise to keep cash in the house," he said, raising his eyebrows. "In Switzerland people are honest, but not in New York."

The transaction went smoothly. I didn't have to feel humiliated and haggle. He produced a recent catalogue with the image of my print. The suggested price was listed below: three hundred dollars. He said he would buy it from me for that amount. Of course I might get more at auction, and he would let me know about future auction dates and so on. Not to bother; I assured him I wanted to sell it today and surprise my husband with the money this evening. He took the print away and came back with three crisp one hundred dollar bills. "Come see me any time," he said, smiling all the way to the door.

Walker was still out when I came home. In a great rush I walked into his study, put the money in the same envelope in the middle drawer, and went to the kitchen to make tea. What a day—what luck—the dealer was honest, a kindly man, really. Now I could tell the story to Vita and Dorothy, they'd get a good laugh out of it. My city came through for me again. It could only have happened in New York.

Chapter 15

We were on the train to Stamford with Dorothy and John, on our way to Eleanor and Red Warren's New Year's Eve party, an annual event in their Fairfield County barn house. After a music-filled family Christmas Eve with the McDonalds I barely had time to prepare myself for this legendary gathering. I had met Eleanor and Red only a couple of times, once at a show of Dorothy's paintings in the Village, and after the opening of Red's play *All the King's Men*, but I had not talked to them or read their books. How would I cope with these famous writers and artists at a seated dinner? "Don't worry, my child," was Walker's answer whenever I fretted over such matters. "You'll be the belle of the ball." By now his compliment sounded more like a put-down and was of little comfort to me.

John, whom I counted as my best ally, was concentrating on finishing Styron's *Set This House on Fire*, a present from Walker, who had just read it and thought it was "damn good writing." Walker was dozing. He had taken off his glasses and cushioned his head against his folded scarf.

"I bet your dress is beautiful," said Dorothy. "You'll have to go shopping with me when the sales are on." Nothing would be more fun, I said, leaning forward, careful not to wake Walker. "I'm wearing a dress I made last fall. It goes like this." I sketched it on the back of a used envelope. "Taupe satin, quite bare on top, and appliqués of French jet embroidery I found in the Memorial Sloan-Kettering thrift shop." "You're so clever," Dorothy said and waved the smoke from her Camel away from my face, though she had inhaled most of it. "I can't even sew on a button." I said I wished I could paint like her; sewing wasn't an art, just something one learned at home.

Walker stirred. "Aren't we almost there?" He checked his watch and turned to Dorothy. "Who d'you think will be at the party, aside from the regulars?" She chuckled, waved her hand and dropped ashes all over her lap. "I guess there're always a couple of new ones," she said, "people they met on their trips, but I like their old friends and the children best." She took a puff and brushed her skirt with the back of her other hand. "I found the cutest presents for them, the darlings. Poor Rosanna, she's still in a cast." Dorothy explained that Rosanna Warren, age seven, was thrown from her pony before Thanksgiving and had hurt her back.

We were met by Red, who was dressed like a farmer in work boots and a plaid flannel shirt. He looked around the platform to make sure no other friends were waiting for a ride. We climbed into the mud-spattered station wagon and drove out into the country, over winding roads along bare fields fenced in by old stone walls. There was enough light to see the barn from a distance. We were close now, and every part of me was tense.

Life in the Warren barn surpassed all my expectations. Beautiful golden-haired children hurried down from their rooms to greet us, and Eleanor, radiant, came up the stairs, her strong voice filling the large space. She was an American beauty, an aristocrat, nothing to do with fashion, as Walker was quick to say. He firmly believed that her fine, intelligent face, the way she moved and carried herself, was achieved by two hundred years of good breeding.

Eleanor delegated Rosanna to show the McDonalds their quarters and apologized for putting Walker and me in the downstairs bedroom where the party guests left their coats. Next year we would have Rosanna's, but since she was still in her cast, it wasn't fair to make her move. The coat room was fine for one night, I thought, and Walker liked having a bathroom nearby.

"Go look around," said Walker, unpacking. "You'll find all sorts of interesting things." I had never seen a house built into a cow barn. Red was an enthusiastic guide. The oldest part, where the kitchen was, dated to the late 1700s, he said. I tried to perceive the structure as a barn, imagine the transformation that took place in front of their eyes. The high living space with its wide, hewn and pegged beams rested on a first story of old stone. Very little was changed on the outside, leaving most of the barn intact. Red spoke of the young local architect who did the drawings, their joint planning and collaboration. Red had used his carpentry skills and Eleanor helped paint the interior. He urged me to go down to the kitchen to see the rest of the place.

Chapter 15

Dorothy was talking to Eleanor, who ushered us into the dining room where two tables were set for dinner. Eleanor's taste was eclectic: silver candlesticks on the big table, fresh flowers and Christmas angels, Italian pottery and the children's art work. I admired the big fireplace and the proportions of the room. It was a delightful mixture of New England architecture and continental flair, resembling the interiors of farm houses and old mills in the south of France. She asked me if I spoke French and Italian, and when I told her I did, she gave me a big smile and wanted to know where I grew up. After a while we had Rome, skiing in the Alps, and the love of snow in common. Eleanor's descriptions and vivid impressions of places I knew made me want to read her book *Rome and a Villa* right away.

Upstairs I rejoined Walker in the living room, where he was having tea with Red. Red's manner was gentle and courtly, and he was a good listener. He offered me his chair and sat next to me. We talked about Europe. He was sorry he hardly knew Switzerland, but he wanted to tell us about Italy, and their life with Rosanna in the sixteenth-century fortress of La Roca, high above the village of Porto Ercole, on a wild peninsula. They worked in the watchtower way up and lived below in the converted stable over an abandoned garden. He missed the views out the barred windows and seeing the ocean on three sides.

I had to concentrate very hard to understand Red. Southern accents were most difficult for me, especially if spoken by men in soft voices.

Rosanna came sauntering in, agile in spite of her cast, and sat down on the rug. Would I like to speak French with her? She had learned it in France. Like two Parisians, we spoke very fast, much to Walker's surprise.

I asked her if she knew the French song *"Il pleut, il pleut bergère, rentres tes blancs moutons"*? She repeated the verses in her lovely voice without a trace of American accent. She knew the words to many songs and her vocabulary was astonishing. When Eleanor called for her to get dressed, I didn't want her to leave, she was such good company.

It was close to seven. We had shed our sweaters and corduroys and changed into our finery, waiting for Eleanor to come down. Red brought us drinks, put more logs on the fire and turned the outside light on. Dorothy looked charming in caramel wool lace. Her small, elegant feet were everyone's envy. She could dance all night in high heels. To be in evening clothes heightened my sense of pleasure, and I knew Walker felt the same. He always bathed and dressed with the greatest care when invitations called for black tie. He listened to *Tosca* or *Bohème* in his bath, borrowed my Swiss shampoo, and asked for the best set of towels. It always touched me: such long sessions in front of the mirror to put on the different layers, the suspenders, the right bow tie, the studs and the cuff links. No wonder the English nobility depended on butlers. "Dress me and pack me" were orders Walker would be delighted to give.

It started to snow. Gabriel came running to tell his father the news. The Warrens were leaving for Vermont in a couple of days. "Take off your boots," Rosanna said to him, and he hurried into the mud room. To celebrate she put bows in her curls and slipped a cream party dress over her cast. "It looks like a nightgown because of this. I can't tie the pretty sash." She drummed on her cast with her fists. "Two more weeks and it'll come off."

Eleanor made her entrance in a long red dress, the right color for her light, shiny hair. Her cheeks were flushed. A touch of lipstick was all she added, her face didn't need makeup.

The cocktail hour was long enough for old friends to catch up with each other, look around and see who else was there. First-timers and former Yale students were given a chance to meet everyone and chat with their hosts and the children. Eleanor and Red were busy introducing newcomers to us, and Walker showed great pleasure when they knew his work. Albert Erskine and his beautiful new wife, the Italian contessa Marisa Bisi, Bill and Rose Styron, Shirley Hazzard and Francis Steegmuller, the painter Peter Blume, the Sandy Calders, composer Alexei Haieff, and Ralph and Fanny Ellison came over and said hello. Jack Jessup and his wife, Eunice, Eleanor's sister, congratulated us on our marriage. I had not seen them since our visit to Squirrel Island. Their traditional New Year's luncheon party was tomorrow. She wanted to know all about the McDonalds on Cranberry, how we liked it, who we met. She was a little envious when she heard that Walker planned to return to the island and photograph. "Dot said they don't even have a library. I doubt if I could spend the whole summer there."

The tall candles and the fire were lit in the dining room. Eleanor directed us to our tables. I found myself at the smaller one, next to John Cheever. Red sat at the head of our table; Eleanor presided over the big table, with Walker on her left. My other table mate was Albert Erskine; he too was enamored of Rome. I felt more at ease without Walker watching me. Let's give it a try, I thought, I might be able to wing it and have fun.

Both men turned to me at the same time, and once more we talked of our love for Italy. Our three-way conversation was spiked with Italian idioms and names of Italian dishes, laughter, and repartee. We made entirely too much noise, and before the dessert was served we agreed to calm down in Italian, *piano, piano,* and behave for the rest of the delicious meal. Like my father, writers were curious and often gregarious, and bored by academic talk. My confidence rose by hundreds of points, and I did not want this dinner to end.

Upstairs our favorite jazz tunes were playing. Wives looked for their husbands, and the first couples moved over to the dance floor. Walker had enjoyed his dinner partners and was anxious to know all about mine. He said he always liked to see Cheever, one of his oldest friends. We danced close together, absorbed in our own thoughts. Would the New Year take us to Europe? I yearned to be in Rome with Walker; he hadn't been to Italy. And my family was eager to meet him. The honeymoon pictures had awakened my siblings' curiosity.

John McDonald cut in, and the next dance was a Glenn Miller tune. He hardly moved, softly cradling me to the beat of the music. I just followed, cheek to cheek, losing myself in the blues.

A short break—just long enough for after-dinner drinks—and I was back with Dorothy. "John says you're a good dancer," she said with a smile and put out her cigarette. "That's a real compliment." I told her I liked his style. The blues were part of my art school days and I was a little homesick. "Oh, honey," she said. She took my hand and comforted me like a mother. "It's that time of year—you'll have to come down to my studio. I'll get Bob and Jack. They love you."

The music started again with a swing tune, and a tall man about my age asked me to dance. He tore through the dancers like a tornado, jitterbugging at lightning speed, whirling and twisting me around. I feared he might tear my dress, his arms and hands were so strong. "Who is this dancing dervish?" Walker asked when I was returned to the group. "No idea," I said. "We didn't talk. Look at him now with Marisa—crazy, if you ask me." "Probably drunk," said Walker and got up. "I shall find out who he is."

I watched the madman dance with another dark-haired woman, and they almost fell to the floor. Sandy Calder got out of the way, his red shirt soaking wet. Louisa, his wife, brought another shirt for him to change into, so he could dance some more later.

Walker reappeared, visibly pleased with his findings. "I got the whole scoop from Eunice," he said. "He's one of Stanford White's grandsons. That explains it all."

Happy New Year! We drank to one other, our glasses spilling over with champagne. Outside the snow was coming down hard. A good omen, I thought, and kissed Walker. He was hungry, and as the guests began to leave he tried to find John to go down to the kitchen for a bite.

Husbands stood around in coats and fur hats, their wives keeping them waiting with their long goodbyes. I watched Ralph Ellison belt his Burberry trench coat and recalled a recent remark of his that Walker had mentioned to me. They were leaving a New York club at the same time and the attendant in the coat room handed them their identical Burberry trench coats. Walker made a joke about the classic British coat. Ellison was quick to point out the difference between his and Walker's. "You can afford to let yours get old and a little shabby," he had said. "Mine has to be spotless."

As each batch of guests departed, the cold night air blew through the open door and I shivered. Then, at last, all was quiet. The only sounds were male voices coming from the kitchen below. Could John be making scrambled eggs on toast at this hour? Dorothy had long since gone to bed.

Much too tired to join them, I went to our room and closed the door. There were still a few coats on the bed. I kicked off my shoes and lay down on someone's fur coat, wrapping the sleeves around my bare shoulders. I must have dozed off. Suddenly the door was flung open and somebody leapt on top of me. It was the mad dancer. He tried to pull down my dress strap, and I felt his sweaty head and hot breath on my neck. I struggled and pushed him away but was too embarrassed to scream. Then, looking over my attacker's shoulder, I caught sight of Walker in the doorway, shaken and unable to utter a sound. Seconds later, his voice a low hiss, he said, "Get the hell out, you bastard." The mad dancer jumped to his feet and ran out the door, past Walker, as fast as he had come in.

Upset and disheveled, I told Walker what happened. He was angry and blamed me: I had encouraged the madman, he insisted. I should never have danced with him. Anyone could see he was drunk. Walker undressed in silence and went to sleep without saying good night.

That wall again, I thought, that impenetrable wall Walker put up between us when he did not want to hear my side of the argument. Nothing would change his mind. Shut out and miserable, I took my rumpled dress off. Why did it have to end this way? The lively dinner, the dancing with friends in the beautiful barn—was I to be punished every time I had fun? I thought I played by the rules. Was every young man a threat, no matter how he behaved?

In the morning we got up without speaking. I washed my eyes with cold water, hoping no one would notice that I had cried. Breakfast at house parties was my favorite time. Today I felt homely inside and out, in spite of my red Christmas sweater. Eleanor's New Year's breakfast table was a treat: homemade breads and muffins, honey and pots of jam, and in front of each plate a walnut dipped in gold, a surprise from Rosanna. I sat between Dorothy and John, protected from Walker's cold silence.

The telephone rang and Eleanor answered it in the kitchen. She talked for a moment and then it rang again. "I guess we won't invite him next year," she said more to herself, when she came back to the table.

"Who called?" asked Red.

"Albert and Bill. I'll tell you later." She sat down next to Walker. I overheard her talk about the mad dancer, how he had torn Marisa's silk ball dress. She was very angry at him.

Would Walker believe me now, apologize with a kiss? Our eyes met across the table. His expression was far better than words. He was sorry, I could tell. I love you, I love you, he seemed to say. But his accusation still hurt, left a bitter taste.

Rosanna lifted my spirits. "You haven't opened your nut," she said. "There's a message in it, like fortune cookies. Open it," she begged. I pried open the nut with my butter knife and pulled out the handwritten message: "You are the fairest in the land and you will have a beautiful baby."

I never had that baby.

Chapter 16

My father wrote to say he had lunched with Alec. Alec had just seen his lawyer, and the bad news was that under Swiss law my Mexican divorce was invalid. Worse, I could be arrested as a bigamist if I went to Switzerland. My father had hired a lawyer for me, but it might take well over a year to straighten it out. He thought it imprudent to go anywhere in Europe with my Swiss passport until Alec's and my Swiss divorce was final.

To cheer me up, my father had decided to visit us for my birthday in late January and go on to Washington to stay with his old friend Gustav Lindt, the Swiss ambassador. He was looking forward to his first trip to the U.S.A., and Swissair gave him a big discount with his press card. He ended his letter in English: "Cheerio, my darling, until then, your Papa."

At first anger, feelings of injustice and loss, raged in my mind. I couldn't concentrate, read, or do anything useful. It wasn't Grenny's fault, he had been a great help, and Walker couldn't have known, but who was to blame? After hours of brooding and getting nowhere, I took a walk down Madison Avenue. People and small shops never failed to distract me. Signs for sales and two-for-one bargains were pasted all over the store windows. It was a cold, gloomy afternoon, and the lights were already turned on.

Now I really knew what it felt like to be an immigrant. I had met so many Polish, Hungarian, and Russian people who thought they would never see their countries again. My Swiss passport, red with its friendly white cross, had always been the envy of most Europeans. I could go anywhere, even to Communist countries. My brother, who was a lecturer at the Free University in Berlin, wrote that he frequently crossed over from West Berlin to East Berlin to see plays at the Brecht Theater and buy books. As long as he was back at Checkpoint Charlie by the arranged time, he had no trouble at all. A German word came to mind that described my new status: *Hausarrest*. I was under

Hausarrest in America. When I lived with Walker I was legal, but now that I married him I was blacklisted and illegal in my own country. It didn't make sense. Sad, I would have to tell my friends in Zurich why I couldn't visit them. And until when? It might even take two years!

I crossed over to the little antique and curio shop above Eighty-Sixth Street. In the window an amethyst pin caught my eye, part of a display of trinkets on a velvet cushion, all marked thirty-five dollars. The pin looked Chinese, with a cluster of baroque pearls and pale green jade beads mounted on top, as if casually spilled over the carved amethyst. It was far more interesting than the gold circles the Junior League girls wore on their lapels. Why not go in and browse? I deserved a present, and my birthday was coming up.

The older woman in the dark shop convinced me that I picked the only good bargain on the velvet cushion. She spoke with a heavy Slavic accent and rolled her Rs. I tried on the pin in front of the round mirror, and ten minutes later I left the shop with my little treasure in a box.

On my way to the French patisserie I looked down Eighty-second Street and saw the Metropolitan Museum. I should stop by and get some information on the exhibits for Papa, I thought. He loved paintings, and Roman and Greek antiquities and coins. Soon I would show him New York, and he'd stride from the East River to the Hudson, thinking it might take only fifteen minutes. No taxis for him. The Frick Museum, the Morgan Library, and the Museum of Modern Art would be next on his agenda, and in Washington he'd have a car and a driver to explore the city. He was promised a meeting with Walter Lippman and, if lucky, he might shake hands with President Kennedy at a reception.

But first he had to like Walker. I wasn't worried, the two men had much in common: London, Paris, American history, journalism and books, good food and wine. They both smoked. Papa was seldom without his Dunhill pipe, and once in a while he enjoyed a Havana cigar. And after all, they were practically the same age. I couldn't wait to see him, after all this time. My heart was jumping. Three more weeks and we'd be together for ten days, longer than I could remember, and I wouldn't have to share him.

I walked faster and faster, up the steps to the Met, gathered folders and a museum map and inquired about special exhibitions.

When I arrived home Walker was having tea in his study. He was wondering where I'd been. I translated Papa's letter for him and he was astonished and upset. Could the Swiss ambassador help? I shouldn't be treated so harshly. I was innocent and didn't know the consequences. But the good news was my father's visit. Walker would do anything in his power to make it a success: take him to the Century, introduce him to our friends and to the editors at *Fortune* and *Time* and *Life*.

On a blustery day toward the end of January I took a taxi out to Idlewild and waited in the international terminal for Papa's plane to come in. All sorts of foreigners, many of them Swiss, were jostling for space in the balcony above the large receiving hall where the arriving passengers had to clear customs. Walker suggested I meet Papa without him, so we could chat in our native "gibberish" on the way back to the city. I had not yet convinced him that everybody in Switzerland, even the president and university professors, spoke Swiss-German with one another. This became especially important during the war, when shopkeepers selling rationed items like coffee and sugar simply ignored Germans who did not speak the dialect.

I felt engulfed by the throng's excitement when the first travelers came through the heavy doors. I moved to the front of the crowd, just in time to see Papa in hat and tweed coat hoist his luggage onto a counter on the far side of the hall. For a second I watched him trying to find me. Then he waved and smiled and blew me a kiss. I fought back tears and waved with both hands. His bushy eyebrows were a little grayer than before, but he was young and strong compared to Walker. Among the many pale and sallow faces, Papa's healthy color stood out. Summer or winter, he never stayed indoors all day. By the end of June he was among the first to swim in the Aare before lunch, and after a big snowfall he loved walking through the woods. Now he looked eager and excited and I knew that he would not be satisfied until he experienced all of Walker's and my New York.

Walker had lit a fire and brought out the ice and the scotch in preparation for Papa's arrival. Right away Papa seemed comfortable in our apartment, with the many books and stacks of *The New York Times*. Vita let me have her spare room for his visit.

I prepared dinner while Walker and Papa discussed Churchill's history of World War II. Papa said he learned English late in life, after the war, and, while now he read English biographies, history, and the reviews in the *Times Literary Supplement*, he still had to look up words. This was not at all unusual even for native Americans, commented Walker. When he read British authors he often didn't know the specific meaning of a word, and in his own writing he liked to have a little fun and use a word or two that others might have to look up. He admired Nabokov who wrote in four languages and sometimes invented words.

During dinner we made plans for Papa's first full day in New York. He had a map of the city and proposed starting with a visit to the Metropolitan Museum, since we were so close. He said he was particularly interested in American artists, Copley and the Hudson River School and Sargent in particular. Did I know his painting of Madame X? Walker laughed and complimented him on his research. Madame X was one of Walker's favorites too, *"très piquant, n'est-ce pas?"* He might even join Papa for an abbreviated tour of the Met.

Papa ate breakfast like a king. He heavily buttered his toast and spread the coarse-cut English marmalade, and after three cups of Earl Grey he finished off the meal with a piece of Gruyère cheese. This was the Swiss German in him, so different from Maman, who ate very little in the morning. As I sat with him and drank my café au lait, he gave me the news of Maman and my siblings. My youngest sister, Anne-Marie, about to be sixteen, was in love with a nice young man, he said, and mentioned the boy's father. Papa always knew how families were related, their males' current and past achievements and status in the Swiss army. He wasn't a social snob, but he cared about peoples' professions and careers. Unlike Walker, he encouraged women to become lawyers and doctors and join the work force. One of his first questions was why I wasn't working. I skirted the truth, but I told him that by spring I would certainly look for a part-time job. He was right, I didn't have enough to do.

On our way to buy the paper I took Papa down Ninety-second Street to show him one of New York's treasures, a mid-nineteenth-century wood frame house embellished with Corinthian porch columns. Papa wanted to know more about the two-block long Jacob Ruppert Brewery on Third Avenue—Ruppert must have been a German, he said. The mixture of architectural styles and the Avenue's plain, old-fashioned shops in our immediate neighborhood surprised him, and I was amused when he read the names of their Slovak, Polish, and German owners out loud. "Most of them have been slightly Anglicized," he said, smiling. "I don't blame them."

Walker greeted us on the landing in his bathrobe when we came up the stairs with the paper, and we all had another cup of tea. He said he wouldn't join us today, but he'd like to make a date with Hermann for lunch at the Century tomorrow. Papa loved London clubs and was flattered, but he drew a blank when Walker mentioned Stanford White. "You're in for a surprise, Hermann," said Walker and winked at me.

The Met was dark and quite empty. A weekday morning was the perfect time to have the galleries to oneself. We began with antiquities, first Greek and then Roman. I could hardly tear Papa away from the small-scale bronzes and gold jewelry, and when he discovered the collection of terra cotta amphoras he was in his element. All through my childhood I had tagged along when he took us to excavations of Roman sites in Switzerland. They always seemed very sparse to me, especially after my stay in a boarding school in Rome.

Lunch was delayed by a pass through the extensive armor collection on the way to the cafeteria, Rennaissance weaponry being another special interest of Papa. "Now I'd give anything for an espresso," he joked after our sandwich lunch and a cup of regular brew. "American coffee will not keep me awake."

In the American painting galleries he knew Copley, Cole and Church, Whistler and Sargent, but he had not seen much of Winslow Homer's work. He was overwhelmed by some of the paintings' powerful realism and dramatic compositions. But where was Madame X, the Sargent he wanted to see most? A guard told us it had been temporarily removed. Papa was not ready to accept this. "We must find out more about it," he said. I suggested we go down to the front desk and talk to someone there. It was déjà vu—Papa's stubborn refusal to accept the inevitable, his need to win arguments at all cost and fight for his rights, to get even with a rude hotel clerk or a taxi driver had embarrassed me when I was younger and made me want to withdraw from him and pretend not to know him. In restaurants he often complained and left a meager tip when he felt the service was poor. Usually he tipped generously and was cordial with agreeable waiters and hotel personnel.

At the front desk he made his special request in polite, well-chosen words. He presented his press card and told the friendly lady that he was here on official business on his way to Washington and that he could come back another day and view the painting then, providing it was in the museum. She nodded, wrote down some numbers for him to call, and said she would see what could be done.

My father eventually won and got to see Madame X alone. It was the only time during his stay that he irritated me. He redeemed himself on my birthday when he presented me with a beautifully wrapped little package during breakfast. One of my happiest memories was in Paris, on my fifth birthday, when he woke me in the morning and placed a small box tied with a pink ribbon on my pillow. I can still see the black patent leather Mary Janes for my doll, Yvonne, so Parisian and well made! The strap had a real buttonhole!

Papa loved to give and receive presents. Walker wasn't up yet, so I couldn't show him the elegant gold watch with the alligator strap. Crocodile was what Papa called it. "It is Swiss-made," he said and squeezed me.

Walker took us to Giovanni's for dinner, and Papa got his double espresso at last. He enjoyed the ambiance and thought the meal was as good as in any restaurant in Milan, a city he liked for its grand opera, art, commerce, and food. "It's almost like a club," said Walker, looking around the room. "Here you can see anyone from Mayor Wagner to close friends of mine who are old New York. Not too many of them left."

My birthday surprise was the Hennessy Five Star Band playing downtown. We took a bumpy taxi ride through dingy, poorly lit streets. The garbage piled high on sidewalks in front of peeling walls made an impression on Papa. European visitors were always surprised to see so many shabby buildings and grimy busses in New York. When Maman was here she asked me why people did not wash their windows.

The taxi stopped in front of an ageing movie palace on East Fourteenth Street. Even before we got through the door the music coming from an open second-floor window drew us in, and I rushed upstairs to join the party. Seeing me wave to our friends, who played their instruments with bravado and humor, encouraged Papa to twirl me around the dance floor before Walker had a chance to introduce him. Papa led with strong forward motions and used his arms to propel me as far as he could reach. Still holding on to me, he let me do

Chapter 16

my own improvisations and pulled me back in to change directions. Just before the music stopped, he lifted me off the ground in a pretty arch for a grand finale.

Verna put down her tuba and applauded and everyone joined in and wanted to meet Papa. He was the new star of the evening, and he danced with many of the musicians' wives. Walker observed quietly and smiled. We stayed until the last tune and closed the party, glowing with feelings of mellow friendship.

Outside, in the cold night air, saying goodbye to the Hobsons, the Jessups, and the McDonalds, Papa declared he wanted to cool off and walk home. It took all of Walker's humorous cunning to convince him to join us in a taxi after a couple of blocks.

In his direct manner Papa asked me the inevitable questions during our last lunch, at Café Chambord, before he left for Washington. He wanted to know more about Walker's health, and what I would do if he needed to be seriously looked after. And did we have enough money? His advice was that I should become more independent and earn some money. But of course I could always count on his help and support.

I wasn't able to give him honest answers. Until this visit, when my father astonished me with his vigor and energy, I had gotten used to Walker's general lack of physical well-being and had come to expect the frequent ups and downs of his delicate health. As to his money, I didn't know then how poor we really were. My aim was to protect Walker and not spoil the good times he and Papa had had together. Complete opposites, physically and in the ways they approached their work and dealt with people and everyday life, they genuinely liked each other.

My father understood Walker's importance as an American artist and delighted in his original, non-academic interpretations and extensive knowledge of his own country. I found it exciting to listen to them talk about the Civil War after dinner and have Walker show Mathew Brady's photographs to Papa. These moments were just what my father had hoped for, and Walker was generous with his time and interested in Papa's spontaneous reactions. He played a large part in Papa's growing love for America, its history and literature.

Like Walker, my father loved the land and the ocean. But while Walker was an observer and shied away from the slightest hint of physical danger, Papa almost welcomed it. He had a bit of Hemingway in him and was always game for fishing and hunting expeditions with a group of male friends. When he came home and pulled the blue trout or a rack of venison out of his pouch, I was proud of him and relived his adventures, smelling the damp leaves and practically hearing the rushing water. He regaled us with stories of moonlit streams, or the specific place in the woods where he shot the deer. The camaraderie of men was part of his life. The time he spent with his troops in the mountains during the first winter of the war was an exhilarating experience for him, a chunk of life he remembered in every detail until his death.

When Walker and I put Papa on the train for Washington, I felt swept up in his enthusiasm. Nothing bad can happen to me, I thought, buoyed by new expectations. And I am not alone.

After my father left, I had many imaginary conversations with him on my walks in the city. We had talked openly about my mother and my lifelong troubles with her. Why, with an ocean between us, did I still feel the need for her approval? Why couldn't we find more people and things we both liked? He urged me to put this all behind me and think of my future; but he obviously saw that I hadn't given the future much thought.

Chapter 17

Winter 1961
 Dear Papa,
 I wish you had a good map of the U.S.A. to look up the trip that Walker and I took to Guthrie, Kentucky. We left New York from Pennsylvania station around 4 PM. It was the longest train I ever saw and it had a fascinating variety of sleeping cars, roomettes, Pullman cars, lounge and dining cars, with nice servants in clean white coats. Walker and I made ourselves comfortable in our own sitting room with a little W.C. for only us to use. The train pulled out of the station into some suburbs and small towns that looked quite beautiful in the pink light of the winter sunset. We read and talked, looked out the window until it was dark. Walker ordered me a double scotch on the rocks, and we both felt that this was going to be a continuation of our honeymoon.
 Later we had dinner, then read some more and had our room made into a bedroom. It was fun to try out all the refinements of the bedroom, turn the air conditioner on and the ventilation off, see whether the water in the W.C. was really hot and play with all the different lights. We had a lot of "fou rires" before we finally went to sleep.
 Sometimes, during the night, I woke up and looked out the window. It was a cold, clear night; snow lay on the ground and I could see some strange towns and rivers, and in one big S-curve in the mountains of Pennsylvania I saw our whole train passing through the snow very slowly with two engines in front of it. We were in the last car.
 At 4 PM, after 24 hours on the train, we finally got off at Guthrie, a small town on the border of Kentucky and Tennessee.
 Tom's wife Ethel waited for us at the station and drove us to their farm. I wrote you about the Mabry family last summer when we saw them in Lyme. They are wonderful people. Tom, same age as Walker, comes from Clarksville, Tennessee. He went east to study at Harvard.

Later on he became a writer and worked at one time at the Museum of Modern Art. It was during these years that he met Walker through Lincoln Kirstein.

The Mabrys' two daughters are charming. Eliza, age 15, is Walker's godchild. Unfortunately they were both away at boarding school and we didn't see them. As you can imagine it must be very hard for Ethel to live on a farm in the south. It is so lonely; the nearest town, though very provincial and limited, is Nashville, sixty miles away. Besides an amateur symphony orchestra there is nothing cultural around.

Together we spent the nicest evenings, talking, listening to music or reading. There was always a fire in the living room. The first morning Walker left with Tom to work and photograph some poor families. I spent the whole day with Ethel, visiting the stables, the horses, Henrietta, one of the huge sows, John the bull, Tremblebug the boar. Bernice, the wife of one of the farm workers, married when she was 14 and has 5 children. It was quite an experience.

That same day we had cocktails in Elkton, Kentucky, at George Boone's house, an eighteenth-century family place, where he lives alone with his old mother.

Elkton is the county seat and has courthouse. George Boone is the local lawyer, a nice young man who is a descendant of Daniel Boone, the American pioneer who opened Kentucky. Of course Mr. Boone knows everybody and everything in his home state. He helped Walker to get inside some houses of the poor.

We drove to Nashville, spent the last evening with the Mabrys, and slept in a hotel in town. We flew via Washington to New York early in the morning.

The Mabrys brought out the best in Walker. He was as fond of Ethel as he was of Tom, which made our stay very pleasant. It was my first working trip with Walker to an entirely new region of America, a place so different from any part I had visited before.

Eager to show me what interested him, Walker had more energy, and the days' impressions, peoples' voices and faces, stayed with me until I fell asleep late at night. When Walker went off with Tom alone, I didn't feel left out. Ethel and I had much to talk about. She was homesick for New York and their friends. I filled pages of my journal early in the morning before Walker got up.

One day, after breakfast, Red Warren's younger brother Thomas called on Tom to discuss some business matters. Thomas lived in Guthrie, where he and Red had grown up. He owned the local grain elevator and silos and was successful in a great many enterprises in the town.

It was hard for me to imagine Red, who knew so much about American literature and history and European civilization, going to school in such a small town in rural Kentucky as a young boy. Walker commented that very few of the best American poets, writers, and artists were born in New York. "Why, look at Hart Crane, T. S. Eliot, Fitzgerald, Faulkner, Hemingway, and me; we all come from provincial places."

Sometimes I wonder whether my father spoke to Walker on my behalf. After the Mabry visit Walker became much more attentive to my needs and encouraged me to form my own opinions on people and subjects that I found stimulating. He listened and tried to please me. Seeing that I was anxious to meet younger people, he introduced me to Kate Roosevelt, who was soon to marry Bill Haddad, a promising young journalist. Walker had met Kate through Ben Shahn, whom she had consulted about photography lessons. Shahn thought Walker was best equipped to help her. She had recently returned from London, where her stepfather, John Hay Whitney, was the American ambassador during the last years of the Eisenhower era. Kate planned to accompany her future husband on a working trip to Russia.

Kate was shy, but she had great warmth and an open, disarming personality. She made Walker and me feel special by being a good listener and complimenting us as a couple. She seemed to think of me as a free spirit and quite brave for marrying Walker. Her intelligent observations and genuine enthusiasm for Walker's work were encouraging to both of us. He was delighted to have a new, young admirer, and I remember basking in her charming smile all evening.

Soon afterward her older sister, Sara, who was married to the concert pianist Anthony di Bonaventura, invited us for an Italian family dinner at their townhouse on East Sixty-fourth Street. Sara greeted us like old friends. She was a tall, dark-haired beauty with flawless fair skin. I was impressed by her regal bearing and natural elegance. We followed her upstairs into a yellow sitting room, inviting and cozy with comfortable chairs and sofas, books, and family pictures in silver frames. Young children in their bathrobes soon appeared, curious to find out who was there. Sara introduced each one, two boys and two girls, and we shook hands. They gave us little shy smiles and waited for us to talk. Their aunt Kate and Mary Carswell, a close friend, arrived, and in no time the children became animated and scurried back and forth between the two, brought favorite toys to show them, and instantly won our hearts. They responded to Walker and listened to his quiet voice. When Mrs. Whitney walked in, Walker's expression and manner changed. He put on his English Lord act—very inappropriate, to my mind, since she knew more than he did about that life, having been surrounded by royalty and foreign dignitaries during her time in London.

Mrs. Whitney's contribution to the cocktail hour was a crystal bowl full of caviar and a plate of toast points wrapped in a linen napkin. Surrounded by her grandchildren, she spread the caviar on the small triangles as the older children waited eagerly until the lemon wedges were on the plate and it was ready to be passed. They went around a couple of times and they munched happily when given a treat by their smiling grandmama. We were all much amused by the caviar-eating children.

Mrs. Whitney said she was only staying for a moment. Jock had a club dinner and she was delighted to be spending a quiet evening at home.

I found her dashing in her raspberry Pucci shirt and velvet pants, just right for an informal drink at her daughter's house. Little clusters of cabochon rubies and diamonds glittered when she moved her hands and pretty head. I thought of her sister, the beautiful Babe Paley, and the three generations in this room—how different Sara's and Kate's lives were and surely would be by the time their children grew up.

Walker believed Mrs. Whitney to be part of a dwindling elite of well-born rich, still influential in the city's cultural institutions, but her daughters, by choosing men "outside their class," as he put it, had already broken away from their mother's social milieu. We would see much more of this in the new decade, he predicted.

Sara's husband Tony joined us for dinner. He kissed the children good night and urged us to move into the dining room. Mrs. Whitney waved and quickly walked downstairs with Kate, who saw her out.

Chapter 17

Sara had cooked the dinner and served us, going in and out of the kitchen without help from Tony. He sat at the head of the table like a Roman patriarch.

After dinner, Mary Carswell and I moved to a corner and talked. She said she grew up on a big farm in western Massachusetts. I couldn't imagine this blond, aristocratic-looking young woman on a farm. It must have been a farm like the Mabrys', I thought, with a big house and lots of land. I told her about my family and my father's visit to Washington. Her husband was already in the capital, she said, and soon she would follow him and look for an apartment. They had no children. I sensed she had known difficult times in her youth. She spoke of a cruel father and a loving nurse who had saved her and her five siblings. Her story reminded me of Henry James; and Lenox, Massachusetts, was Edith Wharton's place, where he often visited. Mary mentioned her grandmother's house there. Would I ever know her secret? I was drawn to her though she loved animals, nature, and poetry, so different from my taste for the worldly and man-made. Was it her ardent manner, her honesty, her engaging laughter? Before we parted we agreed to call each other and meet again.

Back on Lexington Avenue, Walker felt like walking a few blocks. I raved about the evening. I had missed being with intelligent, remarkable young women like Sara, Kate, and Mary, and especially Americans. He promised to take me to Stonington, Connecticut, this summer, where I would meet Lily and Anthony West and Anne Fuller. Fisher's Island was another place he wanted to show me. Eliza Parkinson had already invited us for a weekend in June—this was only the beginning.

These were all his people, I said, but Mary was my find. Would he approve of her if we became friends? Why not? He agreed she might be good for me, and he liked her New England looks. He thought her attractive and well educated.

Before I had a chance to see Mary again, Walker came home one night from a Century dinner and sat down in the living room, full of "remarkable news." These late evening moments with him were my favorite. It was often the only time he was in a talkative mood, and we both loved gossip. My curiosity was at its peak when he said I could never guess what he learned tonight. An out-of-town member from Stockbridge told him all about Mary's family. Her grandmother, though no longer alive, had been a Vanderbilt, and her house in Lenox was in all the books of the region, very grand and next door to Edith Wharton's. The formal gardens of Mary's great-grandmother's place across the road were designed by Frederick Law Olmsted. These were the settings for the parties in *The House of Mirth*. High Lawn, Mary's parents' farm, came close to an English estate. It was one of the largest in the region, with prize cattle and beautiful land.

Thanks to the good dinner wine, he gleefully exaggerated so that I imagined Mary as a child living in a house like the Frick Museum. But why was she so modest about her money, I asked him. At Sara's house we discussed finding unusual fabrics in some hidden shops downtown and making our own evening clothes. I promised to help her, since I had worked with Paris couture samples in Zurich and at Saks.

"Mary, Mary, quite contrary," he said with a laugh, "there's a riddle for you."

At the end of March we flew to Tampa and visited Walker's sister Jane and her husband Tal Brewer in Anna Maria. I had not met them before, and it was my first trip to Florida. We rented a car and made a detour through Sarasota. Walker pointed out the Ringling place, where he had photographed years ago, and the Asolo Theatre. He regretted there wasn't much left of the old stuff. The circus' winter quarters had provided him with wonderful subject matter.

I was rarely able to see the buildings and places Walker had photographed years ago. His picture of an old carved and gilded circus wagon never ceased to stimulate my imagination. It evoked all the foreign-looking people, animals and smells of our Swiss Zirkus Knie when it came to Bern once a year: the waltzing Lipizzaner horses trained by blond, curly-haired Freddy, and Eliane, his movie-star sister, who took one's breath away when she flew through the air, hanging from the heel of her right foot without a safety net. I heard the oompah brass band follow the slow-moving elephants as they performed with Rolf, the older, heavy-set brother, and stood on their hind legs in unison for the finale.

For several hours during the day we could visit most of the animals and watch them being fed and groomed. I hung around the wagons and peeked through open doors. Dark-eyed children looked back at me and spoke languages I didn't understand. They were eating at odd hours. Sometimes a group of acrobats, all siblings, were practicing pyramids outside. Their youngest member, a skinny girl of eight or nine, would climb to the top monkey-style, and I'd see the jewel in her bellybutton shine like a star.

On our drive through Longboat Key, Walker and I discussed the circus and its appeal to so many different types of people and artists all over the world: the eclectic mélange of dancing animals, the fear for the lion tamer and high-wire artists, the sad-faced clowns. All of this, Walker said, and the pure pleasure of watching physical skills, like sports. The suspense around the greens in a golf tournament—and actually seeing Sam Snead sink a long put. People were sick of "phony high art" and "too much talk." And then there was the impermanence of the whole thing—one day the tent was dismantled and all was gone. He said he went to the circus in Paris to look at the spectators as much as the performers.

Most of what I saw through the car windows was tasteless modernity, but as we approached Anna Maria, I felt better about the authenticity of the place. There were no high buildings, and the beach stretched as far as I could see. We passed through the nothing town and Walker pulled over in front of a bait shack. I recognized it as the one in his painting which hung in our apartment. He had used the shack's bold lettering and signs; the colors in the makeshift little building were even more garish than in his painting. I was enchanted and got out of the car to walk around the structure. Nearby stood a couple of improvised road stands, where local growers sold their produce earlier in the day.

Walker had brought his paints along, and I was hoping he would settle down after a couple of days and paint. The few paintings of his I knew revealed his eye for color. I was only familiar with his black-and-white photographs, though he had recently been experimenting with color film. The paintings' compositions were carefully thought through, nothing was accidental. Some reminded me a little of Stuart Davis's early work.

Walker planned to arrive at the Brewers' shortly before six, the cocktail hour being the most congenial time in his mind for me to meet them. He also wanted me to experience the glorious sunset over the water, and the famous green flash.

As soon as we stopped in the driveway of the bungalow-style house with the louvered windows and tropical plantings, Tal came out to help us unload the car. He greeted me in his friendly, low-key manner. He was an older, slim, long-legged man with an attractive college-boy face. His full, dark gray hair was parted on one side. Jane sat in her sunny turquoise living room and smoked. Walker introduced us, and she asked me to move a chair near her, so she could talk to me while Tal was making us drinks. She joked that Walker had not shown her a picture of me but that I was prettier than any photograph he could've taken. I felt embarrassed, and I knew by glancing at him that Walker didn't appreciate her "older sister" remark. The only resemblance between them was their slight build. Jane, who was blue-eyed, must have once been good-looking and petite, but the sun had wrinkled her fair skin beyond her years, and she didn't bother to dye her hair, which was mousy gray, and the haircut was local.

The sun's red ball on the horizon made us all turn to the picture window and count the minutes until the last sliver was gone. But there was no green flash. The pink glow in the sky and over the calm water lasted a while, until Tal announced his daily evening visitor on the beach, a great blue heron, nearly as tall as Jane. Anna Maria was a resting place for birds on their way north in the spring. Jane and Tal knew every bird. They shared a lifelong interest and made a list to which they kept adding new species. "Harmless occupation," Walker once said mockingly, adding that they looked like birds, the way some people begin to resemble their dogs.

Our daily walks on the beach and late morning swims were the best tonic for Walker's health. In a few days' time his face turned a deep tan and his worry-lines smoothed out. He coughed much less during the night.

Jane seldom appeared before noon, and she didn't do any housework. Tal, the chore man, brought her breakfast in bed, broiled steaks and fish on the grill, and washed the dishes. Recently Jane had become allergic to detergent.

Walker took all of us out for lunch to a little seafood place where the Gulf shrimps were cooked in beer and tasted delicious. He lamented the lack of good restaurants in the area, a "culinary desert," he called it, which made Jane furious. Dinners were eaten at home, partly so the cocktail hour could last longer and partly because of

Jane's poor health. She retired early in the evening with her novels and travel books and cigarettes. In spite of her emphysema, clouds of smoke escaped from their bedroom.

To hear Jane and Walker talk about how they would both stop smoking was hilarious. Short of hypnosis and religion they were willing to try everything, including sucking on a peppermint cigarette. I joked that I would send for dark Swiss chocolate ones. Quite a lot of sparring went on between them, especially during dinners. It was usually about their mother. During the war she had come to live with Jane and Tal and was so demanding and bossy that eventually Jane had a nervous breakdown. At the suggestion of her doctors, it was agreed to find a place for the mother in Pasadena, near relatives on her side of the family. Jane was still resentful at Walker's lack of moral support and involvement at the time, and his inability to feel more charitable towards his mother. He had visited her only once in Pasadena, where she lived out her days. But often, to my great relief, the conversation between them was lighter and of a joshing nature, discussing their childhood places, houses, and cars. Funny, thought Walker, how he and Jane remembered things differently.

Right away I became Tal's helper in the kitchen. Everything was instant: mashed potatoes, coffee, salad dressing out of a bottle, Lipton's powdered soups, and canned peaches. Walker brought some good wine and whipped butter, since the Brewers only rarely drank wine with dinner and used margarine for health reasons. Walker said they enjoyed good food and wine during their stays at various New England inns in the summer and on their trips, but at home they couldn't be bothered. I missed the olive oil and good bread, an important part of our daily diet, and cups of strong brewed coffee.

As we meandered, exploring the Keys, Walker discovered a new place with old fishing boats and a tangled mess of gear and buoys he thought he might like to paint. He planned to use casein paints rather than oil. Early one afternoon we went back, and I watched him make a quick sketch of a strong diagonal on a work boat, not the whole scene the way most amateur painters would do to catch the atmosphere. He jotted down some notes on the colors he wanted to try out for the background. This was enough, he said, to paint from memory, and he could always change the colors, for example use raw umber for the first coat. Like Ben Shahn, he preferred to paint on boards rather than canvas.

After two weeks at the Brewers' we started out on back-country roads across to Palm Beach. *Fortune* had a job for Walker to photograph some new and expensive deep-sea fishing boats in the area. We were so relieved to get away from Jane and Tal's place that we joked and laughed like children who had been cooped up with humorless grandparents. I sang old Charles Trénet songs—"*Symphonie, symphonie d'amour,*" amusing Walker with the sentimental lyrics.

He took narrow, bumpy roads through a poor and undeveloped part of Florida. Migrant workers picking vegetables in the hot sun. They were housed in rusty trailers and sheds. Not much had changed here in twenty years, Walker commented. We reached the east coast and he suggested he'd do this job in a couple of days and then book us into the Colony Hotel for a romantic weekend. Palm Beach at its best—he predicted I would be in heaven.

The motel near the marina was a disappointment. Synthetic wall-to-wall carpeting covered the whole place. Around the pool were spiky flowers in pink plastic shells. Our room smelled of cigar smoke. The noisy air conditioner was on and it was too hot to open the windows. Walker telephoned the boat captains and made a date to go out on the water in one of these fast boats. Apparently one could see whole schools of fish, and with luck, a tuna, from the boats' high towers. He'd photograph the boats and their interiors in the morning—just a hack job, nothing more.

We unpacked, changed into white ducks and canvas shoes, and walked to the marina to have a good look at the boats. Among dozens of powerboats we picked the biggest of the three gleaming fiberglass hulls filling the slips closest to the dock and ramp. The Naughty Gal, registered in Galveston, Texas, was the one, said Walker. This was hardly a boat by his standards. "I call it a machine." All that shiny stainless steel, the heavy fishing rods, and a bolted-down vinyl dentist's chair for the fisherman seemed a far cry from Hemingway's sport of catching a big fish. The more Walker looked, the less he liked it. "I'll make them pay for this," I heard him say to himself. *Fortune* had no idea how to use him anymore. There was nothing in it for him. Any idiot could do this.

He became infuriated when we peeked inside and saw a silver bowl with fake fruit on the cocktail table in the main saloon. Naugahyde swivel lounge chairs were part of the decor.

It upset me too that *Fortune* gave him such a mundane job, especially since he had contributed some highly original portfolios to the magazine, like "Beauties of the Common Tool." Now, only six years later, that particular issue was a collector's item.

Tired and discouraged, we dined at Testa's Restaurant. The minute we were seated we realized we had made a mistake. The place was a tourist trap, and the menu featured far too many entrées to serve fresh food, including Maine lobster. Walker avoided frozen foods as a matter of principle. The wine was overpriced and the salad and bread reeked of garlic. We ordered grilled fish. We were just finishing our meal when a minstrel band in bowler hats and fancy vests arrived to entertain the guests for dessert and after-dinner drinks. The performers wore blackface and imitated Negro dialogue and music. Walker and I were shocked and disgusted. This could only happen in Florida, a hotbed of racism, he fumed. Obviously, for the sake of tourism, the proprietors ignored the civil rights movement and the Freedom Riders. It was demeaning and I felt perturbed. Speechless, Walker put down two twenties and prepared to leave, grabbing me by the arm. I was proud of him. It was usually against Walker's nature to openly protest or become politically engaged, but such a display of racism was intolerable to both of us.

Our moods improved two days later when we checked into the Colony Hotel. The staff was discreet and efficient. Bell captains arranged for our car to be parked and took care of the luggage, which arrived on our floor as we stepped off the elevator. The room exuded an atmosphere of quiet luxury. After we hung up our dressy clothes, a chambermaid knocked on our door. She could have been on the London stage in her organdy apron and headdress. Walker ordered tea and buttered scones with raspberry jam and clotted cream. He changed into a light cardigan, relaxed on the chaise with *The New York Times*, and lit a cigarette.

I slipped on the terry cloth robe supplied by the hotel and lay down. The twin beds were pushed together. On my bedside table I found a selection of magazines, among them *Town & Country* and the Palm Beach society rag. Later on, I thought, I would go down for a swim. From our windows the enclosed pool and terrace looked tempting: a tranquil oasis, its walls covered by trellised greenery and flowering bougainvillea. The only sound was a splashing fountain.

While Walker was having his tea, I read about Palm Beach society. Walker said the Bath and Tennis Club and the Everglades Club did not let in Jews. I asked him if the Kennedys were members. He thought that if they were they'd have to resign, now that they were in the White House. It was hard for me to imagine a place where Jews were not welcome. Switzerland had very few social clubs. Golf, ski, and tennis clubs were open to all kinds of members, including many foreigners, as long as they could foot the bill.

My curiosity rose when I saw a picture of the Duke and Duchess of Windsor in the penthouse of our hotel. They had just moved in, according to the caption, and were staying until Easter, the end of the season. Luck might be on our side tonight—I was hoping. Amused and charmed, Walker called the restaurant to reserve a table for dinner on the late side.

We dressed with great care: Walker in cream linen pants, dusty pink shirt and blazer. I tried my best to look like Jackie in an off-white sleeveless dress and strands of pearls. With the help of Revlon I painted on a light tan. My fake eyelashes and a new frosted lipstick did the rest.

Walker slipped the maître d' a twenty as we walked into the restaurant. Large bouquets of fresh flowers, crisp tablecloths, and crystal wine goblets gave the room a soigné appearance. It was all in good taste, not the least bit chichi. With plenty of room between tables, I was looking forward to an intimate time. The clientele was glamorous and well-mannered, but maybe later on, once the dancing started, a younger crowd might drop in and jazz up the place.

We had champagne with our soft-shell crabs and fresh asparagus. Walker thanked me for being helpful with Jane and Tal. Strange how little these siblings knew about each other and their lives. Walker complained that Jane had no idea about the importance of his work. She had never read his and James Agee's *Let Us Now Praise Famous Men*. She would have been happier if he were a stockbroker. Well, it was true of most artists and writers of his generation. The young Hemingway desperately sought his father's approval. His mother scolded him in one of her letters for using foul language in his writing. I was lucky, Walker observed, to have an intelligent, worldly father and interesting siblings.

I told him I hoped he would soon meet my brother and sisters. I was beginning to miss them, and I wanted them to know him. True,

I had longed to get away from Switzerland and to some degree from my family, but I was much less troubled by them now.

Halfway through dinner Walker asked our waiter if the duke and duchess ever came down to dance. The waiter smiled and pointed to a couple of banquettes along one wall and a large round table with half a dozen chairs. "Stick around, they made a reservation for dessert and dancing tonight, a party of twelve. They're dining upstairs."

This was our reward for the ghastly fishing boat job. And—Walker raised his eyebrows, ready to divulge a deep secret—*Fortune* was going to pay for this, champagne and all.

It was close to ten and nobody had left the room. Everyone was waiting. The band arrived, the drums were set up near the baby grand, and the musicians tested their instruments. They began with easygoing tunes, like "It's Only a Paper Moon" and "Candy, It's Gonna Be Just Dandy." When the duke and duchess walked in with their guests, the band stopped, the dancers turned around, and the diners stood up and cheered. The duke waved and their friends walked to their table and sat down. The next dance, "I Got Rhythm," brought the whole group onto the dance floor. As we danced, Walker moved us very close to the duke. The two men were of the same height and were built alike, but the resemblance ended there. The duke's expression had a disillusioned air. My sympathy was with him and not with the hard-faced duchess, though I admired her style and taste in clothes. She was enviably thin. Tonight she wore a most flattering diamond and coral necklace, just the right shade of orangy pink for her jade-green evening dress. She was surrounded by Palm Beach's social elite. I don't think I ever saw such pretty dresses and jewels: billowing chiffons in Monet hues, and large semi-precious stones. What could be more seductive on young blond beauties than aquamarines and turquoises?

Walker and I danced cheek-to-cheek to "Moonlight Serenade." He held me tight and gently led the way. I was floating, losing all sense of reality. Yes, this must be why I married him—these rare moments, when he trusted me and let me get close to him, and I alone counted.

Once again I was under his spell, exhilarated by his talents and charm. I swayed to and fro in his arms, my insatiable hunger for glamour and romantic love satisfied, and forgot all the troubles of our early marriage. We danced every dance and closed the evening with "Tenderly."

That night, drowsy with sleep and champagne, I felt kisses on my breasts, fingers barely touching me, slowly moving down inside my legs. There—it felt good. How well he knew what I liked. My eyes still closed, I guided his hand. He went deeper, so gently, I wanted more. Faster and faster, I felt his tongue, until flashes of pleasure shot through every part of me.

I woke up late the next morning. Not yet, don't open your eyes, not just yet, I thought. Last night's rush of desire—total abandon—it did happen, my nightgown was all bunched up under my breasts.

Across the room, Walker sat at the breakfast table, drinking tea and reading the paper. Should I tell him what an exciting lover he was and to please do it again? Words seemed too meager a praise; gestures were much more spontaneous. I got out of bed, put on the lovely peignoir from our honeymoon, and tiptoed to the back of his chair. Softly, I put my arms around him and kissed the top of his head. "I love you—you are my prince, no comparison with the duke."

Chapter 18

In the spring I took a weeklong typing course. Much to my surprise, Walker encouraged me to do it. With the new schedule I left the house in the morning after I gave him his first cup of tea, and when I returned home, around one, he was gone downtown to the office or to lunch at the Century. This routine suited both of us, since he liked to start the day slowly, thinking and reading, without talking. Pleased at his reaction, I saw a possibility of my getting a part-time job in the fall.

Mrs. Greenblatt, a redhead with a Viennese accent, guaranteed a flawless sixty words a minute for everyone who attended her class daily. Most of her students were young women just out of college and in need of practical skills to get a start working for magazines, museums, or ad agencies. Whenever she passed me, making sure I wasn't looking at the keys, she'd wink and say *"Eile mit Weile!"* ("Don't hurry!") She detected my accent right away and let out a *"Wunderbar!"* when I told her I was Swiss.

The last day of the course a tall, intelligent-looking girl asked me if I would be interested in a twenty-hour-a-week job, starting after Labor Day. She was leaving it for graduate school, and the pay was an easy $2.50 an hour. Surprised and eager to know more, I suggested lunch at a coffee shop nearby, and off we went with our flimsy certificates, proof that we had passed the final typing test.

A week later I walked down Lexington to a basement office in the Sixties near Third Avenue for my interview at Letters Abroad. I didn't tell Walker; if I got the job, I would surprise him with the good news. Letters Abroad, a pen-pal agency run by volunteers, was started up after the war to spread American goodwill among people, especially the young, in war-damaged countries. Mrs. Ulrich, a statuesque brunette of a certain age, met me at ten in the morning and bombarded me with personal questions. Funny and slightly mischievous, she laughed at her own witty remarks, expecting me to catch on quickly.

On hearing that I spoke four languages and that German was my school language, she virtually promised me the job before I was even able to demonstrate my typing skills. Her heavy charm bracelet jingled as she told me stories of her travels in Europe as a child, how curious she had been to know what was under the fig leaves of boy statues in Rome, and whether the bones of saints in glass cases were cut-off arms and legs like soup bones in butcher shops. Then she asked me to translate and type a longwinded letter from a teacher in a village near Konstanz. The region and the grand lake were familiar to me, and I remembered that the area had been heavily bombed because of the Dornier airplane manufacturing plant nearby.

Mrs. Ulrich asked me to come in again soon to meet the volunteers, all "nice East Side ladies who could be my mother," and that I would officially start work after Labor Day at fifty dollars a week.

I rushed out the door so elated that I nearly stumbled over the few steps up to the sidewalk. A regular job—my own pin money—lunching with friends—it all tumbled around in my mind like confetti in the wind. I deserved a treat. Bloomingdale's was down the street, and I needed a new hat, something to celebrate my job and spring. Navy and white polka dots were the rage for accessories, just like some of Walker's ties, though I preferred larger dots, more Parisian.

Time flew by as I tried on scarves, short gloves, costume jewelry, and many hats. I decided on a stitched silk brim with a round crown, like a child's sun hat. I walked up to the main floor to investigate the new eye shadows and nail polish and dabbed Ma Griffe on my neck and wrists. I sailed home in a state of bliss, unaware of the other people in the streets.

The door to Walker's study was closed. He must be asleep, I guessed, a nap before dinner. How best to tell him, not to upset him? He couldn't possibly mind. This was a ladylike job, and only part-time, with the summers off. I'd still be able to cook and have friends for dinner, sew and read and go away for the weekend Fridays after lunch. Nothing would change for him.

I thought of something funny and unexpected and set out to disarm him. As soon as I heard Walker stirring I put on my new hat, turned up the brim and picked up a folded umbrella from the stand in the hall. When he walked into the living room, I struck a Fred Astaire pose, tossing the hat from hand to hand, one, two, one-two-three, snap, snap, stop—and waited until he smiled. Then I told him I had lucked into a part-time job.

"No—how did you do that?" He looked surprised and pleased. "And where did you get this charming hat? I'd like a cravate made from the same stuff. You could sew it for me." I said I'd be delighted to make him one, all I needed was a good pattern and a piece of silk. Something must have gone right for him that day: he approved of my job and the hours as well as the pay.

During dinner he acted as though he had won the lottery. He called it a "windfall," a great "stroke of luck," and said he enjoyed the suspense created by not revealing his secret until I served the dessert. "I have a surprise for you too," he finally said. "We were virtually given a Jaguar by one of Wilder's rich friends. Wait till you see it, a real beauty."

A gift of a Jaguar, his dream car—I thought it hard to believe. But strange and wonderful things had happened to Walker in the past, like his fortuitous meeting with Hemingway in Cuba when the two were young.

We were both lucky: he had his Jaguar to look forward to and I had my job. Slowly I was inching towards some kind of independence, nothing major, a small change that helped me think more clearly how to live with Walker and be more at peace. The friends he loved most, like Wilder, John, Dorothy, and Calvert, asked nothing of him. They liked him the way he was, with all his faults. Women who were bright, gifted in their professions, and not the least bit needy rated high in his mind. Eleanor Clark and Verna stood out as stars. I wasn't trying to compete with them. Their friendship meant a lot to me. What I could do was to develop my sense of humor, keep things light. Lately he responded to that and we were getting along better.

Spring exploded with a succession of openings and parties, the most memorable being a cocktail party at Eliza Parkinson's. Her apartment on East Seventy-second Street was designed by Philip Johnson and the living room could easily hold more than sixty people. A curved white wall and Mediterranean blue mosaic floor gave one the feeling of being on a luxury liner heading south. Fresh flowers were the only decoration, and nothing interfered with the architecture and the paintings. Eliza had a gift for mixing people from her many worlds. She generously spread kindness among her friends, and as a trustee of the Museum of Modern Art, worked like an ambassador. Walker, whom she had cared for and worried about during his last bout of surgery, and helped financially by buying one of his paintings, was a favorite guest in her house on Fisher's Island and in town. He admired her as a true gentlewoman. Sensible as she was, she understood much better than I at the time how self-centered a husband he must be, and she took me by the arm and introduced me around. He usually waited for people to come to him. In two hours I met Sister Parish, Lily Cushing and her daughters, Lily West and Alexandra (now married to Arthur Schlesinger), Mark Rothko, Daisy and Alfred Barr, and many notable others. It was a wonderful merry-go-round and I felt dizzy with new impressions.

Walker seemed appreciative of my social talents. He seldom mentioned Jane, his first wife, but on these occasions he was apt to comment that she hadn't liked New York social life and in the end refused to join him at large parties. Many of his close friends in this particular set had never met her.

I found it strange that Walker didn't allow me to attend one of Dorothy's openings in a small gallery in the Village because Jane and her new husband would be present. (Jane was now married to Winthrop Sargeant, the music critic of *The New Yorker*.) Surely enough years had passed for Walker to get over his strong resentments against Jane for leaving him.

The McDonalds always gave their own parties after Dorothy's openings and invited all their friends back to their small Morton Street floor-through. It was an eclectic group, which after enough liquor was given to heated discussions on political issues, business practices, and the current art scene. During one such evening we talked with William Zeckendorf, Herbert Solow, the *Fortune* writer, and his wife, the Finnish photographer Silvia Salmi (neighbors in Connecticut), the Lionel Trillings, the Wilder Hobsons, Eleanor Clark and Red Warren, Jack and Bob, and the Tworkovs. This was where I first heard of McCarthyism and the Whittaker Chambers–Alger Hiss case. I listened to raised voices and angry retorts, and too many times I saw some man gather up his wife and leave. Walker seldom participated in these debates.

I had to learn a whole new chapter of recent American history in order to understand the fear and horror some Americans had of

Communism. After the war European students became used to it. At home our northern Italian help Teresa, when asked by my mother if she planned to attend Mass on Sundays, proudly answered, *"No, signora, sono comunista."* Some of my art school teachers were radical socialists, and in Zurich I had a room in the apartment of an aristocratic older lady who distributed the Communist newspaper *Vorwärts*. My father had the greatest disdain for "salon Communists," as he referred to the sons of old money who had turned radical left.

After this spring season I was constantly torn between these two groups of Walker's friends. At big gatherings I preferred his elegant friends with their beautiful houses and manners, but as individuals the artists and intellectuals were closer to our lives and more stimulating for Walker.

At the end of June we left town for Lyme in our tan Jaguar, and Walker demonstrated the overdrive between Madison and Old Saybrook, assuring me that the police waited just short of the bridge to catch speeding drivers. At ninety mph the car hugged the road, and the sound of the engine was a comforting purr. I was very excited to ride in such a beautiful, well-made machine. The wooden dashboard had many more dials than ordinary cars, and Walker said he would give me a couple of driving lessons so that I would never grind the gears or ride the clutch.

Summer began with the shocking news of Hemingway's suicide. Walker withdrew to his bunk and listened to the transistor radio for hours. Later that day, he telephoned old friends in the city and asked them to send him everything they could find in foreign magazines and newspapers. During dinner he seemed preoccupied and low in his mind. He only picked at his food.

My only wish was to comfort him, but I was new in his life and had no experience with the earlier deaths of his friends like Hart Crane and Jim Agee. And Hemingway wasn't a personal friend. They had met by chance in Cuba in 1933. Walker had told me the story many times. He was asked to photograph Cuban poverty during the Machado regime for a book written by Carleton Beals, *The Crime of Cuba*. Hemingway needed someone to drink with. Walker had completed most of the work for the book when they met; after a week of evenings spent in bars with Hemingway, his money ran out. Hemingway loaned him a small amount so he was able to stay another week and take pictures on his own. The meeting was a triumph in Walker's early life.

I knew little about death. In my heart my father was immortal and longevity would be his reward for leading a healthy life. No doubt Walker had thought of his own death at the time when he had bleeding ulcers, a recurring condition that had killed his father before he reached sixty. He seldom went to funerals.

Who was I to help? I felt inadequate and sad. Hemingway was one of my heroes, too. Close friends in Zurich, a painter and his wife, who had a house in Spain and saw him in Pamplona in the fifties, described the scene, his entourage at the bullfights. We'd drink Rioja in a favorite tavern and talk all night about him and *Death in the Afternoon*. There were always pictures of Papa and Mary in foreign magazines.

As more stories and details about Hemingway's illness and depression surfaced, Walker seemed unable to get on with everyday life. It was as if he identified with friends long gone and was reliving some of his most difficult times. He was listless and would read lying down for hours. Even an occasional game of golf with his favorite neighbors, Knollie Knollenberg, a retired Sterling librarian at Yale, and his artist wife, Mary, brought no relief. The hot summer days dragged on, and it wasn't until we began our August pilgrimage to Maine and visited Calvert and John, who were both full of new projects, good talk, and humor, that he recovered enough buoyancy and energy to do some work.

Chapter 19

Nineteen-sixty-two was an important year for Walker. The Museum of Modern Art reissued his first major book, *American Photographs*, which the museum had first published in 1938. The new edition's introduction by Monroe Wheeler was largely written by Walker himself. A celebrated classic, the well-designed book with its gravure printed photographs drew much attention among a growing generation of young people interested in Walker's early work and 1930s America.

Always short of money in spite of his recent successes, Walker counted on friends for magazine jobs. With some reserve and caution, he renewed his friendship with Alice Morris, the literary editor of *Harper's Bazaar*, who was a loyal friend of his first wife Jane. In the last years of their marriage, Jane had often escaped to Alice and her husband, the critic Harvey Breit, and spent the night on a cot in their small apartment on East Seventy-fifth Street. Naturally Walker had stopped seeing Alice. Harvey later divorced Alice and married an heiress, and they gave theater parties in their Park Avenue apartment. Forever impressed by celebrities, Harvey invited Walker and me, and at one such gathering I shook hands with William Faulkner.

Alice seemed eager to be back in Walker's life. As a favor she introduced him to Marvin Israel, the new art director of *Harper's Bazaar*, who became very interested in Walker's subway pictures from the years 1938 to 1941. Marvin, a small, rather obsessive man, came up to our apartment and brought us a rare bottle of claret in a brown paper bag. He talked nonstop in a nasal voice, flattering Walker. Thanks to his and Alice's efforts, a portfolio of Walker's subway pictures, entitled "Walker Evans: The Unposed Portrait," appeared in *Harper's Bazaar* later that year.

Walker's subway pictures were praised by all who saw them. The photographs, taken with a hidden camera, made a great impression on me. While Marvin and Walker completed their selection, I kept looking at the many faces, some in trance-like repose, others watchful. These were ordinary New York City working people, most of them marked by years of hard life. What surprised me was their dignity, the trouble they took to look respectable in spite of their meager resources. Buttoned coats and hats and white scarves, heavy hands folded over a newspaper with a catchy headline—Walker missed nothing during his long days and late hours riding the subway.

Alice soon became a close friend of mine. I admired her style and witty manner. Younger looking than her years and unconventional in Claire McCardell dresses and French espadrilles during the summer months, she moved in a hesitant fashion, on long, thin legs, like a shore bird. When I asked Walker what she was like twenty years ago, he criticized her for her lack of judgment, for falling in love with ideas, unpublished poets, and the wrong people, but he always liked her taste. The more I saw of her, the more I enjoyed her company. We often lunched at the Women's Exchange on Madison Avenue, and she brought along books by Pablo Neruda and Virginia Woolf and gave them to me. I loved to walk her back to her office. Catching a glimpse of Diana Vreeland, Ford Agency models, and known fashion editors was such an event that I could have waited behind a closed door for hours. Alice made it all happen in her charming, nonchalant way. She introduced me around, and some pretty assistant would take me inside her cubicle and show me a wall covered with sketches, fabric swatches and photographs by Irving Penn or Richard Avedon. My job at Letters Abroad seemed most pedestrian and boring in comparison.

I lived for Walker's triumphs and growing fame. Every time a magazine published his work, I brought along the issue wherever I went and showed it to friends. On the bus, I often looked at the pages, hoping that someone might notice the pictures and I could tell them about Walker.

During the year, several more of Walker's photographic essays, some on favorite subjects with text by him, appeared in *Fortune*, *Architectural Forum*, and *Vogue*. The color photographs in "Auto Junkyard," an eight-picture portfolio in *Fortune*, were of special interest to me because I knew most of the yards around Lyme, including the lush swamp across the road from our screened porch where Clark Voorhees's son, Christopher, hid his own derelict cars. It was the first time I saw Walker's work in color on the printed page.

He had shown me slides before. A gadget lover, he bought several slide viewers with small batteries, all equally inadequate; I preferred to hold the little frames up against a bare lightbulb while I admired his sense of color.

The two essays on vintage postcards with reproductions from his collection, "Come on Down," in *Architectural Forum*, and "When Downtown Was a Beautiful Mess," in *Fortune*, accompanied by his own text, were a great coup for Walker. For years he had collected these postcards. Motoring in Connecticut, Maine, and Vermont, we would stop in book barns and antique shops and go through the shoe boxes full of old postcards. The ones depicting familiar places that had recently vanished, like Scollay Square in Boston, would soon be valuable, he said.

For days Walker worked on his text, writing all morning when I was out of the house, smoking and drinking tea. "Don't talk to me, I'm thinking," was his early-morning refrain. After dinner he'd often read me the short piece. I envied his facility for expressing an original idea and making a point without belaboring it. Sometimes, when he wasn't happy with a word, he would telephone Wilder, John, or Alice for suggestions. Then words and more words floated through our living room, like musical notes, until Walker, with his very good ear, chose the right one and quickly wrote it down.

Significant changes were taking place in the art world, most of which Walker approved of. He sounded in high spirits one morning when he called me at Letters Abroad with the good news of John Szarkowski's appointment as the new director of the department of photography at the Museum of Modern Art. They had met in 1955, when Szarkowski called on him in his *Fortune* office bringing with him his photographs of Louis Sullivan's architecture, a Guggenheim project for a book on the architect's work. Little did Szarkowski know at the time that Walker had seen his work before and had helped him to obtain the Guggenheim fellowship. In Szarkowski, Walker felt he had an ally, someone who'd value his opinion and like his work and would also share his taste for the work of younger photographers like Robert Frank and Lee Friedlander, whom he thought most gifted. At long last the Steichen regime was over.

Not all our artist friends were as lucky. During dinner at the Calvert Coggeshalls', Betty Parsons, the doyenne of Abstract

Expressionism, was terribly upset over the New Realists show at Sidney Janis' gallery, an exhibit that signaled the arrival of Pop Art. She was alarmed by Warhol's Campbell's Soup paintings on view in Los Angeles, and Lichtenstein's first show at Leo Castelli Gallery. She predicted that many established abstract painters, like Jack Tworkov, would soon be thrown out of their galleries and forced to look for jobs.

Walker was in a funny, slightly vindictive mood that night at dinner and made a few negative comments about too many dribbling women painters, and wasn't it time for something new and provocative? He embraced the use of common objects, graffiti, and cartoons in art, and saw himself as the father of Pop Art. I realized he didn't take this new departure very seriously and was mostly amused, but Calvert and Betty were angry. We left early, and it upset me. I resented his way of making fun of women artists in front of Betty, who had always been nice to me, but secretly I was glad to be at least on the fringes of the new scene and to have a look at the Pop artists. Soon after this unfortunate evening we were invited to the Motherwells' down the street, where we met Claes Oldenburg, who was young, curly blond, and full of charm. After dinner small versions of his food and merchandise sculptures, like a cheeseburger and a slice of wedding cake, from The Store at his Second Street studio, were passed around much to everyone's delight. "Leave it to the Motherwells," said Walker on the way home. "They're not worried about the art scene, they're too intelligent."

It was a tumultuous time, and wherever we went our friends were worried. Our landlords, Vita and Peter, who had business in Puerto Rico, followed every move of the Cuban Missile Crisis. Eunice Jessup, who had a teenage son, was troubled about the growing number of U.S. military in Vietnam. Race riots, Marilyn Monroe's suicide, the death of Abstract Expressionist painter Franz Kline, drugs, Bob Dylan's songs, Stanley Kubrick's film *Lolita*—all this was vehemently discussed during late, smoke-filled, boozy nights. It sometimes seemed as though we were living on the edge of a precipice, soon to be thrown into a world of chaos and violence.

Walker seemed to pay little attention, though he was scared of drugs and violence. He refused to let me go to artist studios in what he called "dangerous neighborhoods," where some of the first "happenings" were staged. I missed Mary Carswell, with whom I could have discussed my own doubts and fears openly and from whom I'd have enjoyed some comfort and encouragement, but she was in Washington.

Bernard Haggin, a friend of Walker's, took me out regularly to performances of the New York City Ballet. He lived near Columbia University and took the subway down and we would meet at City Center on West Fifty-fifth Street. By the time he'd arrive, he often felt hot and exhausted. I would already be in my seat, not knowing whether he might join me for the first ballet, because he wasn't up to it or disliked the principal dancer or a last-minute change in the program. Bernard was a noted music critic, and going to Balanchine ballets with him was an exercise in being tactful and, above all, silent. A few years older than Walker and extremely tense, he suffered from serious depression and had to take a pill just before the curtain rose. In order to concentrate and guard against any distraction from persons sitting next to him, he clamped two dark pieces of cardboard onto the sides of his eye glasses, thus eliminating all peripheral vision. On his good evenings he could be very funny and tell me anecdotes about Balanchine and his favorite dancers. I learned from him to love ballet music, what to look for in a particular movement or pas de deux. He instinctively spotted the most gifted young dancers and watched them in different ballets throughout the season. Once we had just sat down when Samuel Barber and Gian Carlo Menotti took their seats in front of us. Bernard turned beet red and shook his head rapidly and without a word stormed out of the theater and never returned during the evening. Menotti was one of his *bêtes noires*.

Walker's good luck continued with a generous Carnegie Corporation award, "A Year of Reflection," an honor much like a sabbatical. The sum of money he received matched his annual *Fortune* salary, and no projects and reports were asked of him. We celebrated with the Hobsons and the McDonalds, and I was bursting with pride. He deserved it all. At last free of money worries for a while, he'd be able to take a leave of absence from *Fortune*, do work that interested him, and write more.

In October, Walker traveled to California by train. It was his idea to ride the trains and photograph out the window, "before the great trains disappear altogether." I saw him off with a split of champagne in his roomette on the Wolverine to Chicago. He had all his paraphernalia, books, and pills neatly packed in different size cases, and was in a good mood. He called from Denver and was very chatty on the phone. Not long after, a little note arrived, written aboard the vista-dome California Zephyr shortly before the train reached San Francisco:

The trip has been relaxing but a little long. No one to talk to, but I don't mind solitude as you know. I read and slept and thought or something like thought.

Getting a change will be good for you too, good for anyone. At least it shakes up one's ideas and plans.

Alice Morris and I spent a long weekend in East Hampton, where she went to an old inn once a year to relive the memories of her childhood summers. During the week John and Dorothy asked me for supper with Bob and Jack, and John taught me to dance the Twist. Bob, who was an excellent dancer and already knew all the arm and hip movements, practiced with me, while John acted as coach, barely moving to the monotonous beat, until I finally got it. Dorothy said she liked the Twist and might do a painting of a crowded dance floor, but she didn't enjoy the Chubby Checker music.

When Walker returned from the West Coast, Marvin Israel talked about publishing his pictures of street trash in *Harper's Bazaar*. Cigarette butts in the gutter, wire mesh garbage cans filled to the top, crumpled candy wrappers, broken umbrellas—the timing was perfect, he thought, to shake up the fashion magazine audience. The city was no longer a nice place. One evening, as Marvin and Walker were discussing the trash essay over another vintage bottle, Marvin pulled out a folder of photographs by his friend Diane Arbus. Walker had not heard her name before, but we were both mesmerized by her work. These were posed portraits. The photographer knew her eccentric subjects, and they collaborated with her. How daring, a woman moving without fear in New York's underworld. This appealed to Walker as a voyeur, it excited him. He too had been attracted to *les bas-fonds*, especially in Paris, but he was too scared to go near it.

Marvin smiled and lowered his voice, as though he were telling a secret. Would we like to meet her? She was waiting in a taxi in front of the house, he said. We said we would, and he ran downstairs. A few minutes later he returned, alone. "Too shy to come up," he said and shrugged his shoulders. She was tongue-tied, in awe of Walker, he said, but not to worry, he would make it happen soon.

Just before Christmas my father wrote that my Swiss divorce papers had arrived and he would send me the money for the Swissair flight to Zurich. He suggested I come for my birthday. Right now this was better than all the presents from Bergdorf's, Bendel's, and Cartier— my first transatlantic flight home. Snowflakes dancing against the windows of the plane, it would carry me to my family and friends and their young children not yet born when I left Europe. I hadn't seen my siblings for nearly five years.

.

Chapter 20

Monday Jan 28 63

My love Miss Belle,

I'm in the office working away at moving. Last night was the first night alone. I tried not to miss you and this morning I just thought about the coming day, things to do, but it was awfully quiet and empty without you and the usual thing—breakfast tray, talk and chatter. Luckily for me the telephone rang. Barbara Kerr with her Mademoiselle job. She got things mixed up—I'm not doing James Baldwin, but something else! Oh, these lady editors. Never mind, I charge double for their mistakes.

I just write briefly hastily now to get you this letter in the mail. I expect your telegram later today—which is one reason I won't go out to the art party.

Give my best greetings to your family—tell them how I wish I could be there. And a special additional feeling for your sister whom you have made me love.

Much much love my darling to you.

W

January 29th 63

Darling bird,

In Zurich Christine met me alone. She is a dream; lovely face with a perfect figure. She smiles in a most disarming way, and the two of us speaking English, French, and gibberish at the same time and laughing made people turn around in the streets of Zurich. We traveled first class to Bern in a brand-new train decorated with drawings by Surbek. There Maman waited for us. She was happy to see me and she is very nice to me. She waits on me, and I can do as I please. The small town, the streets, the house we live in is exactly the same. Later Anne-Marie, who is not quite eighteen years old, arrived. She was a great surprise to me. She has a lot of style and personality, and I am very fond of her. She showed me all her collections in her room, rocks, pictures from Ireland and of horses, and in an old gold medallion a picture of her blond young man. He looks very sensitive. They love each other. We spent the evening giving presents to each other and loving each other. They adored all the presents. I went to say goodnight to my mother in her bedroom, and she said that I looked very happy and more mature and that I was a beauty. She said it was because of you. I was very touched by that.

I miss you my angel. I think of you and thank you for giving me much happiness.

Tenderleaf

1963

The old poet Robert Frost died today.

P.S. Here is the data on watch I want if possible. The Breitling, I agree with you, is too complicated for my simple uses. I found out that another Swiss manufacturer has a beauty. The name is Wakman and I'm sure your father would know of this. Enclosed is a picture of the black-face model I want. Cost probably around $40 or $50 in Switzerland or less perhaps. Ben wants one too but how can we afford to advance him the price. He will repay you if you happen to be able to get one for him, so he says. Love, again love,

W.

January 30th 63

Bird, my love,

So many things I want to tell you, I don't know where to start. I had a good night's sleep for the first time. At lunch we celebrated my birthday. Before lunch I went shopping with Christine for my present. She took me to an antique store and I chose a lovely candlestick of joy silver. I thought of you, because of its shape. I know you will love it. My birthday started with an early call from my brother. I talked to him for a long time and it was wonderful. The telephone system in the whole of Europe is well organized. Bernard has sent me some Biedermeier glasses to New York that will get there before me. Then Alec telephoned and he sounded fine and natural. He sent me a dozen pink roses with a silk bow.

Angel bird, I walked through the old parts of town and saw lovely antiques. I also look for watches, but have not found a watch with numerals on a black face. Numerals on a light gray face, the color of steel. Would that bother you? Tonight we went to a concert of baroque music. It was very pleasant except for the intermission. Maman knew everybody and dragged me from person to person, which was terrible. Christine can't stand these people, she really suffers from being in Switzerland and living at home. She is like an angel among provincial bores. Nobody understands her and she has lots of problems. She is a real artist and she works with tremendous energy. She loves you and she wants to write to you. Please answer her. I hope Alec is not going to be too much for me. On Saturday I will see him for the first time, but he wants me to come to Basel some time soon. I wish you could help me. Of course nobody understands that we see each other, except my friends and Christine. People here are so dreary and narrow and so disgustingly rich without any style or chic. In the streets they look at me as though I were a white elephant. How happy I am to have you, who understands everything. I missed you on my birthday, angel. Are you well and gay man about town? Your letter just came, how lovely!

I love you.
Tenderleaf

The birthday party invitation was by Joyce's grandson. The date is 1939, Paris

NY 163 E 94
Friday afternoon
2-1-63

Tenderleaf
Your excellent letter telling of arrival was a charmer.

This weekend may be so lonely I'll go somewhere. I have a call in to the Dupees right now, but haven't reached them.

Last night dinner at the Breuers was fun. Everyone asked for you. Eliza Parkinson was there, and Saul Steinberg and his bad little girl, and Pei, the Chinese architect with a nice Chinese wife. I ate between Mrs. Pei and Connie Breuer. Lots of people came in later, none of whom I knew. A real New York professional party—quite brainy I suppose, though I didn't sample any of the stuff—only Eliza and Marcel a little, and Saul. Saul says he was asked to write an essay on me for some magazine, but he failed to bring it off to his satisfaction. Too bad. I suspect he is a writer born, like me, who works visually just to avoid writing, which is so painful and difficult. (Not for you I believe, you write easily when you get to it.)

I may see something of Eliza; but she isn't really stimulating I'm afraid. Just rather charming, and that's not enough for young W. E.

Irmgard is smelling up the place. I'll have to air it out. Humanity!

The United States Commission for the New York World's Fair telephoned me. The man in charge of "design" asked me to talk things over with him. I do not see what I can do but I will think about it. This Commission has already searched the brains of several journalists I know, among them Rovere and Zinsser, whose reports I'm supposed to read this weekend. Guess who are the final big words for this U.S. fair exhibit just under Pres. Kennedy? Only Augie Heckscher and Arthur Schlesinger! If only I didn't detest the bureaucracy and confusion of working for the U.S. government, I'd leave Fortune *again and poke into the White House as the great director of the World's Fair picture division—with Jackie as my assistant. But the hell with it, it would be the same old frustrating penniless story, and I've been through all that under F. D. Roosevelt.*

I cooked dinner Wednesday for Marvin and his strange little photo girl Diane Arbus. It was not a good evening, as she was inarticulate and he in a poor mood. As you know, I am trying to do business with him—fame and fortune—and he is slippery and unreliable, the devil.

That is all the news. Next week the Canadian Broadcasting Corp. men are coming to see me about Let Us Now Praise Famous Men *pictures. Fame and fortune department. I shall describe their visit. I am getting television advice around town, as to what is proper and profitable in such business.*

I have to write officially a sort of accounting to Carnegie Corporation to mark my termination. Rather dread the task. But if I go to Dupees for the weekend I'll come fresh to the task.

Tell me everything, I love your letters as you know.

Sadly missing you,

Much much love,

W.

Chapter 20

February 3rd, 1963
    Bird, my love,
    I am writing in bed in my old room. There is an old big desk in it, books everywhere, a gold oval mirror, my Louis Philippe armchair with faded blue upholstery and a worn dark red Persian rug. Finally I can be with you alone. I knew it would be a strain to come home without you. I can only rest in your arms and now I miss it, miss it terribly. Saturday Alec rang the bell around noon and it was very natural for me to see him. He looked well, very elegant in London tailored tweeds. He seemed overjoyed with all the presents. The New York map and the shirts made a big hit. He asked about you and your work and was very interested. In his car we drove through lovely country and completely unspoilt villages with working farms, real peasants and lots of tobogganing children. It was cold (zero) and three feet of snow everywhere, but the sun was shining and the air was pure. It is amazing how little the country around Bern has changed.
    Alec told me that it didn't make him sad to see me, and I was so glad of it. He spoke about his job and told me that he had in mind to start on his own. Their number one client is Volkswagen for Europe, rather disagreeable German people bossing everybody in the agency, and he is tired of photographing cars. Alec wants me to come to Basel, and I will stay at an old hotel overlooking the Rhine, where my mother and all of us children lived at the beginning of the war.
    Bird, I take sleeping pills every night, so much I miss you. I kiss you and love you.
    Isabelle

February 8th, 1963
    Bird, my love,
    I am so sad that I would like to cry in your arms and have you nurse me for weeks. Yesterday I took a train to Zurich in the afternoon. Marie-Louise, as beautiful as ever, waited at the station and we were happy to see each other. We had drinks in order to be able to go to the opening. The people at the gallery were similar to New York art people except for one big difference, they were my best friends, art school friends and my teachers, and it was too much for me. The paintings were extremely good. Bruno Bischofberger, whose wife Vre you think looks like Oona Chaplin, is very gifted and serious about his work. Like you, he is an individualist,

not part of the current art scene. In this way he reminds me of Jack Heliker. They attract a small group of collectors and connoisseurs, but it is the school of Pollock that has swept the continent. The dinner party after the opening was gay and witty, and I was happy to see my friends around me. They still love me. I missed you, because I don't make sense without you. I drank a lot in order to be confident, but wasn't able to prove my point, justify my divorce and everything without you. I felt that people thought I was an adventurous woman. Alec was placed next to me at the dinner table, and if Christine hadn't noticed my embarrassment and changed seats with me it would have been too strange for words. Later on, Christine, her man Edi, Alec, and I went to Marie-Louise's apartment and had nightcaps. It was more relaxed, and when they all left, Marie-Louise and I talked and were very close to each other. Since her divorce, she has a very hard time living alone with her two children. She is rich and very sensitive, and right now I am alone because she went to her psychiatrist. She loves you; for you she bought this airmail paper. She looked at your book with great pleasure and loves your face in the pictures I showed her. Some excellent photographs that Landshoff made of you last year at my father's lecture at NYU save my life. I will have them copied for you. This morning I went to see another school friend who has three little girls. I used to design dresses and sew with her and stay often at her magic flat in a street of prostitutes. All my art school years came back to me; all the love affairs, the drinking, feeling exuberant one day and lonely and misunderstood the next. It was a rich time, difficult, but we were carried away by art, poetry, and each other. Now many of these friends experience serious problems in their complicated lives. Switzerland for them is hard to take. Some of them have become introverts, lonely and disillusioned, and some have sold their soul, and it shocks me. I understand your love for Paris and the need to be alone there. Paris is for you what Zurich is for me. Isn't it lucky for us that we both had such a similar intense experience? Bird, I am physically sick, my stomach hurts and I would like to fly to you. I miss you, take me away from the world, the reality and people.

 I love you,
 Isabelle

Rhinebeck, NY
Chez Dupee
Monday, Feb 11, 1963

Love,

Stuck in Rhinebeck through unexpected circumstances. Andy, Dupee's wife, has taken the car to town early this morning. Fred worked all night finishing a book review and is now asleep. And the taxi company is not working today for some stupid reason. I shall wait until he wakes up and then get somehow back to New York. I did have a delicious weekend with them all—attractive as ever they are. While Fred was writing Andy took me around various houses which I photographed. Some excellent pictures, I think. I came up here Friday late. Thursday I dined with a large party at the Coggeshalls—many old friends from way back whom you haven't met.

While you're in London get some large English washcloths, I love them. And please note: Wilkinson razor blades. They are marvelous, long-lasting, and a great economy. Buy me several packages, perhaps a dozen, please, and I'll have shaves for a year.

Thanks for telling me about the Sunday Times' USA issue—I'll get it at the Club.

Much love to all, salutations, and a special kiss for Christine.
W.

Paris, February 18th 63

Bird, my love,

This is my last morning in Paris. I miss you so much. I am homesick for you, my darling bird. Come and get me, and together we would enjoy everything much more.

Yesterday, Sunday at noon, Christine left. I took her to the Gare de l'Est. It was raining and very cold. The old-fashioned train was there already. Plain French people saying goodbye to each other. Women kissing, men kissing, children waving, again and again. White steam came out from under the engine and put a veil over the whole scene.

Christine stood at one of the train windows, smiling faintly. She is not as happy as I want her to be. More steam and a sharp whistle, and the train pulled out of the station. I was so sad, because I thought of my departure in two weeks. From the Gare de L'Est I took a Métro to the Bastille and walked through the old Rue Saint Antoine to the

Place des Vosges. The rain had stopped and the sky was very pale gray, lovely with the brick-red of the houses on the Place. Nobody was there. It was like an old dream. The little park in the center, the buildings with their arcades, the small restaurant on the corner. I expected a miracle any minute: Marcel Marceau doing a children's dance with a hoop, or Barrault dressed in a Pierrot costume. I passed through the iron gate into the garden. A woman was feeding the pigeons. I walked around the grounds and found a tiny sparrow that couldn't fly anymore. It was haunting, and I didn't know what to do. I ran away to the opposite corner and tried to forget it. All of a sudden I heard voices, and out of a side street a lot of laughing children ran and jumped into the little park. They chased the pigeons and played games and were a great comfort to me. Then I continued my walk through old streets like Rue des Francs Bourgeois to the Carnavalet Museum. I passed the Parc Royal, the Cul de Sac des Poissonnières, an old fountain, the grand houses of Hôtel Châtillon, Hôtel Lamoignon with their lovely courtyards, old shops, and churches. The light had changed to a pale sunlight when I crossed the bridge to Quai d'Anjou on the Ile. I said goodbye to the parts of Paris I love. Then I went inside the church of St. Julien le Pauvre off Quai de la Tournelle. The small church is still being used, and a strong smell of incense filled the dark space. I walked around and looked at some medieval graves in the wall. Fresh spring flowers were stuck in little frames of pictures of saints. I bought a candle and lit it. On my long walk I didn't see a single person who didn't belong to the quartier, the street or the church. These were the real people of Paris, and to see them on this Sunday gave me great pleasure.

    I love you
    Isabelle

London, February 19th 63

    Bird, my love,

    Shopping in London, what could be more fun! All for you. I decided only to eat ham sandwiches while I am here, in order to buy things. It is fantastically cheap, compared to Paris. First I went to Harrods and got handkerchiefs (not that cheap) and toilet paper (frightfully soft). I looked for washcloths, but they only had small ones. I shopped everywhere for the Wilkinson razor blades. They are so rare to come by that Harrods, Fortnum and Mason, Burlington Arcade chemists don't have a single package. Why, I don't really know. Then I found hand-knitted Shetland socks in just the natural color you wanted, size 10, the smallest size for men. Then a dotted wool tie, the same large dots you have in silk. The letter paper I am writing on is by Truslove & Hanson and also a present to you. Isn't the color subtle? I went to the Briggs shop and got a big flask and a wonderful collapsible goblet with a handle in a pigskin case. It is for tea as well, and you will never have that plastic taste again. The flask was medium expensive, but much less compared to Brooks or Abercrombie. It is only plate. The sterling one was $45, too high for me. The women's clothes are nothing compared to the men's fantasies. Pink shirts, silk dressing gowns, silk pajamas, vests, and everything is half the price as Brooks. I think of you every minute. The big bargain is second-hand silver. I bought for myself a little dispenser for sovereigns, Victorian and perfectly plain for 2 pounds. You can open it up and slip coins into it. If ever we have a little extra money to spend, silver in London is the thing to buy.

Tonight I go to the Old Vic. The buses are marvelous; I always find a seat, and the ticket women are so polite. The cars stop when I want to cross the street. In Paris one has to be very careful not to have accidents. I am in love with London again, and I am happy that the prices haven't gone up as much as in the rest of Europe. There is an inflation going on in London. Everything is empty: the opera, the restaurants, the shops. People don't have money to spend. Almost one million people are unemployed.

It is still snowing, and I pray to see the Sterns. Much love, my angel. I love you and miss you so.

Isabelle

163 E 94
Sat. Feb. 23, 1963
   Darling,
   You are so good about writing. I have four letters from you, three this morning from London, and your tremendously interesting and as you know exciting letter from Paris describing happiness with Christine. You know how I loved reading that. Of course I was present, in effect, with you too. I was so pleased and stimulated

I could do nothing all morning after reading your letter, Almost nothing, that is.

There is so much to remember, when a few days go by I forget some of the things I do. Of course I see someone every evening—could not quite bear being up here alone, without you. When I have no engagement I make one with the Coggeshalls, who have given me a standing invitation to dinners. Calvert and Susie are a comfort because they seem always really to like and want me. Tonight I go to the Carlins, and we are going to have coffee and brandy after dinner at the John Whites. I see and work with Ben and I have had dinner with Bernard Haggin and Alice. The latest is the downfall of Marvin, fired out of his job as Harper's Bazaar *art director. Of course he wanted to be fired. I must say, he was treating me shabbily, recently he assigned and ordered all sorts of things then withdrew and rejected some of the work I did. I'm afraid I got pretty angry, and told him so. In fact I fired him first. But now that the harm's done to me I feel not vindictive. He's not trustworthy, though, and I'll never work for or with him. As a matter of fact I shall have a tough time over money because of him, because he led me to count on some fees that will not now come in. The World's Fair people blew up too, damn them. They changed their plans away from having a big photo show, and won't need me. Darling do not worry, we can be poor but happy for a time: then I'll be rich and famous again, later, as usual.*

Your letters say so much, I'm fascinated by everything. Good for Jimmy and Tania to call you. Will you meet ever I wonder! I'm busy trying to determine where to write you now. It seems correct to send this to Bern. I don't think I could catch you at Bernard's.

The Canadian Broadcasting Corp., at least, seems still interested to buy pictures from me. And of course very soon I'll be back on the Fortune payroll. The speed of time is staggering. You'll be back before we know it. What a joy to see you again and to live with you again, my love. My delicious love.

W.

On the train from Göttingen to Frankfurt
February 25, 63

Darling bird,

I have so much to tell you, where shall I start? With Jimmy and

Tania of course. It was Thursday the 21st, and I was to meet them in a gallery off Burlington Arcade. All morning I walked around London. First I looked at the newly arranged costume department at the Victoria and Albert. Lots of clothes by Worth, some wonderful Chanels and 1920s dresses and small, exquisite showcases of eighteenth-century boots, bags, traveling cases, hats, and jewels. You would have loved it.

Then I went to Westminster Abbey. The sun was shining, and there couldn't have been a more interesting light in the nave of the abbey. I walked to the Thames and loved the gray river with the dark freighters. What a city, what style and atmosphere! We should live here, bird, it is the right city for us. Slowly I made my way back to Piccadilly. I passed Queen Ann's Gate, Birdcage Walk, and through the lovely park. Then through Burlington Arcade to Cork Street to the Redfern Gallery. My heart was jumping when I entered the gallery. Nobody was there and I looked at the paintings, rather conservative. Finally a most handsome man with gray hair, lovely tweeds, and a wonderful face came in, talked to the gallery man, and looked around. I looked at the pictures some more, nobody spoke to me. After ten minutes a girl came over and asked me about my name. Then this most attractive man nodded, smiled and shook hands with me. We sat down and Jimmy asked all about you, your work, your health, your car, our apartment, your habits, your flasks, your tweeds, and more. We had a wonderful time. I am in love with him ever since I saw him and more so since he kissed me goodbye in Waterloo Station.

We left the gallery and went to Sotheby's to look at the antiques and pictures. I told him all about you, and we laughed a lot. For tea we went to Brown's Hotel. I was dream-walking and so happy that Jimmy liked me. I wore my black velour hat with the wide brim and my gray cape.

Finally Tania returned from shopping. They have not been in London since Xmas because of the cold weather. Tania talked and talked and wanted to know all about you, Vita, Harvey Breit, the Kronenbergers, McDonalds, Hobsons, etc. She is nice, very German, and I had the feeling that she bored Jimmy just a tiny bit. Then Kiki West joined us for the most delicious tea. Jimmy kept filling my plate with sandwiches and every so often he'd wink at me kiddingly, all while Tania was talking, talking, just like Vita. I went with them to

Waterloo Station, where we had drinks in a bar, laughed and joked some more. They are full of love for you and homesick for their New York friends. You must write to them more often. We have to visit them in Tisbury. The house sounds lovely. Bird, I was so sad when they left me to catch their train.

Othello at the Old Vic was a marvelous performance with a black Othello, a superb actor. I was moved and shaken by it.

I was glad to leave London the next day to visit my brother. I flew to Frankfurt, took a train to Göttingen. I will write all about the weekend. It was a great experience. 20 below (Celsius) in the German countryside. Now I am on my way to Zurich where my friends will give a farewell party for me. Soon I'll be home, and soon in your arms. I am so homesick, I can't tell you, darling. Jimmy made me homesick for you, more than ever.

I love you,
Isabelle

On the train Zurich–Bern
February 26th, 63
  Darling bird,
  Let me tell you about the weekend in Göttingen. From London to Frankfurt I took a Lufthansa plane. In Frankfurt I had to wait a few hours for the train. So I walked around the town, Germany's number one financial city, rebuilt from scratch after the war and worse than Miami. Money, money, fat red faces, new Mercedes; it is where that movie about the spy girl was made. We saw it with Calvert. It was called Rosemarie, *and it is a true story. The girl was shot three years ago in Frankfurt.*

  Well, with mixed feelings I entered a first class compartment in the train going north to Hamburg. Göttingen is exactly half way between Munich and Hamburg, 4 1/2 hours from Frankfurt. Five businessmen traveling on big expense accounts sat in the compartment. I snubbed them by pretending to be French. Everybody speaks English in Germany. The level of the conversation was lower than low. After three hours I got depressed and when I arrived in Göttingen around 8 PM I felt like crying. It was 20 below zero (Celsius), dark and unfriendly. My brother kissed me and took me in his arms, and tears rolled down my cheeks. Soon I was in his apartment full of the loveliest books, records, drawings, flowers, wine, and food. He was so sweet; he had arranged for me to stay in a room in the same house. There were flowers on the night table, and a little welcome letter. He wanted to know all about you. I told him everything. He has mellowed and matured very much, and to my surprise he is very critical of Germany. He knows the works of E. E. Cummings, Henry James (including Edel), Auden, Edmund Wilson, etc. Traveling with an English aristocrat related to Jean Campbell, he has fallen in love with England and Scotland. Paris has always been his second domicile. You would like him. He took me out to dinner to a lovely place. I couldn't believe my eyes; everybody in this inn had a nice, intelligent face. It could have been in Harvard Yard. Teachers and students were drinking lovely wine and talking away. Göttingen is a world-famous university, and the whole town revolves around the faculties. The university was founded in 1735 by the English King George II. The first building he gave to the university was a beautiful riding academy for the young lords. The town is medieval with painted wooden houses, gothic churches, and wonderful walks. The student body is international. It is here that the atom was discovered. Bernard took me around. I saw the libraries, the rooms for the seminars, the old church where the main lectures are held, the campus, the excellent book shops, etc. Whenever a new book appears, a messenger is sent out to bring it to my brother's apartment. He is now the chief assistant of the German department and he decides when a book has to be bought, when students are ready for exams, etc. His professor, Walter Killy, was for two years a guest professor at Harvard. I met him. He is charming and he wrote a booklet on German kitsch that is excellent. He collects trivia and he gave me his book when he saw American Photographs. *Everybody is crazy about the book. Bernard thinks it could be a great success in Germany, if published in paperback form. He will get you in touch with publishing houses as soon as you find out whether the Modern would be agreeable to such a plan. Everybody knows about Agee. These young people are so knowledgeable and so sincere, it is a joy. The students are very poor, but brave, brave! Studying means everything to them. They are so critical of their own country. Whenever one makes a complimentary remark about Germany, they deny it. They have horrible guilt feelings, because they know that Naziism is not dead to this day.*

I was sad when I had to leave my brother. I didn't know that we loved each other so much.

Yesterday I arrived in Zurich. My friends had arranged a lovely dinner in a Spanish restaurant. We laughed and ate until midnight. I missed you because you already belong together with my friends. They want to meet you. I spent the night at Marie-Louise's. Her children tried on all my clothes and cried when I left. Lunch at Vre's; her little girls told me their secrets and wanted to wear my perfume. Now I am on the train to Bern with the flu.

I love you,
Isabelle

163 E 94
Feb 28

Love

Thank God your letter from Frankfurt came this morning. I hadn't heard from you for days. The mail is irregular. I know you meant to space letters, but three from London arrived all together, then several days nothing made me worry. On top of that Jimmy had written about your visit but not you—I mean his description of seeing you came immediately, but your letters from London were mailed before you saw him. Now all's well again and I am happy that you are writing and are all right. I have already written to Bern. I just skipped Göttingen. Are you flying the 4th of March? You said you thought you would, but later made no mention. Of course I have to know. Cable me as soon as you get your flight number and just give me the day and flight number so I can telephone Swissair for time.

How I long to see you. Our separation has been a little too long and painful and it has disorganized and demoralized me! Thank God you told Irmgard to come often.

Now what have I to tell you—not much, as I haven't kept track always. Sara di Bonaventura telephoned two invitations, one for both of us Mar. 15 which I accepted.

The Shaws gave a dinner party for ten, I sat next to the Museum [of Modern Art] photo director and talked business. I think as a result of it the Museum will buy some of my prints.

The Canadians offered me a mere $350. Yet that is a one way fare to Europe. Let's go together soon, to England as you suggest. I was *fascinated of course over your opinions of both Sterns. You were so accurate. I love T. but she does bore everyone. And I knew you would fall for Jimmy and he for you. I told you!*

Alice is lonely, poor dear. She is coming here for dinner. Perhaps Vita too—the two lonely lovelies. Or Bernard Haggin, another loner. My pictures of parties are much appreciated. I did Barnes most successfully—like a movie sequence.

Now if you're arriving Mar 4th I'd not go out much. I have a chest cold but it is not severe. I'll go to the office tomorrow because it is Mar 1st (Friday). Back on the payroll by God. Did I tell you I had packed and was ready to go to Anna Maria to the Brewers but that I called it off due to weather there, bad plane connections, and shortness of time. Tuesday I even got as far as the Air Terminal only to find it was impossible to get there without great inconvenience, doubt as to return, and expense. No jets to Sarasota, only Tampa.

I can't think of anything except your arrival and am excited as a schoolboy-bridegroom at the thought of seeing you. I feel we are certainly married. You and I—don't you?

Now I hope this letter gets to you fast. I'll send it special. Enclosed, probably too late, is another choice of watch which Ben found. Note this is pictured white face but can be had same model, black. Here too is a check in case you can get one for Ben. He will repay me Mar 1st.

I've seen The Eclipse, *film by Antonioni. Not his best.*

Dwight Macdonald has taken me up, I'm pleased as I like him. So I take him up and shall ask him to join the Century, with Dupee too. Will have a trio.

Write, wire, cable, telegraph! Often, a lot, tell me all plans and all happiness! Your ever ever lover in all ways.

W.

Chapter 21

Walker met me at Idlewild. Standing in line to clear customs, I found him at once on the balcony all bundled up in a warm coat, tweed hat, and a wool scarf hanging from his neck. We smiled and waved and blew kisses across the crowded space. I was so happy to see him and be back in New York. Soon I'd be able to distance myself from my many new impressions and emotional turmoil, quiet down, and settle into our routine of being alone with each other for a while. He looked a little drawn because of his cold. Over and over again he said how much he had missed me.

Too tired to talk, I leaned against him in the taxi all the way home. Dirty snow lined the streets, and after having enjoyed the early spring in Switzerland and the bright sunny days, the city looked winter-worn and gray. Once inside our apartment I felt relieved. It was spotless and full of surprises: white roses on the dining table, chilled champagne in the icebox and food for supper. Invitations, magazines, and unopened mail were sorted out in neat little piles on my bureau. I was home—home was here and not over there, and all was well.

We had a fire after dinner, and Walker merrily gathered his loot. To find the right presents for him was a challenge, but nothing gave me more pleasure than to see his expression of childlike wonder over the perfect gift, something he really wanted. It might have been his love for everything English, but all my presents were a success. Each one had a little story attached to it, and as he listened, he had asked me about certain favorite London shops, hotels, streets, and squares. Revived by his humor, the brand of which is rather unusual in Switzerland, and the champagne, I was soon laughing and chattering with him, and it must have been four in the morning my time when I finally went to sleep.

Our carefree days were few. Soon after my arrival home, Verna called with the alarming news of Wilder's massive hemorrhage. Walker was shattered. He packed a bag and took the next train out to

Princeton. I was back working at Letters Abroad, so I joined him for the weekend. Wilder lay in the hospital's intensive care unit, and other than his family Walker was the only visitor allowed in. We stayed with neighbors and friends of the Hobsons, Percy and Nancy Woods. We spent the evenings with Verna and their children, Eliza and Archie. Countless friends called and stopped by. Everyone who knew Wilder had such a need to talk about him, to fend off the inevitable.

Wilder died that spring. Walker stayed in Princeton for three weeks. I came out from New York for the funeral, in Wilder's favorite church. The choir sang spirituals, the songs he knew and loved. Afterwards we gathered outside the church in the pale sunlight. There I saw Jane Sargeant, Walker's first wife, for the first time. Walker went over and kissed her hand. Every ex-wife was there: Via (James Agee's first wife), Peggy (Wilder's first wife), and Jack Jessup's first wife, and all were introduced to me, except Jane. I observed her and Walker and thought how different she was from me. She seemed shy and reclusive. Later, at Verna's house, friends spilled out into the yard, and food and drinks were passed as though it were the biannual luncheon party before the Yale-Princeton game. Many of the same people were there, and in my mind I saw Wilder throw out the ball for the enactment of the first touchdown, a ritual among his Yale friends accompanied by shouts of pleasure and anticipation of the game.

Without Wilder we were so much poorer. Verna was an example to all of us. Gallant and courageous, we knew she'd help us go on in his spirit, embrace life to the fullest. There had been no slowing down for him.

With Wilder gone, Walker had no desire to go to museum openings and parties. The spring season was just beginning, and we were asked to many gala events. He wanted to see only his old friends, those who had known Wilder, or have lunch at the Century. The familiar, slightly worn rooms were a comfort to him. Wilder had spent so many late afternoons there, meeting friends and drinking his martinis before catching the train to Princeton.

Walker was losing weight, and even the warm sun and the approaching season of weekends in Lyme made little difference to his depressed state of mind. Something else I noticed one afternoon: Walker pulled his new London flask out of his pocket and poured a little vodka in his tea. The flask was always with him. He must have filled it in the morning when I was at work. This 80 proof burning liquor couldn't possibly be good for his stomach. I began to worry and told Dorothy, who promised she would mention it to John. Dr. Leland might put an end to this, she said quite firmly. She and John missed Wilder too, and nobody wanted to lose Walker.

My life was much changed. I took care of Walker as though he were a patient, fed him and covered him when he felt a chill, answered the phone, and mailed his letters. We seldom talked, and the vodka became a habit. He encouraged me to go out without him, and occasionally, when he had a Century dinner, Alice and I would go see a new foreign film, like Fellini's *8 1/2*. We'd discuss it afterwards over an early supper in a small bistro on Third Avenue.

One memorable evening I had dinner with Mrs. Whitney and her daughter Kate, after a Royal Ballet performance with Margot Fonteyn and Nureyev. Mrs. Whitney, during her husband's ambassadorship in London, had befriended Margot Fonteyn and she promised to bring Kate and me backstage to meet her.

The whole town was talking of Nureyev and Fonteyn. In April, a Cecil Beaton photograph of them dancing appeared in Vogue. I had seen Fonteyn in *Cinderella* at Covent Garden in London and admired her style, expressive movements, and brilliant technique. Her strong brow, large, dark eyes, and pale, translucent skin mirrored her feelings in so many nuances while she danced. I hung on her every turn and gesture. During her innumerable curtain calls, her fans shouted bravos and showered her with flowers, and tonight I was going to see her up close in her dressing room.

It was an elegant audience. Heads turned when Mrs. Whitney, Kate, and I took our seats. C. Z. Guest came in late, and Mrs. Whitney whispered a disapproving remark in my direction. Everyone was tense, waiting for the great moment.

There could not have been a more fervent partner for Fonteyn than Nureyev in *Marguerite et Armand*. Years younger than she, he enveloped her, transformed her into a young Marguerite, and together they gave the most passionate performance of lovers. The contrast was an exciting surprise: this wild Russian with loose, flying hair and a touch of the Tartar in his face had the grace and strength of an animal when he leapt through the air; and Fonteyn was the refined, mature dancer whose emotions were heightened by his energy and charm. Never before had I seen a theater full of New York society react as enthusiastically.

We stayed until the last curtain came down. Mrs. Whitney rushed us backstage, and we were let in in front of the long line. Fonteyn was still in her costume and stage makeup, her dressing room filled with fresh, sweet-smelling flowers. Mrs. Whitney kissed her and praised her and introduced Kate and me. We shook hands, and I didn't know what to say, except that she was wonderful, or some such obvious comment. She looked exhausted and very pleased with tonight's success. She held nothing back, a great and most generous artist.

Mrs. Whitney's chauffeur drove us home, dropping her and Kate home first, then delivering me to my front door. I rode comfortably in the backseat, reliving the evening moment by moment. The thirty blocks were not long enough.

Walker was sound asleep when I came in. I was disappointed—I missed our late evening talks. I sat in the living room by myself, still too exhilarated to go to bed. I discovered a new bottle of vodka on the tray, a different brand. How quickly this all happened. Had he been drinking vodka during the whole time in Princeton because it was Wilder's drink, or did he need something stronger than wine to dull the pain? I could not see myself in the role of caretaker quite yet, but what should I do? He certainly would not want to discuss any of this. Where was my life going? I was married, yet more and more alone.

One day in May, Walker declared that the stairs were getting too much for him. He wanted to move out of Vita and Peter's house and live on the first floor of a brownstone, somewhere on the Upper East Side. I was totally unprepared for this, since he had not mentioned it before. A first-floor apartment to me meant a dark place. No sunlight ever came through Alice's on the ground floor on West Eighty-sixth Street. I so loved our sunny bedroom overlooking the gardens and the handsome living room with the three tall windows and the black marble fireplace. My conversations with Vita during the day made me feel at home, and Vita was the only friend with whom I spoke German.

I begged Walker to think it over during the summer. He would feel stronger after the restful weeks in Lyme and the long afternoon swims. Bob and Jack had invited us to stay with them on Cranberry Island, and he would be stimulated to do some work. Our lease ran

Chapter 21

until the end of October. I couldn't face the idea of apartment hunting in the hot weather.

Later I found out that the stairs were only an excuse. Walker referred to the "check incident" more than once and how it had upset him. Vita, who sorted the mail, placed our letters on a shelf near the front door. Walker was expecting an "important check" from a magazine job. It was probably the end of the month, and he needed the money. A week went by, and the check still hadn't arrived. When he telephoned the magazine's office, he was told the check was mailed ten days ago. He asked Vita, who said she would look among her papers. The next morning, the envelope with the check was on the shelf with Vita's written apology. Walker was furious. What a scatterbrain, he called her, he wasn't going to be subjected to this kind of behavior any longer.

Chapter 22

On June 12 Medgar W. Evers, field secretary of the NAACP, was assassinated in Mississippi. Walker worried there would be race riots in the city this summer. He had only one thought: get out of New York.

I didn't understand his anxieties and irrational fears of what might happen in New York. Obviously things were changing, but it had been his town for so many years, and he had friends in every intellectual and social group. Was he so shaken by death that he had to leave? Was Lyme so much safer? Our friends there were building bomb shelters, outfitting them with sleeping bags, first aid kits, and jars of peanut butter.

We packed the Jaguar and settled down in Lyme two weeks earlier than usual. A few days after our arrival, our friend and neighbor Clark Voorhees, wandered in to greet us. Pleased to see him, I made another pot of coffee and we sat around on the porch. Walker asked about Billie, the Knollenbergs, and many others in the area. Clark did not seem very talkative. A couple of times he hesitated, then let Walker do the talking. There was something on his mind. Just as he got up to go, he scratched his head and looked down. By the way, he said, he had met a very nice woman and he planned to live with her. They were looking at a place in Weston, Vermont, an old house. He wasn't going to leave tomorrow, but by this winter he hoped to be gone.

Walker asked if he had told the children. Yes, he said, he had. Christopher was going to stay here, and Michael would eventually go to college. Nothing was said about Billie.

This was a blow for Walker, losing another close friend. I, too, was sad to see Clark go. He was a kind, helpful neighbor, and he knew all the pleasures and chores of country living. How would Billie take this? She was already in such bad shape.

Luckily some old friends from Stonington called, and we spent several evenings with Anne Fuller and her eccentric entourage of artists, *haute bohême* and people who had reinvented themselves.

The setting for these unpredictable evenings was a Greek Revival church that she had transformed into part art gallery and part living quarters. Her flair for mixing primary colors and finding unusual pieces of furniture and decorations was enviable. Having lived in Jakarta with her late husband and great friend of Walker, Charles Fuller, she was gutsy in her room compositions of Asian and European antiques and contemporary objects, made even more playful by an odd piece of American folk art, something she might have found in a junk shop.

Quite the opposite was Anthony and Lily West's Rhode Island farm near Westerly, a place to write, garden, bring up young children, and keep sheep. Their home-cooked, unfussy lunches around a kitchen table invited good conversation. Walker was always eager to talk to literary critics and hear inside stories.

At least once a summer, Eliza Parkinson invited us to Fisher's Island, where we might see Lily West's mother, the painter Lily Cushing, Eileen Maynard, her son Robin, and his young, blond wife, Pam. I enjoyed beach picnics and gatherings with the children of Walker's friends. Eliza and Eileen, thoughtful as they were, always invited the young on my behalf.

At the end of July we flew over to Fisher's in a small plane for a swim and a luncheon party at the Whitneys'. The plane was Walker's idea. He seemed unafraid of small machines, and he thought he might be over his fear of flying. It was Sunday, and we arrived before Mrs. Whitney had returned from church. A member of the staff showed us in and gave us towels and a guest room to change in. We swam in the saltwater pool overlooking the bay, and dressed for lunch, which was outside on a flower-filled terrace. I sat at Mr. Whitney's table, and when I told him I was interested in modern art, he said I should have a look at a Picasso painting in the living room. It had just been sent from a New York gallery for approval.

I was glad to see Walker regain some of his appetite for social life, since I so loved it. When Helen Levitt telephoned and said she would like to come out for the day, I had to convince him to invite her. We had met only briefly, but right away I felt a rapport with her. I was drawn to her photographs of children in the street—in motion, using trash-filled vacant city lots as playgrounds, finding big cardboard boxes and throwaways for toys—she showed the children's exuberant innocence despite their poor surroundings. Her pictures of children's chalk drawings and graffiti revealed her acute sense of humor.

She arrived by train and we picked her up in Old Saybrook. Petite and dark haired, she looked younger than her age. Walker had told me that he had met her in the thirties, when she occasionally worked for him as an assistant. By the time we reached our place it was close to noon. I had prepared a niçoise, sliced tomatoes with my own basil and fresh berries. Walker was hungry and asked Helen if she wouldn't mind an early lunch. She said to please go ahead but she would eat later. I felt awkward eating with Walker while Helen sat at the table without a plate. For once, I felt, Walker could have waited and pleased our guest. After lunch he took a few puffs of a cigarette and asked to be excused for his nap.

Eventually I served Helen her lunch, and we talked about New York and how we wouldn't live anywhere else. I told her how worried I was over Walker's recent feelings of uneasiness about the city. I couldn't imagine living in the country year-round. She invited me to visit her in her apartment off lower Fifth Avenue. I took this as a great compliment and thanked her.

When Walker woke up we all had a cup of tea, and he suggested a drive and a late afternoon swim. He would take us out for lobster. He assured Helen that there were plenty of trains running from New London at the end of the day.

Helen sat in the front seat next to Walker. He drove toward his favorite barn, with the faded Coca-Cola sign. He said he was determined to get that sign one of these days, before someone took it down. The roads were bumpy and I did not hear every bit of their conversation. They talked about people I didn't know. She asked about the new edition of his book and how it was doing. We rode along past familiar houses and crossroads. The heat made me sleepy. I was beginning to doze off when Walker said something like, "You know I don't like women painters." Helen raised her voice and sounded extremely irritated. "You don't like women," she said. "You never have. And I want to go to the station right now. Just get me there, I want to go home."

Nobody spoke on the way to New London. When we reached the station, she opened the door and left. I was very upset. Surely Helen wasn't a women's libber. Betty Friedan's *The Feminine Mystique* was just out and was causing quite a stir, but didn't Helen know better than to take Walker's every word seriously, after all these years? Maybe she had a bad day, and Walker hadn't been very gallant to her when she arrived. But then, one didn't have to be a feminist to disapprove of his opinions on women. He often put me down. Sad, he could be so charming when he felt like it.

Labor Day came too soon, and with it the dreaded chore of finding an affordable apartment. Walker was busy photographing Pennsylvania Station before the great main room, the copy of the Bath of Caracalla, was completely demolished. He was already having trouble with the lighting in the darkened space, but he managed to take enough black-and-white pictures for a portfolio. Sadly none of the protests by architects or the indignant articles written by preservationists and well-known critics like Ada Louise Huxtable were able to save this majestic Stanford White monument.

Every day after work I'd walk through different streets in the upper Seventies and Eighties between Second and Third Avenues to Lexington and Park, looking for signs advertising floor-throughs in remodeled brownstones. Whenever I saw workmen going in and out of a townhouse, I walked right in and asked them if there was anything for rent. Our budget was under three hundred dollars for a two-bedroom unit, and Walker insisted on a working fireplace. By the end of the week I knew every shop on Lexington in these ten or fifteen blocks beginning with Seventy-fifth Street.

Not far from Lascoff's old-fashioned drugstore, a place that reminded me of a London chemist with its decorative apothecary jars, I discovered a hand-painted sign in a fish market. It was a narrow white board about four feet high, with the names of every possible fish painted in fancy red letters—a free, spontaneous attempt at calligraphy. Even the spelling made me laugh. "Halabut" was just one of many errors. I thought of Walker—he had to see this sign, it was a true primitive, and maybe it was for sale.

As I continued my walk, I turned onto Eighty-fourth Street and headed toward Park Avenue. A cardboard notice advertised a vacant first-floor apartment. I stepped down to a small door and rang the bell. A short, wiry, gray-haired man named Mr. O'Donnell answered and asked if I was interested in the apartment. The painters were still in it but the kitchen and bath were done. All new appliances, a working fireplace, hardwood floors, and a garden, lovely. "Come along, dear," he said and led the way up, half a dozen keys dangling from his key chain.

As I expected, the apartment was dark, and the garden was a dreary rectangle planted with sickly ivy that was barely surviving the lack of light and air. The two bedrooms were small and faced the courtyard. I was instantly depressed but I told Mr. O'Donnell I'd confer with my husband.

When Walker saw the apartment, he went straight to the agent and put down a deposit for a one-year lease.

That evening, during cocktails, he announced that we were moving at the end of October. I was speechless with surprise and anger. We had an argument. He had no right to ignore my wishes and put me in that dungeon! It mattered a great deal to me where I lived. Sunlight and my surroundings were most important, since I spent many afternoons at home.

There was no possible way to reason with him. In a glacial voice he answered that he was tired of climbing stairs and we couldn't afford to live in a doorman building with an elevator. Mr. O'Donnell would be a great asset, would help him pack the car on weekends and carry his camera bags into the hall. He had already discussed it with him. Crash—the impenetrable wall came down again and he withdrew to his study and closed the door.

I stood alone in the kitchen, preparing dinner. The only thing I could think to do was to write him a letter after I calmed down, express my feelings clearly, and appeal to his own sense as a civilized man. Extreme selfishness was not part of a gentleman's character.

Vita and Peter were very sorry when we left their comfortable house.

One afternoon soon after we moved, the phone rang and I picked it up. It was an executive calling from the Container Corporation of America, asking to speak with Mr. Evans. All our phones were on long cords, so I dragged the phone over to Walker, who was busy unpacking his books. I took in bits and pieces of the conversation. At one point Walker said quietly, "That will be ten thousand dollars." After he hung up, he raised his arms and clapped his hands. "Did you hear that? We're rich and famous! I'll buy you a fur coat for Christmas."

A fur coat didn't give me back our old, charming place, but it was a friendly gesture, and something I'd always wanted.

The search for the perfect coat became quite an obsession during the following week. In my previous job at Saks, I often tried on coats in the fur department after the last customers had left. Mink, everyone's favorite, in novel shades of champagne, pinky beige, and navy, looked bulky on me. I wasn't tall enough to carry it off like Lauren Bacall. Now, on my twelve hundred-dollar budget, mink was out. Just for fun I went back to Saks and fell in love with a charcoal-gray broadtail coat by Révillon of Paris. The collar was cut away from the neck à la Balenciaga, and it fit me perfectly, but the price was astronomical. Where to go, what to look for? I was hesitant to try the fur district, for fear I would be talked into a coat I didn't really like.

Time was running out if I wanted my coat for Christmas. On a gloomy November afternoon on my way home from work, I was attracted by a single red coat in the window of a new boutique above Bloomingdale's. As I examined the coat I saw that it was made of moleskin fur, countless small pieces artfully sewn together to create a velvety texture. The coat had patch pockets and shiny red buttons like a cloth coat, spare and chic. Walker wouldn't like red, but the style was right for me. No one was in the shop when I stepped in. I quickly ran my hand over the back of the coat and was surprised at how soft it felt. What did moles look like? Wasn't there a mole in *The Wind in the Willows*? Didn't moles live below ground, so their fur wasn't exposed to the elements—was it warm and durable?

A fair young man with the palest blue eyes appeared from behind a curtain and smiled at me. The modern jazz on the radio, a leather apron around his narrow hips, and the fact that he was wearing clogs gave me the impression that he was both the owner and designer. I asked if I could try on the coat.

"Yes, of course," he answered in a shy voice. "I detect an accent—are you from Europe?"

"Yes, Switzerland." I said, trying to place his accent—Swedish? No, he was Dutch. Ah, the clogs—I should have guessed. He pointed out that the moleskins were also from Holland. The coat felt light and comfortable around my neck and shoulders. I put my hands in the pockets and looked over my shoulder at the mirror. Dashing—the coat was a charmer, nothing too furry or opulent about it. The furrier complimented me and then named his price: twelve hundred dollars. My lucky day—now all I needed was a better color. What about taupe?

"Yes, why not?" he said and nodded approvingly. "The natural color, more or less. I have a sample." He disappeared behind the curtain and returned with the little piece of fur. I asked if I could take it home to show my husband; tomorrow I would place the order. He slipped the sliver of fur into an envelope and we made a date for a fitting. I thanked him, smiled, and shook his hand, blushing with pleasure.

I walked up Lexington and passed the fish market. Walker had seen the sign and now he wanted it at all cost. "See if you can buy it from them," he said with a wink, challenging me. "I'll go as high as fifty."

I went in and bought some fish for supper. Just before leaving I told the man behind the marble counter that I was married to an artist who admired the sign. Would he possibly sell it to me? He went and asked the boss. An older man in a checked flannel shirt came out, looked me up and down, and shook his head. No, he said, the sign had been painted years ago by a friend at the Fulton Fish Market. He couldn't possibly replace it. His friend had passed away.

Don't give up, I thought, there's got to be a way. I wanted to surprise Walker with the sign for Christmas. It would be equivalent to my fur coat, a luxury and something he coveted.

At home I drew the coat for Walker and showed him the fur. Taupe was one of his favorite colors. He seemed pleased with my choice. "I'd like a lining of the stuff," he laughed and rubbed the fur against the back of his hand.

I wasn't able to concentrate at work the day of my first fitting. I left the office at one o'clock and did all my errands first; I even delayed things and spent time in Bloomingdale's before getting to the furrier. I was barely through the door when he stormed through the curtain. Breathless, he stammered. "K-K-Kennedy's been shot in D-Dallas—right now—it's on the news. Listen." He went back behind the curtain and turned up the volume. I sat down on the settee and listened. Moment by moment the tragedy unfolded: shots were heard in rapid succession as the president's motorcade drove past the Texas School Book Depository....

I almost forgot where I was, stopped breathing, until the furrier came to sit next to me. Our shoulders were touching. Tears rolled down my cheeks, salty, comforting. I leaned against him. He took out his handkerchief and gave it to me. We sat like that for a long time, numb and lost in our own sad thoughts. When I got up and turned to him I saw that he, too, was in tears. I squeezed his hand, thanked him, and left.

On my way to Third Avenue I remembered the coat. No, not today, I thought. The bus stop was crowded with women crying. People were leaving work early, anxious to get home to their television. Some had transistor radios glued to their ears. Where could I go? I didn't want to be alone in the apartment—too depressing, and we had no television. The world was a lonely place without our young hero and friend. Poor Jackie, poor children, where will they go?

In January we had a blizzard. Walker decided not to go out during the heavy snowfall, since he was constantly plagued by bronchitis, so he spent the two days on the sofa instead, reading in front of the fire. While I was at work in the morning Mrs. O'Donnell often came in and made him a cup of tea. By now he had established a friendly master-servant relationship with the O'Donnells. I was aware that he gave them very good tips, but their servile manner got on my nerves, so I stayed away from them.

Winter in our apartment was bleak. Even the Beatles failed to cheer me up, though we both liked their songs. I missed seeing the pictures of Jackie in her elegant clothes. With Lyndon Johnson and his Lady Bird in the White House, I felt that cultural sophistication and good taste were once again taking a backseat, and Vietnam loomed ominously in the background. The foreign papers, especially the French, were spreading anti-American propaganda. Walker and I felt gloomy and the only event to look forward to was my brother's arrival on my birthday. It was his first trip to the U.S.A. He had been asked to teach the spring semester in the German department at Harvard. He had married Renate, a young German woman, also an academician, whom I had not met. She would join him later in Cambridge.

Given Walker's ambivalent feelings about academics, I worried that he might find Bernard too serious and literal. I was much relieved when the two developed a strong rapport and were able to laugh with

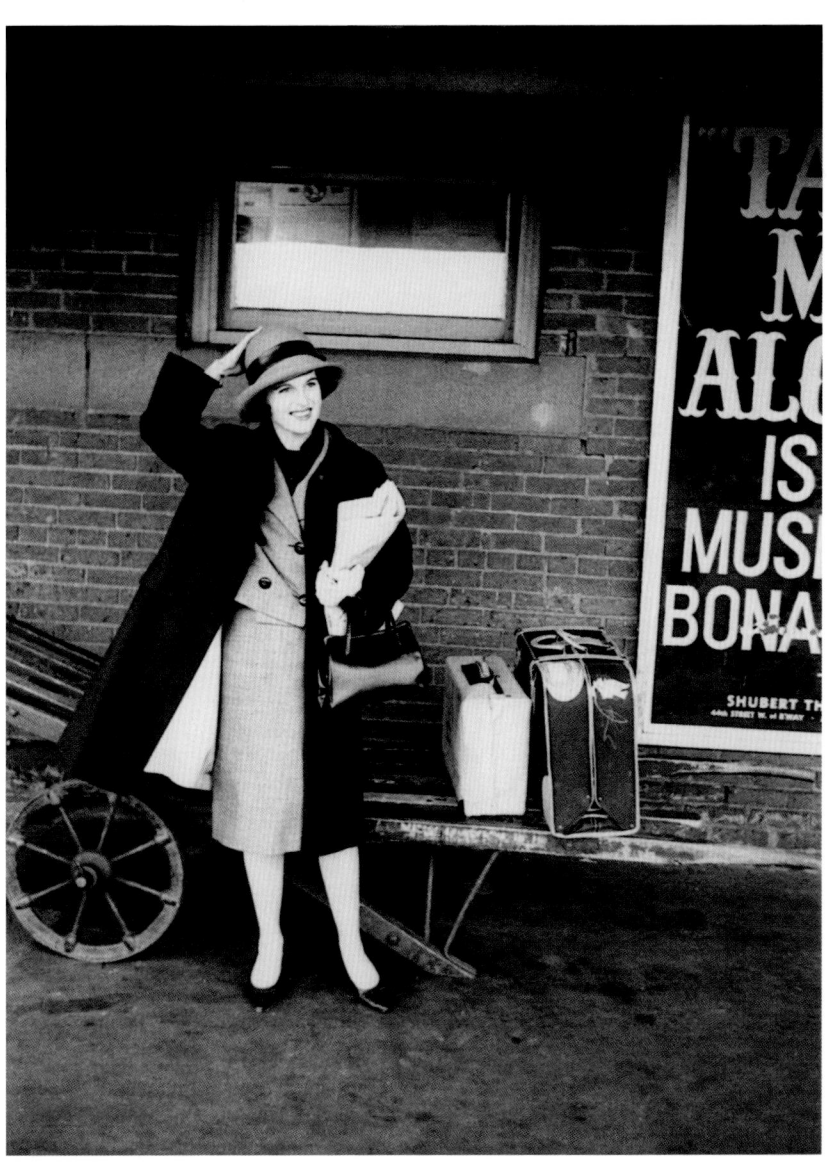

On our wedding day, October 29, 1960, at the New London station, waiting for the train to Boston.
Photograph by Walker Evans

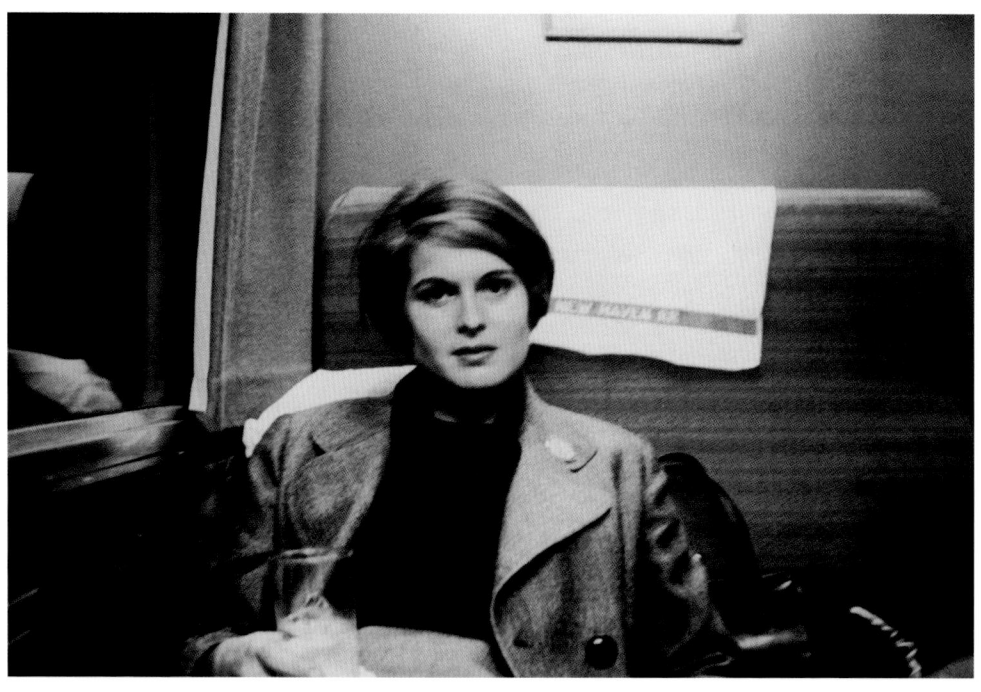

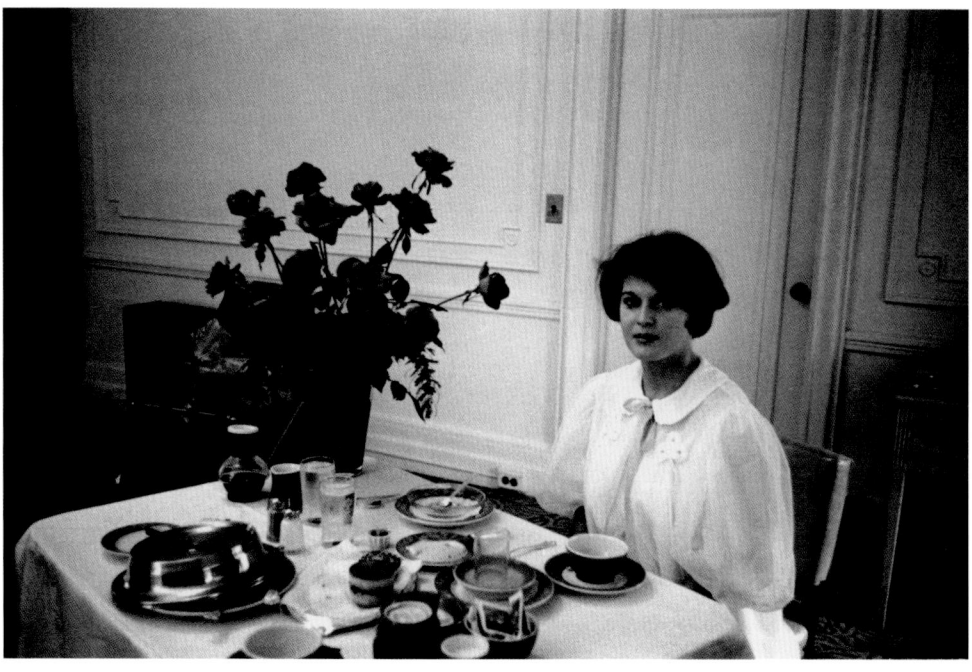

In our roomette on the Boston train. Photograph by Walker Evans
On the first morning of our honeymoon, wearing the peignoir Walker gave me for the occasion. Photograph by Walker Evans

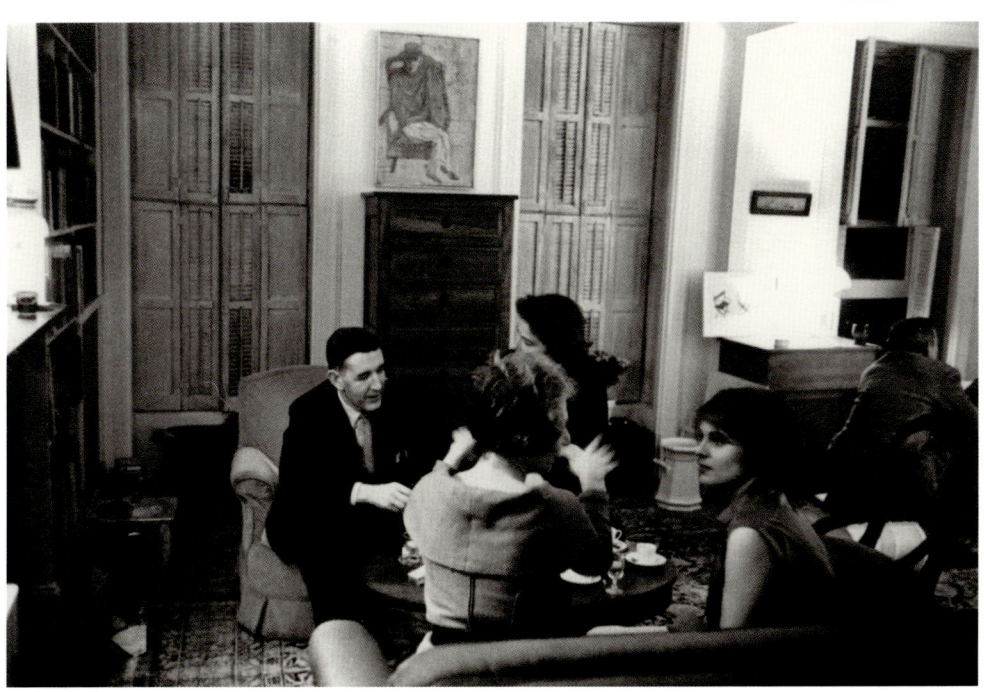

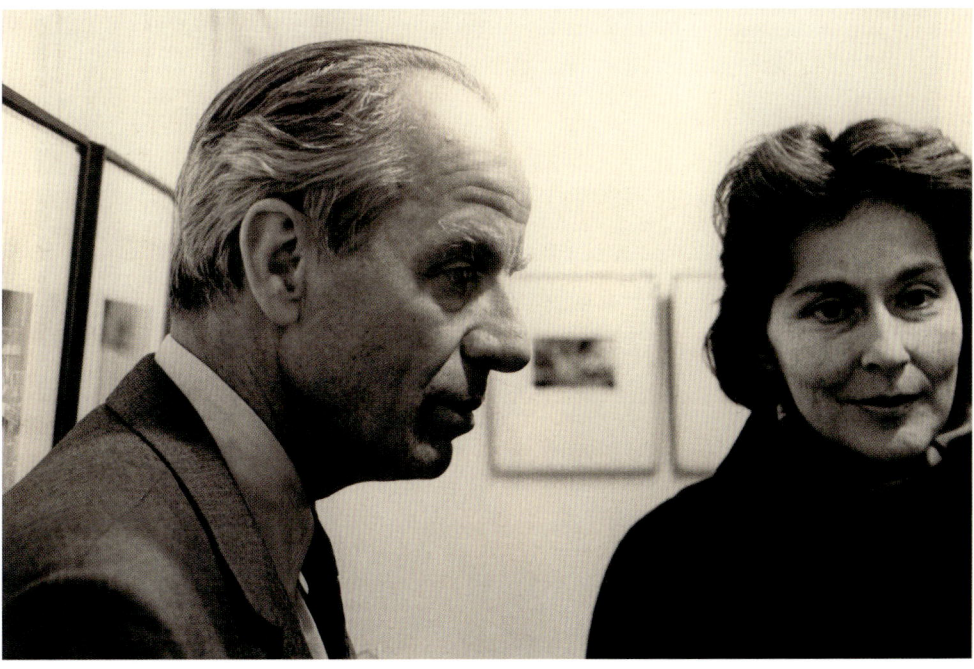

Vita Petersen, Alfred Kazin, Dorothy, and me at the first dinner party in our apartment on East Ninety-fourth Street, 1960. Above the tall chest of drawers is Ben Shahn's portrait of Walker, painted in the thirties. Photograph by Walker Evans

Our landlords Peter and Vita Petersen at the opening of Walker's exhibition of the subway photographs at the Museum of Modern Art, 1967.

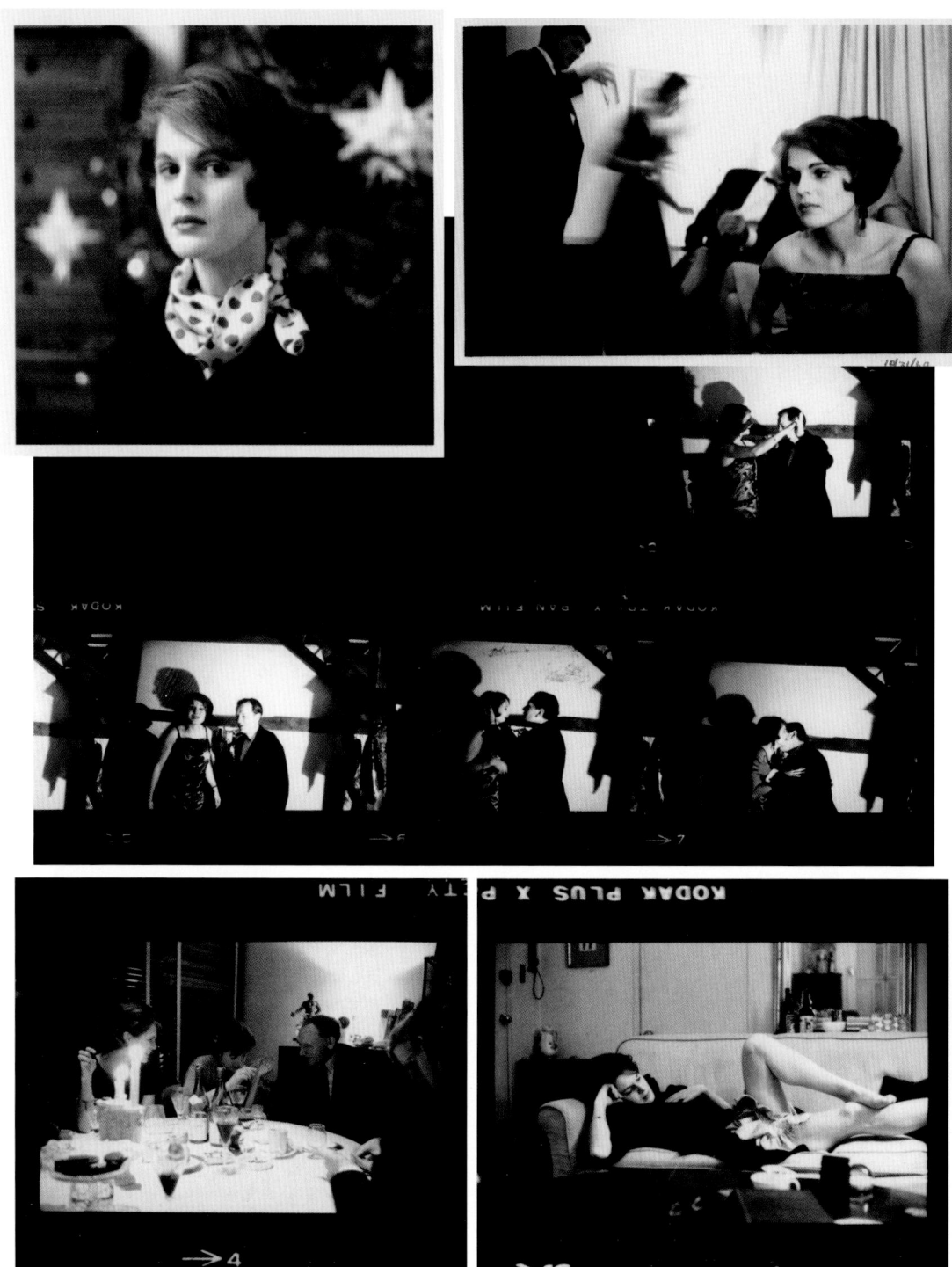

First Christmas on Ninety-fourth Street, 1960. Photograph by Walker Evans
Party at William H. Whyte's new apartment, New York, October 21, 1960. Photograph by Walker Evans
Dancing with John McDonald at the Warrens' New Year's Eve party in Fairfield, Connecticut, 1960. Photograph by Walker Evans
At a dinner party at the Motherwells' with Robert Penn Warren and Helen Frankenthaler next to me.
The Motherwells lived on our block on Ninety-fourth Street. Photograph by Walker Evans
Late evening, after the last guest had left the party, New York, early 1960s. Photograph by Walker Evans

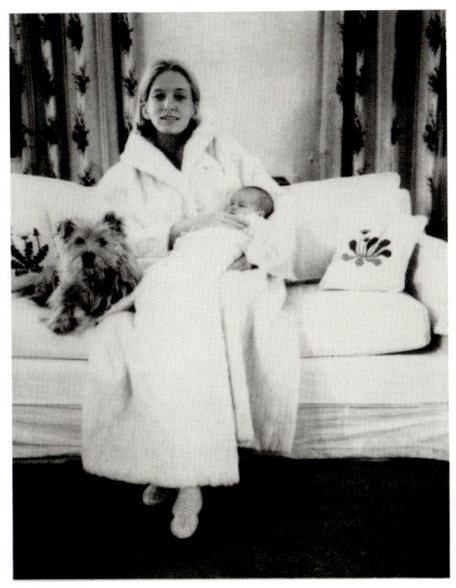
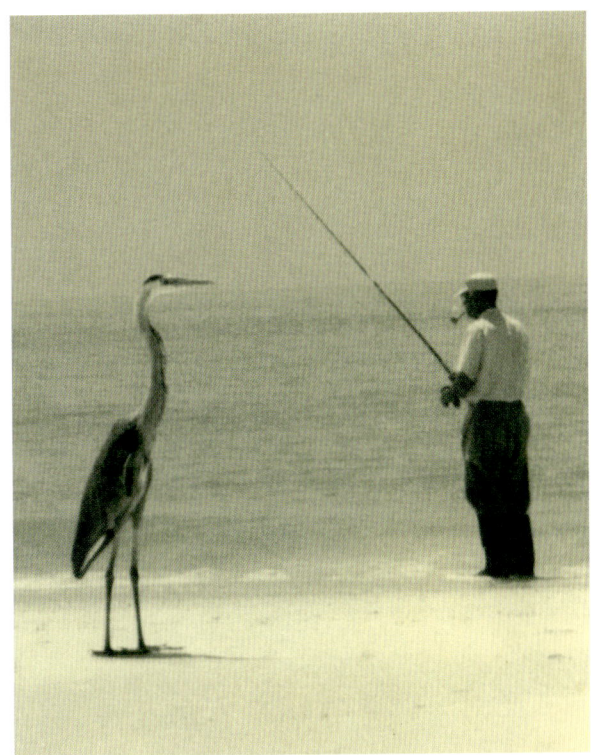
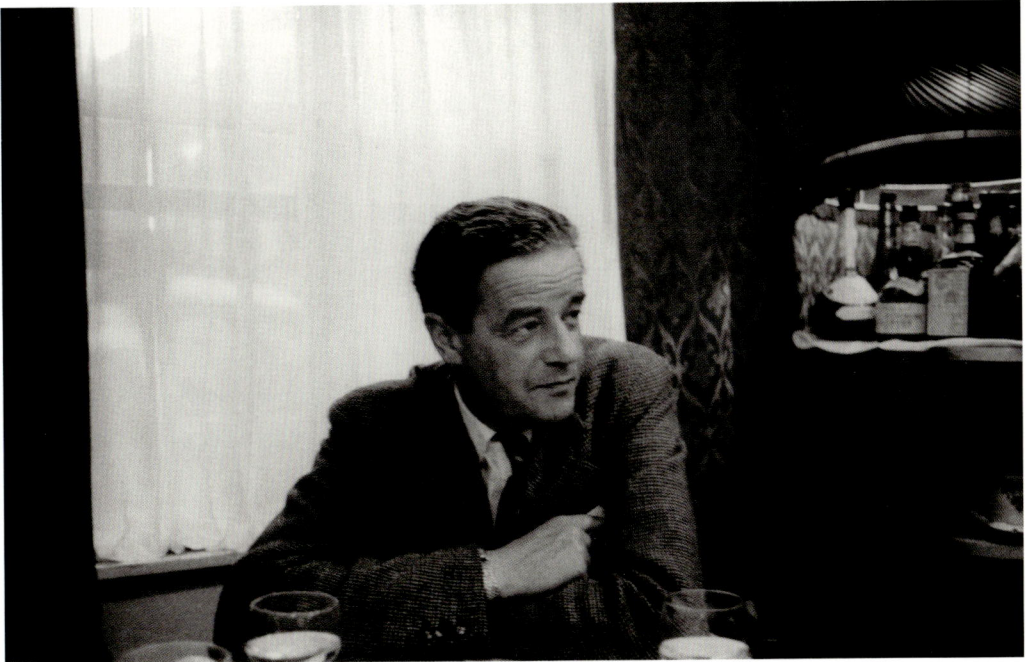

Mary Carswell with her daughter Kate in New York, 1968.
Anna Maria, Florida. Walker was amused by this picture and kept it in his collection for years. Photograph by Talbot Brewer
Jimmy Stern in a London bar, 1950s.

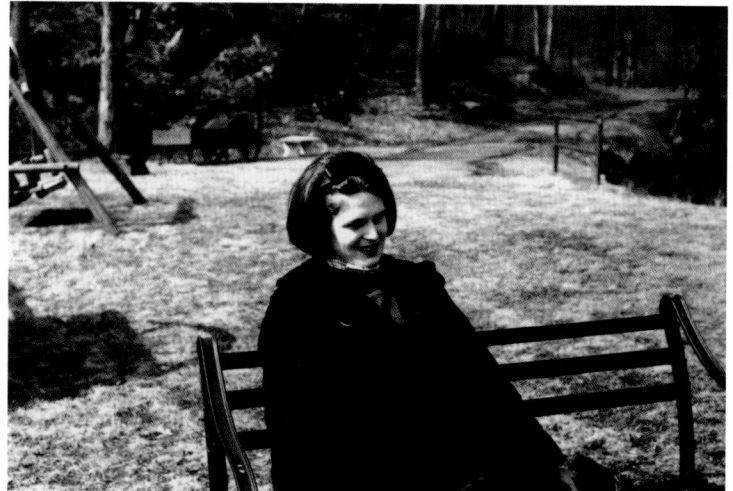
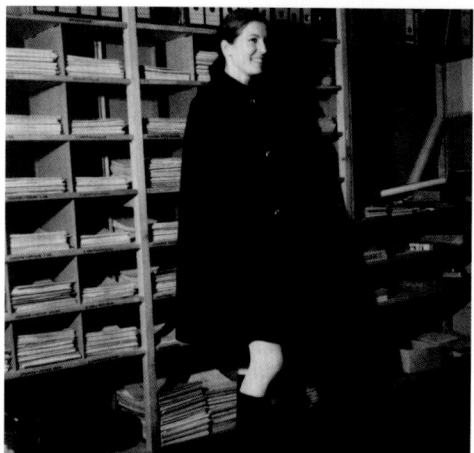
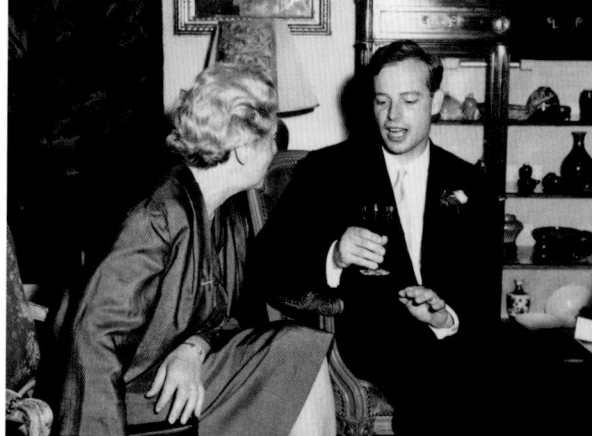
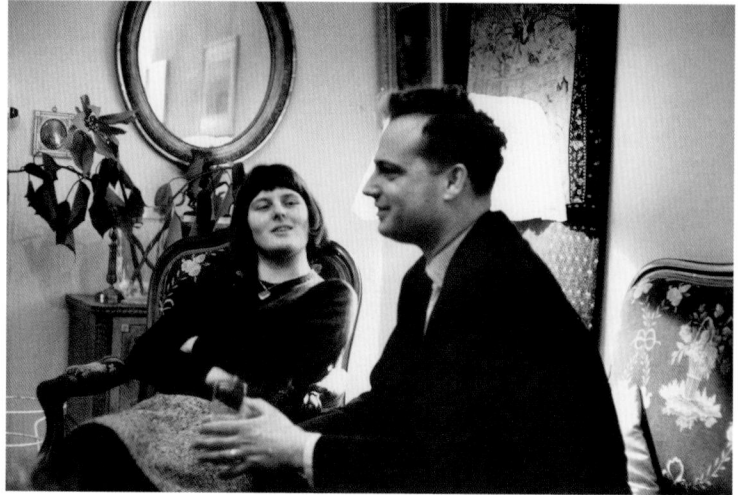

In my new fur coat during a winter weekend at Stonehenge, Connecticut, 1964. Photograph by Walker Evans
My sister Christine in Zurich, 1960s.
My brother Bernard at his wedding reception, 1963.
My youngest sister Anne-Marie with Bernard, 1964. Photograph by Walker Evans

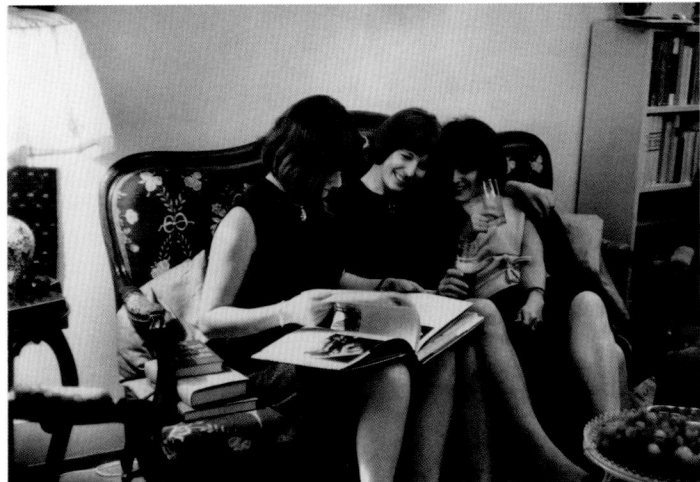
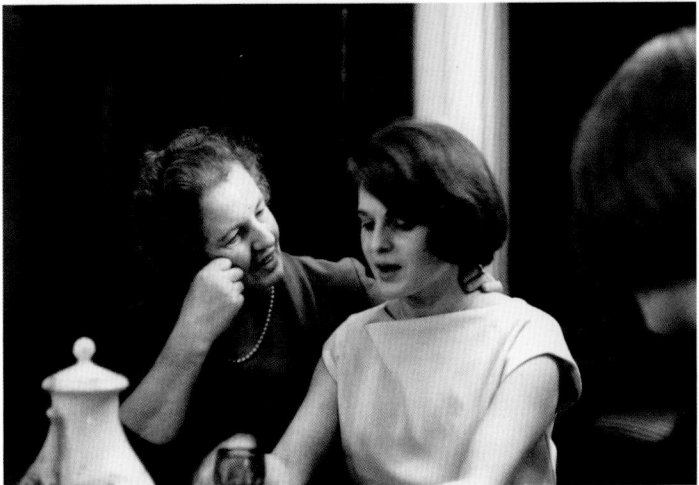
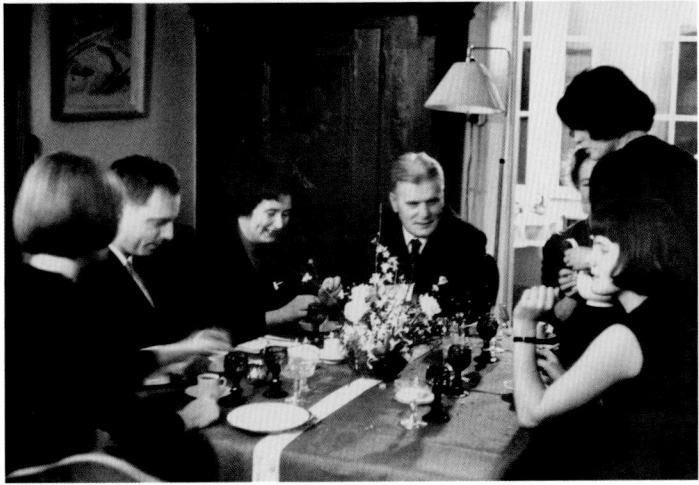

Christmas *en famille* in Bern, 1964, when Walker met all my siblings for the first time:
With my two sisters, Christine and Anne-Marie. Photograph by Walker Evans
With Maman. Photograph by Walker Evans
At the dinner table. Renate, Bernard's wife, is next to Papa. Photograph by Walker Evans

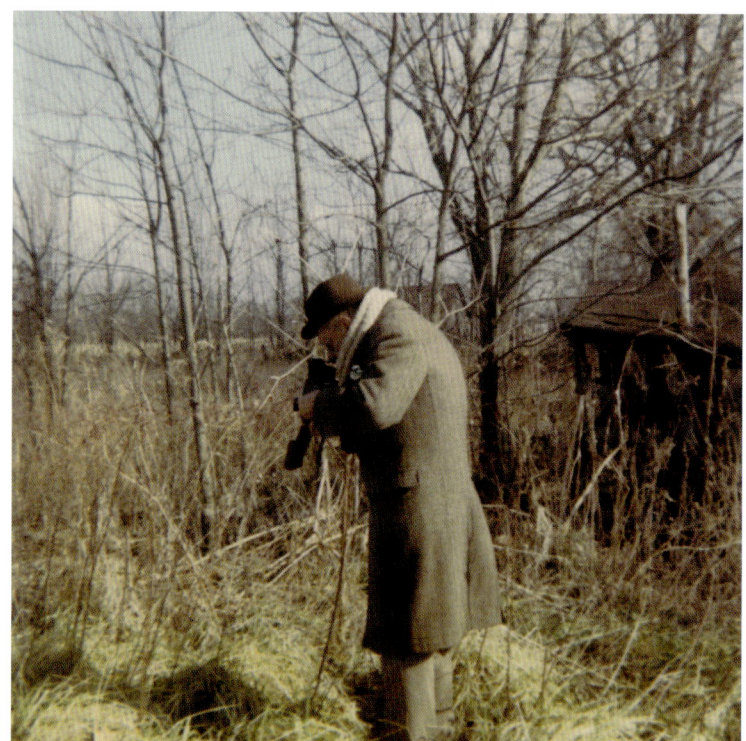
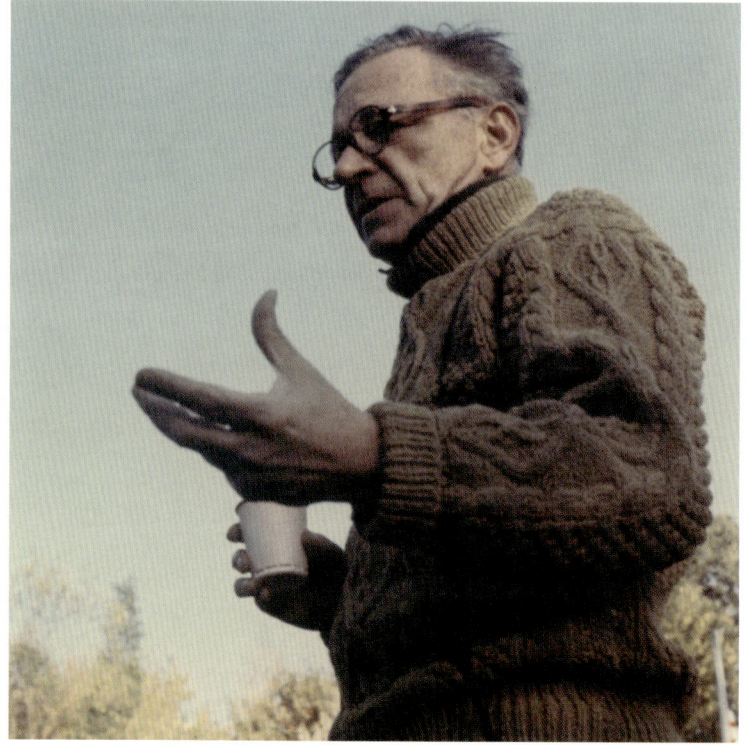

Walker photographing near the Mabry place in Allensville, Kentucky. Photograph by Eliza Mabry
Walker in a boccie tournament, Lyme, Connecticut, 1965.

each other. Bernard, a Germanist with a Greek and Latin background as well as a thorough command of French, did not know English very well. So when he was searching for a specific word he often made it up, combining a potpourri of languages, with highly humorous results. These Bernardisms, as Walker called them, sent him into fits of laughter, and he wrote them down.

Showing Bernard New York was a learning experience for me, albeit strenuous. His appetite for sightseeing and museums was enormous. We explored Staten Island and the whole length of Manhattan and traveled by subway and bus to the Cloisters, where he knew every detail of the history and the sites of the French and Spanish monastic cloisters imported and reassembled there. I would return to Walker happy and dead tired, but Bernard still had enough energy left to go to a concert or an opera.

I could hardly wait for Renate to get here and become a fan of my city. We were exactly the same age, and I was hoping to gain not only a sister-in-law but also a friend. How on earth would she calm Bernard down?

Both Walker and I took to her right away. Her subtle sense of humor, so unlike most Germans,' and her love of the English language, which she spoke flawlessly, were but a few of her special qualities.

One evening, before Renate was here, Robert Beverly Hale, a good friend and contemporary of Walker's, and his young wife, Nicki, invited the three of us to dinner. Bob was the first curator of contemporary art at the Metropolitan Museum and taught a life drawing class at the Art Students League. He mentioned that Marcel Duchamp and his American wife would join us. Bernard was in ecstasy. Walker, the magician, was producing miracles for him.

We took a taxi to Central Park West and arrived early. Nicki, an art historian of Greek origin, greeted us warmly, and we found ourselves in a stark, high-ceilinged white living room with one large Abstract Expressionist, black-and-white painting. Bob smiled and asked us to guess who the artist was. Knowing that he had bought the first Pollock for the museum, I thought this might be one, too. Walker winked at me and guessed right. It was Bob's own work. Bubbling over with new impressions, Bernard fell into conversation with Nicki. The two talked about Greece and the classical period and Greek mythology, naming the gods and goddesses as though they were living today.

We all had drinks and waited for Duchamp. Walker was getting hungry, and eventually he told Nicki that his poor stomach "desperately needed sustenance." We sat down to her delicious Greek lamb. Towards the end of dinner the telephone rang and Bob took the call. He reported that it was Duchamp, who sounded very apologetic but was playing chess against himself and couldn't possibly stop until the game was finished. As disappointed as we all were, the evening ended with a flurry of jokes and witticisms, such as Walker taking the title of Beckett's play and changing it to *En Attendant Duchamp*.

Chapter 23

Back on the *Fortune* payroll after the Carnegie Corporation award ran its course, Walker seemed discouraged with the magazine, and with the editors' lack of interest in his work. When the Century asked him to give a lecture, he leapt at the chance and used it to elaborate on his already published and very successful postcard portfolios. Jack Tworkov, who had just become the head of the painting department at the Yale School of Art and Architecture, heard the lecture and suggested Walker as a possible lecturer for a series put on by the School and organized by architecture professor Charles Brewer.

On March 11 we drove to New Haven and put the Jaguar into a garage near the school, where we checked in at the desk. The school's recently completed building designed by Paul Rudolph was a fortresslike structure made of bush-hammered concrete, not at all like the architecture of Corbusier, Gropius, and Philip Johnson that I admired.

A student brought us up in the elevator to the penthouse suite, our quarters for the night. We settled in as best we could. Walker thought the large, bare space most uncomfortable. He looked in vain for a bedside lamp; I tried to open a window, only to find that the floor-to-ceiling glass panels were sealed shut. After a lengthy search I found a floor vent that could be opened. I lifted the cover and looked right down to the street many flights below, so frightening that I pulled back in alarm. The opening was just wide enough for a child to fall through and the screen had not yet been installed.

Walker was nervous, reviewing and rereviewing his material, and I made him a cup of tea in the kitchenette. Finally it was time to go and meet Jack, who introduced us to his colleagues, and we walked over to the Yale Art Gallery building, where the lecture was to be held. Walker handed his slides over to an assistant, who seemed pleased to be of help and treated him like a great master. We chatted outside the hall, and in no time the large formal auditorium was packed. I went in and sat with Wally Tworkov, my heart beating faster and faster. This was a new experience—Walker lecturing at a prestigious university, he who was self-taught and left Williams College after one year.

Soon my fears were gone. In "Lyric Documentary," Walker's title for the lecture and one of his favorite subjects, he discussed his taste for vernacular images like the picture postcard and its unstudied attempt to document the commonplace. The last slide he showed was one of his own photographs, *Westchester, New York Farmhouse, 1931*, which prompted a round of applause. Walker's talk was exactly what these graduate students and the many artists among the faculty were waiting to hear, and as different from any academic theory as possible.

If *Fortune* no longer knew what to do with Walker and considered him an unnecessary luxury, Yale certainly did know. Soon after the lecture, Alvin Eisenman, a professor of graphic design, called Walker repeatedly in an effort to persuade him to teach in his department, where photography was one of the subjects. As encouraged and pleased as Walker felt by being wooed, he took his time to respond. In the end he agreed to teach one day a week for a year.

The first signs of spring appeared and the sun came out; Walker's health improved and he seemed less dependent on his vodka. In May, John Kowenhoven, a much-respected historian and an acquaintance of Walker, recommended him for a commission to document Brown Brothers Harriman & Co. for his book *Partners in Banking; A Historical Portrait of a Great Private Bank*. Walker took the commission and soon got used to working with the partners on Wall Street; he'd amicably refer to them as the Brownies and the Harries.

Yale called again. Starting in early July, Walker was to be one of the visiting artists at the Yale Summer School of Music and Art, in Norfolk, Connecticut. Some of the faculty members were only a few years older than me, and the students weren't much younger. I looked forward to being with a new group of intelligent, gifted people of all ages.

In July we drove across the state to Norfolk. I was surprised to see the change in the landscape. Much greener and hillier, it resembled the Berkshires and parts of Switzerland. The two most important buildings of the Battel-Stoeckel estate, where the school was situated, were a rather grand mansion, known as the White House, and a beautifully crafted music barn with the best acoustics. Concerts were regularly given by the student orchestra with excellent soloists.

We were welcomed by the painter Bernard Chaet, who ran the school that summer. Our guest suite was in the mansion, which suited Walker very well, since its architecture and furnishings were Victorian. We had cocktails with members of the faculty, who moved around very casually in sweaters, enjoying the cool summer air. Students were urged to meet Walker and join in the conversation. Some asked me where I was from and knew of my school in Zurich.

The next morning Walker let me have the Jaguar while he went to look at the students' work and talk to them informally. I drove through new territory, along trout streams and fertile farm land, and stopped in small towns, visited every antique store and book barn, and even shifted into overdrive for a fast stretch of the road. (Walker never allowed that when I was driving with him.) The car gave me a sense of power and adventure. It was made for these curvy country roads, so much like England, and I practiced my downshifting to perfection.

I returned to the mansion and checked our room to see if Walker was back. Not finding him anywhere, I went down to the kitchen and made tea, prepared a tray with milk and sugar, and started on my way to the studios, balancing the tray through narrow paths and down some steps. A handful of students sat around in what looked like a small yard enclosed by stone walls. I asked if they had seen Walker. I could tell from their amused expressions that they knew something I didn't know, but wouldn't tell. Oh well, maybe we had just missed each other, and he might be back at the house. Feeling rather foolish, I carried the tray back the same way I had come.

Just as I reached the front porch, a snappy red sports car with the top down sped up and stopped on a dime. Walker and a tan brunette with long pretty hair smiled at me from the front seat. "Delightful spin, thanks very much," Walker said to the girl with dark glasses. Without introducing me he got out of the car and vrrum, vrrum—off she went, waving goodbye. *Merde alors*, I thought! How silly I must have looked with that stupid tray, like a dutiful housewife. Who was she, anyway? "Oh, just one of the students," Walker said, lighting his cigarette. "Not very talented. You know how much I like sports cars. She just took me on a tour of the town." New girls—and so many, how could he resist them? This one seemed aggressive, the way she smiled and drove off looking quite pleased with herself.

In the fall, Monday was Walker's teaching day at Yale. In order to get a good night's sleep he would leave Sunday afternoon, take the train to New Haven, and stay at the Hotel Duncan, a rather run-down place near the school. In the beginning he said very little about the students and his approach to teaching photography, but as I got to know a few, I found out that he urged them to read Flaubert, Henry James, Proust, and Nabokov, all authors "with an eye." In order to gain an impression of his students, one of his first assignments was to make a self-portrait. He discouraged them from using tricky techniques and color, which he thought vulgar. Once pinned on the studio wall, these photographs were most revealing. Weeks passed before he showed me the picture of a girl's nude slender back, her version of the portrait. Later, in his critiques, by engaging them in conversations and asking questions, he was able to help them focus more directly on subjects that interested them, which were often their immediate surroundings, and come up with an original idea. He was quick to dismiss work that resembled his own. His unobtrusive non-method reminded me of my best teachers, all working artists, in Zurich.

Sometimes when he came back from New Haven, hungry and all tired out, I felt jealous of his students. They obviously knew how to squeeze every last bit of energy out of him. It was then that I noticed he was once again filling his flask.

Chapter 24

Three days before Christmas, we flew on Swissair to Zurich and took the train to Bern, where my father met us. He had booked us into a comfortable hotel under the arcades and made it clear that we were his guests. Walker found the hotel well-run but without charm. As we strolled down to the old part of town he commented on the solid, provincial architecture and the bourgeois atmosphere. But the shops, which were filled with optical instruments, Swiss watches, fountain pens, and German cameras, made up for his disappointment in my hometown. I could hardly tear him away from the luxurious displays.

All through my childhood, Christmas Eve was our family celebration without relatives. The help had the day off, and Papa went shopping for our feast of smoked salmon and eel, terrine en gelée, celery rémoulade, and a ripe vacherin cheese. For dessert we always had fresh pineapple, a great luxury at the time, and Maman's homemade Christmas cookies in the familiar shapes of heart, star, and sickle moon, which we helped cut out, year after year. My siblings and I would sit around the table with Papa, sipping champagne and cracking open walnuts and almonds, while Maman quietly disappeared into the living room to light the beeswax candles on the tree. Finally we'd hear the little high bell, her signal to come in.

Tonight, my first time *en famille* with Walker, the smell of the candles and the fresh spruce after years of absence filled me with great longing and a sense of loss. Had I traded all this for a life without family and children? I was lonely at times, but I could never admit this to my family. This was no time to be sad, I thought. Bernard sat down at the piano and we all joined in, high and low, in perfect harmony, Christine's beautiful alto with Maman's soprano, Anne-Marie, Papa, and Bernard. I remembered the words and sang softly. I turned to look at Walker and saw tears rolling down his pale cheeks. You, too, I said to myself, and moved over and took his hand. I love you, don't we love each other?

During our few days in Bern, Walker became interested in our family life, and especially in Christine. The moment they met he sensed the artist in her, and she responded with her whole being, so pleased to find someone who seemed to understand her. He was attracted by her vulnerability, quick humor, and changing expressions. He also must have seen signs of her difficulties, for he wanted to help her. He later called Grenny in New York and put her in his will.

When we checked out of our hotel in Bern, I offered to pay the liquor bill, not wanting my father to see it. I was shocked: it was more than the room bill. A frosted bottle of Russian vodka had been brought up with the breakfast tray every morning and returned empty at night. Papa asked me a couple of times if I had reasons to worry about Walker's health, but I assured him that Walker's drinking had to do with the Christmas season and his excitement of meeting our family and friends.

We went to Zurich, where Walker met all my friends and saw Alec at various gatherings and dinners. Everyone was charmed by his wit and intelligence. Drinking, literary conversations, and bantering lasted late into the night. We were often so stimulated that we lost hours of precious sleep, and by the time we arrived in London, just before New Year's, Walker was weak with exhaustion. At Waterloo Station we caught the train to Tisbury, where Jimmy Stern welcomed us to Hatch Manor with more drinks and the news of a White House telephone call for Walker. "You're famous, old pal," was his greeting with a tap on Walker's back, so pleased to see him after several years. Tania threw her arms around us. Walker was alarmed at first, until he found out that the White House call was from President Johnson's cultural team asking Walker to be an overseer of photography in the U.S. "Overseer?" he grumbled. "Now what the hell can that mean?"

We had dinner in the kitchen and toasted one other and our New York friends. Jimmy kiddingly told Tania to shut up every time she interrupted him and Walker in their recounting of old memories of James Agee and funny *Time* magazine stories. Frequently, between cigarettes, Walker took a swig from his flask. Jimmy's vodka was only 60 proof.

Observing Jimmy and Tania, I saw what I thought a real marriage was. Hard to explain, for they certainly had strong opinions and disagreements. Trust and honesty were most important, and simply liking each other day in, day out, and being kind even when one didn't feel like it. *La politesse du coeur* described it perfectly. Finding humor in small things always helped, and lots of touching and cuddling. I wanted to stay in this kitchen with them and rest in the warmth of the Aga stove that Tania kept going all winter.

It wasn't until the following morning that I stepped outside and looked back from the wintry garden at the sixteenth-century stone façade of the house. We took a walk through winding country roads with Jimmy and were enchanted by so much ancient stone in this pastoral Wiltshire landscape.

The days passed all too quickly. There were several rituals to observe: Jimmy was in his study with the door closed until about eleven, working. Then he posted his letters and we went for a walk. Dry sherry or a Guinness before lunch, and long periods of napping and reading afterwards. Late afternoon, just before cocktails, Jimmy would move from the fire in the sitting room to his study and open the liquor closet. The second day, he offered me a black velvet, a drink of Guinness and champagne, and much to my surprise I liked it very much. Soon all four of us were in his study, holding our drinks. Always curious how people lived, Walker snooped around on Jimmy's desk and looked at the books. It was a man's room, and it smelled of old leather and cigarette smoke. Tania gave me the signal to follow her downstairs to the kitchen and leave the gents alone. We had a chance to talk—"motorboating," as Jimmy called the way Tania threw in whole German sentences to bolster her English, and nobody could talk as fast and as much as Tania. She wanted to know how New York was changing. Had Beatlemania swept the nation? Were mod clothes the rage? And long hair? London was going to hell.

I told her about the Black Panther Party, and the young people's increasingly rebellious attitudes towards the Vietnam War, and the free speech movement at Berkeley. Times were more serious than in London, from what I could tell.

She changed the subject and asked what had brought on Walker's drinking. It was many things, I ventured: depression over Wilder's death, feeling unappreciated at *Fortune*, lack of energy, lack of money. She nodded. She knew only too well how artists and writers lived. The Sterns' walls were covered with their friends' paintings, drawings, and photographs by the likes of Alexander Calder, Lucien

Freud, and Berenice Abbott. Every time Jimmy showed us a book, it was a first edition amicably inscribed to both of them by the author.

"You must do something," she said, "before it's too late." No doubt she was thinking of Agee, their close friend. I took her remark as an intelligent and sincere piece of advice from a wise and caring woman, but I pointed out that no woman, and certainly not a wife, could tell Walker what to do. I explained that I had not been able to talk to him about what he called "disagreeable subjects," which included virtually everything that mattered in life. I felt I knew her well enough to ask if she was able to control Jimmy's drinking. No, she said, looking down, slightly irritated. He was very bad at times, but they were always able to talk when he was sober, and that was one of the reasons their marriage had lasted.

Did she think our marriage had much of a chance, the way Walker was behaving?

Tania smiled at me with such warmth and sympathy, I no longer needed an answer. Even if I didn't feel loved by Walker, I now had three sets of parents who loved me: my own, Dorothy and John in New York, and Jimmy and Tania at Hatch. I couldn't have asked to begin the New Year with better friends.

Chapter 25

Walker went back to New York early in January, and I stayed on with my family to hear Bernard's inaugural lecture as a tenured professor of the University of Geneva. It was a grand occasion. The lecture hall was very crowded with faculty members, friends, and students, and Bernard spoke for three quarters of an hour in perfect French, looking relaxed and in charge. The subject was Rousseau's influence on the German poets Hoelderlin, Richter, and Kleist. Though much of it was over my head and might have been too academic for Walker, I was sorry he wasn't there as a member of our family. It seemed that I had to get used to living much of my life without him.

Walker wrote several letters while I was in Switzerland. He expressed his sentiments on T. S. Eliot's death and Churchill's funeral, and he discussed his plans for his retirement from *Fortune*. Time, Inc. hired outside people to help employees make the best financial decisions, and Walker called for an appointment. The money from his time-sharing plan amounted to less than $40,000. Courtie Barnes arranged for Walker to have lunch with a Wall Street broker, who told him that he didn't have enough money to invest in the stock market. It depressed him to have worked all these years for *Fortune* and have so little to retire on.

I came back in early February. Walker was in a low mood and talked again of leaving New York and living in Lyme, closer to Yale. In one of his letters he had complained that he didn't "really like the tone or something about university life" and that he had only two exceptional students out of thirty. Some were intelligent, but he regretted that very few were "well-bred, so perhaps that was a thing of the past." Unlike many of our friends with their outrageous teenage children, he was not amused by the exuberant young with their crazy haircuts, pop fashion, and loud music. At dinner parties, after Johnson had ordered the bombing of North Vietnam, the talk was of the war, or the assassination of Malcolm X and racial violence.

Walker, who was not engaged in politics, would withdraw and we would go home early.

I rushed about town alone and spent less time at home. The Carswells were back from Washington and were settled in a duplex above the Whitneys' garage, with a large terrace overlooking the gardens of the grand double townhouse on East Sixty-third Street, which was built for the Whitneys in time for their return from London.

I often visited Mary after work. She was fixing up their apartment and showed me samples of curtain fabrics and color swatches. We took walks through her neighborhood, discovering new antique shops and boutiques, the Tender Button store being the best find. As the weather got warmer we brought picnics to the park. Mary, who had grown up in the country, loved trees.

Mary seldom asked questions about Walker, she just knew how I felt. She could tell by looking at me. I had missed her very much when she was in Washington. Several years of intense living had passed without our seeing each other, and yet we communicated about our experiences and families as though we had not been apart at all.

There was always some excitement going on next door at the Whitneys'. Mary knew the butler and Mrs. Whitney's personal maid, who took care of her couture clothes. Mrs. Whitney approved of Mary, and after a while she was given Mrs. Whitney's best Givenchy hand-me-downs and tried them on for me to see. Beaded velvets and satins passed through my hands, and Mary asked my opinion. Sometimes I pinned up a hem of a ball dress, or we made small changes in front of the mirror and put on Kenneth J. Lane's fake baubles, laughing all afternoon.

I also made friends with the whole Tworkov family. Hermine, their older daughter, an artist who lived with the painter Robert Moskowitz, frequently asked me to join them at loft and gallery parties in SoHo, and with them I experienced a whole new world, danced through wild nights with artists and filmmakers, saw the first video art exhibit of works by Nam June Paik, and watched Andy Warhol perform with the Velvet Underground. Walker was fond of Hermine and Bob. He trusted them and was confident that I would not smoke marijuana.

At home I had no place to sew and make things; the bedroom was too dark and small. Walker's mind was elsewhere. For days I wasn't able to communicate with him. In the afternoons, I often found him asleep in his study, a book lying open on the floor. At dinner he ate poorly and talked very little. It was like living in perpetual darkness.

Walker left *Fortune* at the end of May. No one seemed to care. There were no farewell lunches with colleagues, no celebratory retirement dinner given in his honor. His last *Fortune* portfolio, "American Masonry," seven color photographs, was published later that year.

Nothing seemed to be going right. In June, Walker attended President Johnson's White House Festival of the Arts and returned from Washington incensed that Norman Mailer was among the writers and artists picketing outside the gate. Walker grumbled that if Duke Ellington was there as an honored guest, he saw no reason why he shouldn't have gone, though several of his friends had declined because of Johnson's escalation of the war in Vietnam. Later, few were surprised when Arthur Miller refused to be present as Johnson signed the Arts and Humanities Act. Walker's name never appeared on the long lists of protesting writers and artists.

We left for the country as soon as the first hot days became unbearable in our apartment. But summer in Lyme was not the same without Clark. His garden was overgrown and the land was untended—the place reflected Billie's condition. We had enough to worry about without taking on Billie, but we both felt guilty not to see more of her.

Swimming and playing golf with the Knollenbergs, Walker was able to relax a little. Through them we met several younger couples with children, and soon we were invited to join this group at parties and sporting events. A gregarious, carefree bunch, busy making money during the week and playing hard on weekends, they were curious about us and couldn't believe we lived in a shack. We became friendly with Barry Gourlay, a maverick Scottish architect who had fought in the war in his late teens, and his wife, Mimi, a soft-spoken Philadelphia debutante. Mimi's younger brother Bob Busser was in his last year of studying architecture at Yale. A shy and thoughtful young man, he once in a while came by on his own and visited with us. He discussed his design projects with Walker and me, and we got the idea that we might be able to afford a modest contemporary house with a studio on our small piece of land. A new house filled with light and enough space for living and working had seemed a pipe dream, and yet Bob thought it could be built for $50,000.

At night, in bed, I imagined the shape of the house: tall windows, a clerestory in the living room perhaps, my own worktable, and a studio with a darkroom for Walker. But no—I mustn't be tempted by a new house in the country, I reasoned, even though it made perfect sense, since we couldn't afford anything decent in the city. But it would mean leaving New York, the city that freed me from conventions and helped me think for myself, where I found new friends and everything I loved. What would I possibly do in the winter, during the dark, gray months, without the street life, the ballet, and zillions of people to look at? I would shrivel up and fall down like the leaves in the yard. In Lyme, most women my age had a station wagon full of children and a young husband.

New York always gave me hope. It was human, unexpected things happened, and no explanations were needed. I could even talk to strangers on the bus, my favorite pastime, or strike up a conversation in a museum, and hear the children laugh in the Central Park Zoo. The whole city was mine to explore, from the fabric places on Delancey Street to the Ninety-second Street Y, where Alice and I heard Auden read his poems. Oh yes, and the skyline at night, the bridges with their garlands of light, and the slow-moving rivers. How could I ever give it up?

I wrote to Jimmy and asked him if he missed London. He answered that the reason they chose Tisbury was the two-hour train ride to London. They spent at least a few days a month, from September to early June, in the city. During the summer months the garden kept them busy, and he couldn't bear to stay away from his roses for very long. I could tell from the tone of his letter that he thought I was too young to bury myself in Lyme. And it was different for them, they did things together. Walker had his work at Yale, but where would I fit in?

There was no time to agonize over it. In August, the superintendent of 1681 York Avenue, Walker's fifth-floor tenement studio, called him in Lyme to inform him that there had been a bad leak. The owners were anxious to clean up the mess and plaster and paint the apartment; he needed Walker's key to get in. Evidently Walker had changed the locks to protect his camera equipment.

Walker wasn't well enough to brave the heat and the dust. He hadn't used the studio for a year, and I had never set foot inside it. I volunteered to go down and sort out what could be saved, on the condition that he would let me fix it up to use as our pad in Manhattan if he decided to build the house in Lyme. Walker hesitated at first, realizing that five flights were a hard climb for him should he need to spend time in the city, but finally he gave in. For $120 a month he couldn't argue very much.

It was ninety-eight degrees when I arrived at the smelly, airless walk-up. The rusty water–stained ceiling was still wet, and occasional drips drummed on the metal file cabinet. Handfuls of damaged prints and negatives were stuck together, beyond recognition. I spent the entire day going through the contents of a second file cabinet that had narrowly escaped the floods. I sorted out the valuable stuff among obsolete timetables, magazine articles, and old newspaper clippings and pictures.

The second day was worse. Drawers of old letters, some without envelopes, strained my already burning eyes. I felt compelled to read the endings and find out who they were from. A manila folder with pencil-written letters on cheap yellowed paper in very small handwriting forced me to move into the grilling sunlight near the windows in order to decipher them. They were Agee's letters to Walker, written from his hospital bed in Santa Barbara in 1951. Agee was recovering from a heart attack after a stint in Hollywood where he had been working with John Huston on the script of *The African Queen*. He wrote of his passionate affair with a screenwriter and his feelings for his wife, Mia, whom he loved and was hurting.

I had no business reading these letters, but I couldn't stop. I grew more and more depressed over the lives of Agee and Mia and their children, Jim's guilt, his second heart attack brought on by heavy drinking and smoking—I panicked that this could happen to me. Walker won't survive, I thought, all choked up, my mouth dry, my eyes smarting. "You must do something," Tania had said. But what? Please tell me, I need help.

By the end of the day I knew I was allergic to the dust, because I had a hard time breathing. I tried to call Walker but the phone in the studio was dead. I packed up and called Jim Leland, Walker's doctor, from a phone booth. He ordered me to hurry over to Doctors' Hospital, where he treated me right away. He gave me a shot of cortisone and I spent the night there.

I felt much better in the morning. Jim came to see me and I took this opportunity to bring up Walker's drinking. He pulled up a chair and sat down, looking very serious. Walker had come to him in the spring, he said, feeling listless and depressed. "Of course he doesn't tell you these things." Jim's voice sounded irritable. Alcohol was certainly the main reason for his depression, Jim continued. He had warned Walker about the dangers of drinking the hard stuff, and had given him the names of two or three places he could go to dry out for a couple of weeks. Then he'd need some program with regular therapy and treatment. He realized Walker would not want to go to AA meetings, "but he won't do anything unless it gets much worse."

I asked if I should talk to John McDonald, who was also Jim's patient. Jim thought it might be a good idea. He saw me out and said to call him anytime and not to go back to the studio until the weather turned cool.

Walker's sister Jane had died the summer before, and Tal, during his first visit to Lyme as a widower, felt kindly towards Walker and me, and lent us $10,000 for the house. Together with the money from Walker's time-sharing plan and a small inheritance from my grandfather and my savings, Walker felt confident that work could be started in the late fall and finished by April.

After Labor Day Walker met with his new students and spent more time at Yale. I persuaded him that we should move into the York Avenue studio, once it was made habitable, and not renew the lease for our wretched apartment.

The ladies at Letters Abroad were waiting for me to come back. During the work week I hardly had time to see my friends, hurrying to York Avenue to check on the workmen and running errands for Walker. Sometimes when I came home after one o'clock he was still in bed and had not eaten anything. Taking care of him gradually put me into a Florence Nightingale state of mind. He depended on me, and I felt needed day and night.

Why, in this time of crisis, I took on another patient, Margaret Marshall, an old friend of Alice and Walker whom I hardly knew, was unclear to me even then. I must have liked myself in this new role of caregiver. Margaret was undergoing shock treatments and needed someone to take her home afterward and sit with her until she could be left alone in her apartment. At the time she was working at Harcourt Brace. Before that she had been an editor at *The Nation*. When she felt well she told me stories of her childhood in Utah, how she and her many siblings had traveled long distances in a covered wagon. She showed me pictures of their homestead during a sandstorm of such violence that the roof blew off. None of her brothers and sisters, all Mormons, were alive, but once in a while a distant Mormon cousin would look her up and try to reconvert her before it was too late for her soul to be saved.

One evening, a very charming man came to call on Margaret while I was with her. He seemed to be a good friend of hers, though much younger. She introduced us, and he made me and himself a drink, moving around the apartment with great ease. It was Leslie Katz, who had just started his own press, the Eakins Press, and was eager to meet Walker, black-and-white photography being one of Leslie's many interests. He took me and Margaret out to dinner and we talked about books, jazz, and Brooklyn, where Leslie and his wife, the poet Jane Mayhall, lived. When he brought me home in a taxi, I assured him I would do my best to have Walker get in touch with him. "I can't promise, he isn't very well right now," I said as he walked me to the door, keeping the taxi waiting.

Leslie, a man of infinite patience and tact, finally managed to have lunch with Walker, but he saw right away that Walker needed to get better before he could approach him with the idea of a book published by the Eakins Press.

I spoke to John and Dorothy about Walker's drinking problem. We kept in close touch and I was anxious to see them. They agreed to come to our place for dinner. I spent the latter part of the afternoon arranging flowers for the table, cooking and serving Walker his cups of tea in the study.

The McDonalds arrived late because of traffic. In the middle of dinner, Walker excused himself, saying he wasn't feeling well. He retired to the bedroom and stayed there. Then John got up to look in on him. I couldn't hear a sound coming from the small room. Dorothy tried to comfort me and said John had already spoken to Jim Leland, and it was just a matter of time now. Jim was looking into Regent's Hospital, a private clinic in the East Sixties with an excellent doctor and expert staff. When John returned to the table he said very little.

He never had much color in his face, but tonight his cheeks were white and he looked drawn and worried. They left earlier than usual, and nobody drank anything after dinner.

I went to the bedroom, helped Walker into his pajamas, and covered him with an extra blanket. He was always cold and so thin his clothes just hung on him.

Cleaning up was therapy for me, like all busywork. Alone in the kitchen I talked to myself. Why were we building a house when Walker was unwell? It didn't make sense. How could he hold on to his Yale job the way things were going? Winter was coming. There wasn't even snow on the ground and he already walked like an old man.

It must have been past eleven when the doorbell rang. It was John. "I just dropped Dot off, how's Walk?"

"He's asleep," I said.

We sat in the living room for a while, quietly, not talking. I had been fighting tears for days, but now I could let go; it was all right to cry. John lit a cigarette and waited until I calmed down.

"He'll make it," he said softly. "He told me tonight he wanted to go to the clinic."

On the ninth of November, a Tuesday, Walker was scheduled to check into Regent's Hospital. He was planning to take an afternoon train from New Haven. It was a triumphant day for me, as though I had won a battle, and I wanted to make it as pleasant as possible for him. We had arranged to meet at the hospital. I packed a bag with what I thought he might need. The day before I'd gone to Regent's to examine his room. It was very well appointed with mahogany furniture, good lighting, and a private bath. There were comfortable chairs for visitors. The resident doctor took time to explain the procedures, the injections Walker would be given, and how he might feel. I knew it wouldn't be easy, but anything would be better than these past weeks.

Maybe a luxurious eau de toilette might cheer him up, something refreshing with lime. Bloomingdale's was close to the hospital; I took the bus down Lexington. I passed the fish market and saw the sign in the window. Tomorrow I would buy it, no matter what the cost—a present for the new house.

I entered Bloomingdale's and I headed for the men's department. I looked at all the shirts, just in case I should find a particular blue or dusty pink chambray, Walker's favorite weave. I bought a pair of cashmere socks to go with his new London slippers and meandered through the tie section to the men's colognes. Nothing sweet or too spicy; Walker was fussy and he didn't like sprays.

I was just about to make a decision when all the lights went out. The voice over the loudspeaker told us to stay where we were and we would be escorted to an exit. Soon flashlights were handed out to salespeople, and I joined a group of shoppers following a friendly young man to the doors on Third Avenue. It was getting dark, and except for the car headlights, nothing was lit. People were pouring out of office buildings and stores, aimlessly crossing the avenue, not knowing where to go. I walked to Regent's.

There the lights were on—the hospital had its own generator—and I was greeted with a smile by a friendly woman who led me up to Walker's room and told about the giant power failure all over the East Coast. Why didn't I stay here for the night, she suggested. "Your hubby will show up in the morning, fine with me." I turned on the radio and listened to the reports on the power failure. How lucky I was. People were trapped in elevators and in subway stations, pushing and pressing against each other, apartment lobbies crowded with people who couldn't walk up the many flights of stairs, and this was only the beginning. I couldn't reach Walker, and it would have been impossible for him to get to a public phone. His train must have come into Grand Central just about when the lights went off. I called Alice—no answer. Then I tried Margaret. She was in one of her high moods and invited me for dinner with friends. "Come on down, sweetheart," she said in her silver bell voice. "I've lit all the candles and I'm cooking with gas."

I left Regent's and told them that I'd be back later. The night was mild, and since the commuter trains weren't running, the suburbanites had decided to party. The streets were full of people strolling arm in arm, laughing and coming in and out of candlelit bars and restaurants. Civilians directed traffic, and some kind of order prevailed all through the evening. I felt perfectly safe walking down First Avenue to Margaret's apartment near the United Nations, and on my way back to Regent's, the moon cast a bluish light over the darkened city.

Walker called in the morning. He sounded tired but was quite excited about his blackout adventure. His train had just rolled into Grand Central when the lights went out, and he was loaded down with a briefcase. Luckily he carried his transistor radio and knew at all times what was going on. It would be his last night in a bar, he laughed, so he decided to camp out at the Vanderbilt Hotel, first in the bar and later in the lobby.

When he turned up at Regent's, he seemed in a cheerful mood, in spite of looking disheveled and in need of a bath. "I guess this'll be my hotel for a while," he joked with the nurse. Relieved, I left him in the hands of the medical staff and promised to visit later in the afternoon.

As soon as Walker felt better, John and Leslie visited every day. John brought greetings from old friends and his own version of the "Talk of the Town." Leslie, ardent and admiring of Walker's work, talked about a book. He had a way of falling in love with people, and Walker took to him the way a wilted plant responds to rain. They discussed photographs of interiors. Walker suggested pictures from his recent Chicago exhibition, newer work few people had seen. Leslie mentioned some of his favorite interiors, the Ringling circus wagon and the Alabama fireplace, both vintage photographs. I delighted in their animated exchange, the best cure for Walker. Leslie always included me and asked for my opinion, and after the two weeks at Regent's I couldn't imagine our lives without our new friend. "Things are looking up, Boo," Walker said to me one evening. He was feeling more like himself again. "We're going to the Ritz in Boston after I leave here. You deserve a break."

Chapter 26

The winter months flew by in a frenzy of activity. We stayed at the Ritz in Boston during Walker's recovery and had dinner with Lovell Thompson and his wife Kay. Kay wasn't well but Lovell never said much about it. She seemed frail, almost transparent, next to him, with his large head and bushy eyebrows.

Walker, who was on antabuse, spoke freely about his experience at Regent's and how it didn't bother him when his friends drank. He said he wanted to stop smoking but that it would be much harder than giving up drinking. Lovell mentioned the subway pictures. He thought the timing was right and that Houghton Mifflin was interested in doing a book. If the success of *Let Us Now Praise Famous Men* was any indication, then this new generation would certainly want to see these pictures.

Back in New York, Leslie and Walker spent long lunches on Leslie's account, designing the book of interiors, luxurious and gravure-printed. I suspected that Leslie's overgenerous advance had paid for the Regent Hospital bill and the Ritz as well, our last extravagance for a while. We were saving money and had moved into the York Avenue walk-up. I put our furniture in storage and pretended the studio was a beach house. White walls, straw matting on the floor, blue canvas chairs, and some of Walker's Florida sketches gave the sun-filled sitting room a light, carefree appearance. It was like living in a Dufy painting. Walker couldn't believe the change. I didn't mind that our pad was in a tenement. It would be a place to come back to when we needed a change from Lyme. I was still heartbroken about leaving New York, but I knew the move was right for Walker.

That winter we made several trips to the site of our new house with Bob there to answer all our questions. The transformation from blueprints into three-dimensional space was so exciting that I jumped around in the water-filled basement, and Walker pantomimed hanging pictures on imaginary walls. At home I cut out little squares of sofas and tables to scale and moved them around the fireplace in different configurations. Was it preferable to have two seating groups rather than one wide circle?

Mary and Bob Carswell were also building a house in the country, on a generous piece of land with a grand view over hills and valleys in Great Barrington, Massachusetts. Mary and I compared elevation drawings, plans, materials, shapes, and wood stains and promised to visit each other's new dwellings in the spring.

On a mild afternoon in April, I packed a couple of pillows, some sheets, towels, and a blanket, and we drove up to Lyme to spend the first night in our new house. Bob had telephoned and sent us a solid brass key to the heavy front door, which had a custom lock chosen by Walker.

As we drove down Grassy Hill Road I saw the shadblow in bloom in the bare woods. I had never been in Lyme this early in the season. It was getting dark. Neither of us spoke. We knew every turn in the narrow road, and yet it was different tonight, we were on our way to a new place—so important it almost took my breath away. Would I be happy here? Was this a new beginning? I could take the train to New York anytime. My pad would always be there.

The outside light was on. Our footsteps on the bluestone entry hall echoed through the two-story living room. We walked in the darkness through the house to the sliding door onto the deck and stayed outside for a while listening to the night sounds. The moonlight gave the gray wood siding of the house a bluish wash. As we went back inside we saw stars through the clerestory windows. The moon was rising. Shadows appeared on the white walls. It was like a muted stage set. We stood there in wonder.

I turned on the lights in the kitchen to look at the new appliances. Everything sparkled. After years of scrubbing old stoves in various city apartments, I could hardly believe my luck.

The next day, before lunch, the moving van arrived. Walker spent the rest of the day in his studio. I moved furniture around and unpacked boxes in the kitchen. We had an improvised dinner in our dining room, looking out to the huge dogwood tree.

All spring I nested, listening to jazz while I sewed pillows and bedspreads on my solid worktable in the bedroom. Outside, behind Walker's studio, I discovered a pile of rocks left over from the excavation. Wouldn't a rock garden be a good idea, I thought, and ordered a truckload of loam. If Maman could see me now, planning our garden. Gardening was her pleasure, and so far in our family none of us had much enjoyed it as adults. I studied my new Christmas garden books. Visits to different nurseries became more adventurous than shopping for clothes at Saks. I missed Clark, who knew how to cultivate plants.

By early June the Knollenbergs put us up for the Old Lyme Country Club, the little "cowpatch" nine-hole golf course where Walker liked to play. A new clubhouse made it a good place to have lunch. Walker suggested I take golf lessons. After a few lessons I knew golf would not become a passion of mine. I liked to play by myself, early in the morning, when the rabbits and woodchucks were feeding, or at cocktail time in the summer. I wasn't going to join the ladies' golf on Wednesdays.

I got to know Walker's Yale faculty colleagues much better: John and Dorothy Hill, the Alvin Eisenmans, the Norman Iveses, Dean Gibson Dane and his wife Ilse, and some students. Esther Kirschenbaum and Chris Pullman, Walker's star students, were engaged, so they always visited together. Both were graphic designers. Esther also knew how to bind books and make boxes, a superior craft in Walker's eyes. As a house present for us she sewed a set of green and dark pink striped cotton placemats. I was touched.

Nobody in the department was more helpful to Walker than John T. Hill, who was a photographer himself. I always enjoyed being with John and his wife Dorothy, a graphic artist who had wonderful taste and a gift with color. She cooked the most delicious dinners while Walker and John were engaged in irreverent conversations. John's sense of humor certainly matched Walker's. Now that Walker wasn't drinking I liked to see him have a good time with new, younger friends who admired his work and were undemanding. He deserved to be treated like a famous artist after the *Fortune* years.

Alice Morris was our first weekend visitor from New York. She praised the house and was much interested in my barely emerging plants. She knew all the names of ferns and wildflowers and carried a set of binoculars for a bird-watching expedition across the road on the edge of the swamp.

Walker brought out the pictures for Leslie's book and showed Alice the format, a fourteen-inch square, the charcoal linen for the case, the buff endpapers, and the elegant typeface. She was delighted with the selection of familiar photographs, like the church organ in rural Alabama, and new work she hadn't seen.

"Give me a title," said Walker, pleased with her reaction. "Come on, Alice, you're good with words." They each lit another cigarette and tossed words around as if they were playing a fast game of ping-pong. There was lots of joshing, and then a long pause.

"Interiors," Alice mused, "they're all interiors without people, but we know they're either inhabited, or were. What's the message?" She inhaled her smoke and wrote something down. "I got it, hurrah! *Message from the Interior*. As simple as that."

Walker thought it brilliant. "Just right. Thank you, my dear, you're a genius. I'll telephone Leslie."

The more time Walker spent in the studio, thoroughly absorbed and excited with his projects, the more I felt that something in my new life was wrong. At night I was tired from weeding the garden and moving rocks. Falling asleep was no longer a problem, but my mind was seldom fully engaged. I missed my friends, our conversations, my city freedom. We had only one car, and when Walker was gone—he always had an excuse to drive here and there—I was stuck.

I sensed what was in his mind: he had given us our beautiful house; he liked me working around the place, sewing and gardening, swimming and playing golf with him, and entertaining friends. In his professional life he was regaining lost time, and he thrived on being courted by publishers, museum curators, and institutions. The new studio and darkroom gave him an opportunity to invite Yale students out to Lyme for a couple of days and help him print and mount pictures under his close supervision, a pleasant and efficient way to get things done.

Summer would soon be over, the garden dormant, and then what? Where was I going? I began to worry with every passing week.

An airmail letter from Zurich arrived, offering me a teaching position for the fall and winter semesters, I felt exalted: my innermost wish had been granted! A real job, in a place I loved, with people I knew—there was no question that I would accept it. My father sent a congratulatory note, encouraging me to take the offer. Obviously, the school had asked him for my Lyme address and mentioned the position.

But I couldn't leave without Walker's blessing. The term from late October 'til Christmas wasn't such a long time, not now that he was so busy. The second separation, from January through March, might be more difficult for him, but his friends at Yale would take care of him. In New York he had the Century and all his old chums. It was my turn now, and besides, I was getting a decent salary. I'd be off his payroll, except for our Christmas vacation.

Walker reacted more reasonably than I had expected. He was proud of me for getting the job. He'd checked it out: all the faculty members in his department knew my school, which rated very highly in the field of graphic design.

I spent the first part of October in New York, putting together a small collection of books and museum catalogues of exhibitions showing fashion accessories, my special teaching assignment in the department of textile design.

Hats, bags, gloves, shoes, and costume jewelry designed by Americans would certainly impress my students, who, I imagined, were probably looking at Mary Quant and Courrèges' white boots and Yves Saint Laurent's nude look. I was ready to surprise them with Rudi Gernreich. I'd been so hungry for the city, and now I had a reason to use it—to view fashion, film, and art through the eyes of my future students. I saw Warhol's *Chelsea Girls*; went to a performance of Klüver and Rauschenberg's *Art and Technology*, which fused music, painting, film, dance, television, and advanced technology; and gathered all kinds of material that would have interested me when I was at the school.

I left for Zurich around the twentieth of October with Walker's best wishes. He and some friends saw me off at Kennedy Airport. I was glad he had company for the rest of the day.

Chapter 27

Walker's first letter arrived in early November. He seemed in good spirits. He was and busy and had new plans for an exhibition at Robert Schoelkopf's gallery on Madison Avenue. Schoelkopf was a close friend of Leslie's, and there was no doubt in my mind that Leslie had made this possible. The exhibit was scheduled for December, before Christmas: thirty prints, all beautifully mounted, he wrote, mentioning money and how much he will miss me, my friends, my list-making, and my help in hanging the pictures.

He had other news: Lovell Thompson had phoned to tell him that Houghton Mifflin and the Museum of Modern Art were planning a joint party on December 1 to celebrate the publication of his new book, *Many Are Called*. The party was going to be "good and big" and he was going to ask everybody. This too I would miss, but it couldn't be helped.

The last paragraph reported depressing news from Jack Tworkov. Jack said that Kingman Brewster, the Yale president, apparently doubted that painting ought to be taught at the university. Walker's response sounded disturbing: "Poor Tworks. They don't have much future. Jack has no gallery and a dwindling following. Wally is worried." I was sad because I was very fond of the Tworkovs, and they deserved better.

As I began my new life in Zurich I missed Walker very much, and I longed to hear and speak English. The daily *Herald Tribune*, which I bought at the train station kiosk at great expense was a small comfort. Writing letters in the evenings in my cozy hotel room became a much-needed diversion after a long day of working with my students. I had a small group of seven, all girls between the ages of eighteen and twenty. They were rather cool and blasé, and wore bell-bottom pants and boys' caps. I made myself elegant just for them and told them about fashion in New York and what I thought the essence of fashion was. "It is never artsy craftsy, but terribly fast and contemporary, of today." Walker would have approved of my statement, I thought, knowing how much he disliked muumuus and Marimekko clothes.

On the third day, Vre Bischofberger, who taught fashion design, invited my students for tea in her class and we all discussed the upcoming fashion show, our joint spring event. The meeting was successful, but there was an enormous amount of intrigue and rivalry between the different department heads and the textile and fashion design classes, so we had to keep quiet about the fashion show. The students understood this and were stimulated by it and willing to work longer hours if necessary. As long as I stuck with Vre, who knew the school's director very well, I felt I'd be all right.

I was planning a small dinner with Vre and Bruno for Walker to meet Director Baumann. They all knew and admired Walker's work and they had also met John Szarkowski. Photography books published by the Museum of Modern Art were in great demand at the school, but it was very difficult to obtain them. I asked Walker to send some softcover copies of *Message from the Interior*. Everyone was eager to see the book.

All Walker wrote about were these parties: "How we shall need you, both at the Museum and at the gallery. One does need a wife, especially a pretty one!"

I wanted to know what prints he was selecting for the Schoelkopf exhibition and was eager for more details about the small, carefully designed catalogue. This was his first New York gallery exhibition since we were married, and I felt frustrated not to see it. I asked him if he would keep a set of duplicate prints so that I could reconstruct the show. Half joking, I wrote that I would gladly sell my few jewels and the fur coat to fly to the opening.

It upset me that he thought of me primarily as a decorative accessory and girl Friday, especially now with my new job. And I was anxious to hear his answer to a more serious question. In these first weeks in Zurich I was overcome with doubts and a certain malaise about living in Switzerland. I felt torn between my satisfying work and my close Swiss friends, and America, the country of my choice. It was a disturbing state of mind to be in, and I felt ungrateful. Under these circumstances my professional life seemed just as uncertain as before. In a long letter, I described these feelings to Walker:

Chapter 27

It is Switzerland that gets on my nerves so terribly, I don't think I could stand much of it. I think I am going to make myself an American. I would feel better. This back and forth and living in two continents is hard on one's soul.

I received a thoughtful response from Walker, who said he had spoken to John Kouwenhoven about me. John knew people at the Rhode Island School of Design and thought I might be able to teach there. This news made me very happy. The school was similar to my Swiss school, and I could easily drive there from Lyme. The future didn't seem as bleak anymore.

"State of crisis—over money," Walker wrote from New Haven at the end of November. His gallery exhibition was scheduled to open on December 20, so money from the print sales would not arrive in time for our Christmas vacation. Also, the Brown Brothers job was progressing more slowly than anticipated, and with various difficulties, and how he hated all this now. He described a weekend in Lyme with his students Chris Pullman and his bride-to-be, Esther, working at full speed, mounting sixty pictures for the show. The photographs still had to be spotted and framed. Chris and Esther were wonderful, he reported. Esther cooked every meal, roast beef and chicken, and the sleeping arrangements were solved easily. Esther slept in the guest room and Chris on the studio couch. They both loved the house. He ended the letter telling me not to expect a very luxurious vacation—he hadn't the money, unless something came up.

I was used to money worries. It made little difference whether I earned money or not—Walker always overspent. He was generous to himself and rarely considerate of my needs. I was living frugally on my own in Zurich, staying in a modest hotel near the Jung Institute during my days of teaching, and spending free time with my family in Bern. I realized how different my parents' and friends' financial arrangements were from Walker's. The Swiss were conservative. Money was not spent before it actually came in.

It was already December, and the ever-changing winter weather brought on colds and flu. The first snow covered the roofs of the old part of town, and then, much to my surprise, was gone the next morning because of the Föhn, a warm wind that blew down from the mountains. Everyone felt lousy and complained of headaches and fatigue. After living at sea level for so long I was badly affected by the dismal Föhn, but the productive work at the school made up for it. The students surprised me with clean, uncluttered designs, and new materials and color combinations. I helped them solve technical problems. Some patterns for hats and scarves had to be cut on the bias to hold their shape or drape properly when stitched by machine. The finishing touches were most important, and hours were spent on achieving perfection.

Every so often I tried to lighten the workload by playing the most recent American music on an inexpensive record player one of the students brought in. They all loved jazz and knew most of the American musicians. Duke Ellington was one of their favorites. Broadway musicals like *South Pacific, West Side Story*, and *My Fair Lady* were less familiar. As a group the young women touched my heart, and they were affectionate and never tired of my New York stories.

Providence
Dec 4 1966

Darling BooBoo

I must tell you about the Museum reception. It was a great success, I assure you, and I certainly needed you by my side. You'd have loved it. About 150 people, and all had a good time, for an official party. The new book just got there in time, and 50 copies were sold—all they had in the store downstairs. I ate supper before going, and stood the storm well. Everyone asked about you, of course.

Who was there: alphabetically: Mia Agee, (I'll skip people you don't know or care about) Auchincloss (Lily), Barnes, Barr, Martha Blake, Carlins, Carswells, Coggeshalls, Guy de Lesseps, D'Harnoncourt, Kate Haddad, Sara and Tony, Grenny Emmet, Father Fly, Robert and Mary Frank, Lee Friedlander, Brendan Gill, Grotz and his awful wife who made a fool of herself, Verna and Arch Hobson, Marvin Israel (uninvited), Leslie Katz, without Jane, Barbara Kerr, Esther Kirschenbaum, Helen Levitt, Dan and Peggy Lindley, John and Dot McDonald, Herbert Matter, Alice Morris, R. Motherwell, Elodie Osborne, Eliza Parkinson, Betty Parsons, Geoffrey and Helen Platt, Leslie Saalburg, Ben and Sheila Schultz, Liz and Sam Shaw, Steichen and wife, Robt. Stultz, John Szarkowski, E. M. M. Warburg, Lily West, Alexandra her sister, Betsy Zogbaum, and all the Tworkovs, Helen newly arrived. Many of my students came from New Haven. Of course I talked a little to everyone, and a lot of strangers too. Lovell

Chapter 27

Thompson couldn't come. I'm afraid Kay is quite sick. I'll find out more about that. The party was well catered, with two bars, several hot food casseroles, and lots of hors d'oeuvres and sandwiches. Some came in evening clothes to go on out somewhere else. It was supposed to end at eight, but people had to be shooed out by dipping lights. No one got drunk and the only contretemps was Dorothy Grotz, who was simply impossible. I think she must be mad. Afterwards I went to the Shaws, impromptu with only the Dwight Macdonalds, Szarkowskis and Betsy Zogbaum who was asked by mistake as we were standing waiting for taxis.

Love,
W.

Walker was coasting on a high and I felt happy for him and pleased that he was well enough to enjoy this wave of success. He had waited long enough and endured lean years. But why was I prevented from being part of the festivities? I wrote to him, complaining:

I really thought you would invite me to fly to it, and I am still upset that you didn't. You know that I have a great sense for special occasions, and such an occasion! I think you should have felt this, and what is $350 compared to a celebration for you?

He would have to make it up to me in London. In a couple of weeks we would be there together. I knew he missed me and thought of me. It was all in his letters and he even sent the copies of *Message from the Interior*. My mother looked carefully at every picture and said, "Only a great artist can be so direct and so simple."

Chapter 28

Walker met me late in the afternoon at Heathrow in a chauffeur-driven Rover and before he gave me a chance to hug him, he apologized for not getting a Rolls-Royce—they were all booked over the Christmas holidays.

He looked frail and so much older than he had sounded in his dashing, breathless letters. If I had stayed home he wouldn't have had to go out every night. But I couldn't let guilt ruin our few precious days. I was bubbling over with news, and yet we were both silent. It wasn't the right moment—maybe later, over a cup of tea, once we were settled in our cozy room.

On our way in from the airport, most of London was muted gray, until we reached Kensington Gardens. There, in the light of old-fashioned street lanterns, the gilded coat of arms on the tall gates, century-old trees, and shiny holly were among the first signs of the London we both loved. Dusk fell quickly during these days before Christmas, and it was hard to see through the constant drizzle. In spite of the bad weather, there was no other place I would rather have been with Walker.

I was delighted with the Hyde Park Hotel. We had a large room that looked over the park. Again, Walker apologized that it wasn't the Ritz, where we'd dine tonight, special surprise, rather early, because he was famished.

The tufted chaise, tea table, and reading lamp were for me, declared Walker, who preferred the club chair and the kneehole desk for his books. I opened the mirrored closet doors, walked over to the bathroom, and turned on all the lights. Walker followed me in. He approved of the accoutrements, especially the Pear soap in the bathtub tray and the thick towels folded on the heated rack. "The English know how to bathe," he said, smiling and looking more like himself.

At dinner I envied young couples on my right and left. They seemed to have an easier time talking and being themselves. Walker observed everybody who came into the dining room, sized them up jokingly, and tried to guess who they might be. Normally I would have laughed and happily played his game, but tonight I had hoped for more. Judging from his letters, his life had been full of major events, and praise for his books and exhibitions. It was a time to celebrate. But it seemed as if he didn't want to include me; he wasn't interested in hearing about my work, and I was too afraid to bring up the subject. Had we lost each other in our two months' separation? Was my job threatening him? It certainly filled a great need in my life. Maybe he sensed this and felt displaced.

The next morning Walker didn't feel well. It wasn't his stomach, he said, just general fatigue. After lunch we took a short walk in Hyde Park and watched the children play while nannies in sensible shoes hurried their prams through the penetrating mist.

One of my presents was tickets to the ballet, with Fonteyn and Nureyev at the Royal Opera House. I loved Covent Garden, the market, and its surroundings. Walker wasn't sure he could make it. I suggested high tea at the hotel instead of rushing through dinner. The same driver was hired to pick us up in his Rover with plenty of time and bring us home. Nothing would be stressful, I assured Walker, and begged him to come. He'd be enchanted by the dancing and the elegant audience. Everyone dressed up: opera capes flying, top hats, furs, and jewels.

Curled up in his chair with a blanket, Walker worried he wasn't up to it, didn't think he'd last through the evening, he didn't want to spoil it for me.

If I couldn't change Walker's mind and dress for him, I'd put on my velvet Paris suit and dangling paste earrings for the dancers—they deserved the best.

As soon as Fonteyn and Nureyev appeared on stage I felt tears rolling down my cheeks, unable to stop them from gushing like a waterfall. All I had was a kleenex, no sunglasses to hide my bleary eyes. There was such tenderness in Fonteyn's movements: her arms extended, head tilted, she seemed to draw arabesques in the air while her legs were in constant motion. I watched her dip backwards in an arc-like curve, Nureyev holding her close, then twirling her faster and faster before lifting her high above his head, triumphant in youthful exuberance.

No words to disturb all my longings, pure dance, movements and gestures shaped by music—ballet became a substitute for love. I would have given anything for a hug. Walker seldom touched me, and he often pulled back when I tried to kiss him. I thought of his subway pictures, those plain faces turned inward, they were not seen with exploitative eyes. I knew Walker was capable of love, but he kept it for his work and for a few friends who asked nothing in return.

After Christmas, Walker decided we should move to Dukes Hotel, because it was less expensive. First he telephoned Tom Matthews. Upon hearing that we were planning to move to Dukes, Tom's sympathetic wife Pam drove to the Ritz in her town car, helped us pack, and drove us to their house in Chester Square. A light, comfortable guest room on the second floor was made up in minutes, and we were waited on by the most efficient staff. That night we dined with the Matthews at home, chatted amicably in front of the fire and went to bed early. Walker, Tom, and Jimmy Stern all had been close to Agee during the forties at *Time*, and until his death in 1955. I learned more about Agee from Tom and Jimmy than I had from Walker. Even after I had found Agee's letters, Walker was close-mouthed when I mentioned their contents. Agee belonged to his previous life, as did Jane and so many others.

New Year's at Hatch with Jimmy and Tania was my real present. The moment I walked into the house, the fire burning in the living room and the stacks of new books made me want to stay for a week. I was safe with my allies, and Walker's mood seemed to improve, though Jimmy's patience was tested right away when Walker asked for a Virgin Mary on ice. Not only was the Sterns' fridge a vintage model with a minute ice compartment, but in Jimmy's mind cocktails were uniquely American and he never offered them to guests at Hatch.

Drinking was so much a part of Jimmy's life with his close friends that I grew worried on behalf of Walker. At first Walker joked and said not drinking made no difference to him, but after a couple of evenings he became very demanding. I was carrying tea trays up and down the narrow stairs, bringing him breakfast in bed, night snacks, water for his many pills, and more. In the morning he found our bathroom too cold. Could I fetch an electric heater and warm up the room before his bath and keep the door closed?

Jimmy winked at me and called me "nursy" when we crossed on the stairs. Thank God for his sense of humor and Tania's generous nature. By the end of our stay they were both astonished at Walker's behavior towards me. Downstairs, in the kitchen, Tania asked if I was being punished for having accepted the job at my school.

We went to Bern and stayed at the Bellevue Palace, the grandest hotel, with suites reserved for heads of states and foreign dignitaries like Queen Juliana and Churchill. My father disapproved and found it extravagant. He wondered where all this money was coming from, since I often had to borrow from him. I couldn't tell him that our whole trip was charged on the American Express card, and a basket of unopened bills would surely be waiting for me when I returned to Lyme.

Again Walker photographed my whole family. Anne-Marie's baby Annette appealed to him, and he took many pictures of her with her young mother, quite touching. I had not seen any such pictures by him before. I often mentioned to Walker how fond I was of Annette, the first grandchild in our family. Papa had spoken with me not long ago and said he would help me educate a child, if I thought I could have one. I was still young enough, and now that we lived in the country it might be easier. A baby all my own, a warm little creature who depended on me, someone I could love always, like all my friends' children. No, no, it wasn't too late.

We spent our last evening in Bern with my mother and sisters (my father had already left for London). Annette was passed from arms to welcoming arms in the living room before dinner. Her large eyes were wide open and she seemed to observe everything around her without smiling. Walker thought she wasn't a conventional baby and predicted a remarkable future for her. We all played at guessing what she might become: a dancer, a famous architect, the first Swiss woman president....

After we said goodbye to everyone, Walker felt like walking back to the hotel.

It was a clear night. A layer of new snow silenced our whole neighborhood of old houses and fenced-in gardens. There were no cars to spoil the fresh snow. Everything glistened. It was the perfect night to show Walker our hidden path down to the river and cross over the wooden footbridge. As children we often took this shortcut into the oldest part of town. Across the river the lit-up Gothic cathedral soared above the row houses, their roofs heavy with snow.

Walker found it quite beautiful in itself, though not to photograph. "The French painters were good with snow," he said. "It requires great skill."

During the war the cathedral was always dark at night. I used to be a little frightened in that part of town, because it was so old and empty. My steps would echo in some of the narrow passageways, and it scared me. Most people preferred the high bridge with the trolley cars and wide sidewalks.

"Let's hope little Annette grows up without a war, such an adorable child," Walker said quietly, more to himself.

Now was the time to tell him how I felt; I had little to lose, he was in a mellow mood. "We could have a child just like her. Lyme is a good place for children, and Papa said he would help us."

We walked in silence for a while. I couldn't see his expression when he finally answered: "You can put this idea right out of your mind. Forever." His voice was as cold as the air. "A child of mine would have to be educated at Groton and Harvard, and we don't have the money."

I separated myself and walked ahead. How could he say such things? Didn't he know what children needed most? It certainly wasn't Groton and Harvard! He was still troubled by his own miserable childhood—surely he must realize that by the time a child goes to Groton and Harvard it's way too late if he hasn't been loved well and nurtured years before.

Strange that I longed to have a baby at this moment in my life, when my marriage was so unstable. Any friend who knew our situation would have advised me against it, but I remembered, from the war years, that to bring a child into this world is seldom a purely rational decision.

Walker's Way My Years with Walker Evans

Chapter 29

Walker flew back to New York on a crisp, snowy morning in the middle of January. I waited outside the departure lounge at the Zurich airport and watched his plane rise up into a clear blue sky, a welcome change from the usual wintry gray.

I spent most of the day wandering aimlessly in the narrow streets of the old town, poking in and out of antique shops and bookstores. I ate an early dinner in the deserted hotel dining room and felt terribly lonely. I was grateful for my Churchill book, a present from Walker. In the chapter I had just started to read, the young Churchill was at Harrow, and his letters were often touching, a mixture of passionate love for his rather cold mother and an ingrained snobbery and precise knowledge of his privileges and social position. I read until the church bells struck midnight. Tomorrow I would be surrounded by my students and would hear about their new projects.

On my third day teaching, Director Baumann asked me to his office and told me how pleased he was to have me there. Did I intend to return in the fall? I said I would be delighted, but only if my students could be integrated into the class of fashion design. He readily agreed that the design of fashion accessories and clothes should be taught in the same class.

I wrote Walker about the director's offer and how I had dealt with it. I begged him not to worry, since I had no contract with the school. I assured him I would do what was best for us. It seemed wise not to close any doors connected with money at this time in our lives. I also mentioned my great pleasure in reading Churchill after work and back and forth on the train. Living without a household was a new experience for me. I asked him if in the future he could give me two hours a day of perfect peace for my reading; no cups of tea and no phone calls. Summer in Lyme with the house, the garden, friends, and golf was a full-time job, and my books were left unopened.

Walker sent me a hasty note written from Ben and Sheila Schultz's apartment in New York. Ben had been fighting cancer for months, and I knew Walker was very concerned that Ben might not last through the winter. It was so unlike Walker not to mention Ben's health in his note, but he only referred to my letter. He sounded harassed. Yes, he agreed, it was unwise to close doors, but in the light of his new feelings about being with me, he didn't think we ought to spend another year with the same separation. In fact, he had already decided against it and he was sure I would agree with him. His advice was to say nothing definite to the school, not yet.

My birthday, January 30, failed to cheer me up. The world news was too depressing: the catastrophe with the Apollo 1 astronauts, the war in Vietnam, and the anti-American feelings growing so rapidly all around me. In Zurich, the falling stock market was on everyone's mind. Land and house prices were dropping, the boom was over. I feared that we might have to sell our house. Walker assured me that things weren't so bad and that we would be able to manage, but his mind was elsewhere. Once again I hoped for decisive answers to my most pressing questions:

> *I feel happy that you miss me so much and I don't mind your making up your mind for me, as long as you are responsible for the whole show. If I have to earn money, I prefer doing it here, where I can step right into every job I like. I have never felt privileged in getting interesting work in U.S.A. I would prefer having a gay New York winter any time, but I would hate to type away in some stupid office.*

Walker sent me a cable and a check for my birthday. But a letter describing the changes he made in our New York walk-up, because he needed more work space, infuriated me. How dare he crowd the small kitchen with yet another table, and put a heavy chest of drawers in the bedroom, where I had carefully placed a narrow piece of furniture to make the room more airy! I considered our little apartment to be my creation, but wherever we lived I had to fight against his clutter. He had no respect for my ideas of design, or my collections. I complained and sent an angry reply:

> *As to the bedroom, I reserve my rights not to like the new chest, since I haven't seen it. You certainly would do the same. I showed you the Limoges china*

before I arranged to have it shipped, even though I inherited it from my grandmother. If you really cared about my feelings you would never have done such a thing. If your study is too small, it is because you should clean things up.

I felt guilty as soon as I mailed the letter. Other than my work, nothing was going well. Walker sent news of Ben's death, the February blizzard on the day of the funeral, and his feeling ill due to this "rocking experience." He wasn't able to attend the service. A couple of days later, Robert Frank drove him to the burial in Paramus, New Jersey.

Poor Walker. Death, and especially the loss of a devoted younger friend like Ben, depressed and frightened him for long periods of time. And now I wasn't near him to envelop and comfort him. I worried about his delicate health. The winter weather, the lack of home-cooked food and small comforts were enough to bring on a major bronchitis or an upset stomach. He could not afford to lose weight.

Toward the end of February Walker reported on making some progress in the studio in Lyme: "order at last." He was planning a big summer's job printing and mounting photographs for his next exhibition, which was going to be a large retrospective at the Modern. To help Walker, John Szarkowski suggested a young assistant paid for by a foundation grant. In March he dined at the Szarkowskis and John revealed that the museum was eager for Walker to do a book for them. Walker, disillusioned about money, complained that the museum never paid enough or sold enough books, they just tempted him by letting him do what he wanted and then reaped the prestige of a beautiful and distinguished job with their name on it.

I, on the other hand, was overjoyed with the news of a big, important show and a book. The Modern was my temple of worship, and I disliked Walker's critical attitudes. Again he spoiled my pleasure with talk of money. He had barely managed to pay the most pressing bills, he said, and had borrowed to the hilt to do so. His little income was overdrawn and he couldn't celebrate my return handsomely, as he felt like doing. But he was careful to assure me that no bills were directly connected with me, since I had been off his payroll for months, except for the London vacation.

Just as I had made up my mind that we couldn't stand such a long separation another year, I was torn between Walker's constant lack of funds and my ability to earn a good salary here in Zurich. There was little hope of getting a job at the Rhode Island School of Design, and the prospect of a jobless winter in Lyme was too depressing. I loved my work, the students, the excitement. I tried to communicate my enthusiasm to Walker:

Now I must tell you about our fashion show. 200 people came to see it. We had three models: one tall, extremely thin one, one little, very pop looking one, and a charming "jeune femme" for the more ladylike things. There was music, and flowers decorated the white-walled bare room with mirrors as the only refinement. Both Vre and I wore suits and looked very businesslike when our guests arrived. Our director gave a little speech at the beginning and called me a rare consultant from U.S.A. He also said he hoped I could repeat my splendid performance. Then the show started.

People applauded all the time. The clothes and hats looked extremely new and well-designed. The show was full of ideas. In the intermission we served drinks and people became gay and funny. The end was charming. We received flowers and our public gave us a standing ovation. That day, the 9th of March, I was on my feet from 8 AM to 12 PM.

The press was full of good reviews of the show, and Elle *magazine plans to use one of the evening ensembles for their cover.*

Spring vacation was about to begin. I was free to fly back to the U.S. in time for Easter. I asked Walker if he could lend me $250 to pay for my flight. The school was going to reimburse me for this amount and some other expenses, but it always took time dealing with Swiss bureaucracy.

I was angry when Walker wrote back that it was precisely that $250 he needed to pay the Country Club, in order to keep us in. No mention of the fashion show, no praise for a job well done. Money, or rather the lack thereof, was what ruled our lives. I wasn't able to book a flight, and I didn't intend to borrow from my father to save face for Walker. Not after his choice to stay at the Bellevue Palace during our last visit in Bern. My father would not have understood that Walker lacked the $250 to bring me home.

Chapter 30

When I arrived at Kennedy Airport, Walker was not there to meet me. My legs hurt from the long flight, and it was quite a struggle getting my four suitcases through customs. The Swiss lace dress I designed and sewed mostly by hand became the subject of a vehement discussion with two officers. I wasn't going to pay duty on something I made from scratch. In the meantime, the limousine to Connecticut had left and I had to take the later one.

Walker sounded a little annoyed on the telephone. He'd wait for me in the station parking lot, but he warned me that his back hurt and he was corseted again and couldn't lift anything.

The closer I came to New Haven, the more I was haunted by doubts and worries. I tried to breathe slowly and close my eyes. My disappointment would show—on the plane I had imagined and relived the moment a dozen times; to be back with Walker in the country. Why didn't he give me a loving welcome?

The air smelled fresh, as though cleansed by a gentle spring rain. I loved seeing the water, the palest green in the woods, the big spaces— I felt so much more at home in America.

But Walker acted harassed and looked drawn. We barely kissed. He was in a hurry to get going. I lifted the suitcases into the rented car, stepped in, and he drove off. Too tired to start a conversation, I waited for him to talk.

"You can't imagine what a hard winter I've had," he said and lit a cigarette.

"Mine wasn't as easy as you think. I loved the work, but it was trying at times."

"I won't let you go again. It's out of the question." He inhaled deeply, in spite of his recent chest cold.

Oh, why bother to answer—nothing would change his mind. I was back in my cage.

The lights were on in the house. Walker went ahead to open the door. I unloaded the suitcases and carried them into the hall. I noticed that things were different in the living room—furniture moved, objects I cared for missing. I hurried from place to place, where my treasures had been—this wasn't a mistake, it was done on purpose. I heard myself scream, "Where's my opaline bowl, my French mirror, my drawings—answer me!"

"You left—I felt deserted—and I was sick." Walker's voice sounded artificial and hollow, like that of a robot.

In the bedroom, my dressing table was bare, nothing of mine left. I closed the door, rummaged in the cupboard under the bathroom sink, and found some of Walker's sleeping pills. I took three or four—sleep, deep, all-erasing sleep—not thinking, not feeling.

I lay in bed for two days, and when I woke up, the sun was in my face. I couldn't remember how I got there, what had caused my long sleep. Walker was sitting in the chair by the window. I was thirsty. He went out and came back with a glass of ginger ale and some biscuits. "That'll do you good. Dr. Saunders wants to see you later on. I'll run your bath, all right?" He was slightly bent over as he walked to the bathroom.

Soon I felt better. Walker drove to New Haven and said he'd stay in town for dinner. Most of that day I played in the house and put everything back the way it was before I left. After lunch I went into the garden. There nothing had changed. The daffodils were up and tulips had sprouted everywhere. The lilacs and dogwood looked healthy, their buds still tight. In the rock garden tiny irises showed their pointed leaves, and the grape hyacinths were beginning to bloom. My plants were alive—they deserved my care, and tomorrow I would rake the lawns and clean up the winter debris.

I wrote to Jimmy and Tania, read *The New Yorker*, and put on some jazz. Right now Jimmy and Tania were probably out in their garden, looking like scarecrows in their torn hats and wellingtons, weeding and clipping. A long, quiet day, how I had missed the country, our small piece of land, the stone walls and trees.

Lately Walker slept in his studio. Alone at night, I was attacked again by the racing thoughts, worse than ever. Usually it started with a real worry—the tray of unpaid bills on Walker's desk, or his incessant smoking. Then imaginary disasters like fire, roof leaks, and accidents crept into my mind, spiraling and circling at an increasing speed until I lost all power to resist. When at last the spinning came to a halt, I experienced the dizzying motion of slowly falling through space and drowning.

I couldn't tell Walker; we seldom talked.

On weekends students often came out for lunch and provided laughter and entertainment. They always had to do something for Walker first—lift a piece of heavy equipment or help in the studio. One Sunday a new student appeared, one of Walker's favorites, Alston Purvis, who drove up in a Cadillac, bringing with him a fellow South Carolinian, a tall, flamboyant man with flying white hair. His name was Ben de Loache, a baritone singer and voice teacher at Yale. There was a reason why Alston wanted Walker to meet Ben. In the thirties, on one of his photographic expeditions, Walker had stayed with Julia Peterkin at Old Lang Syne, her plantation in South Carolina where artists and writers were always welcome. Peterkin, nationally known then for her books *Scarlet Sister Mary*, *Roll, Jordan, Roll*, and *A Plantation Christmas*, published in 1934, had paid for Ben's education at the Curtis Institute in Philadelphia.

Walker and Ben were in high spirits, telling stories about people and places they both knew. Ben remembered names, dates, and the families who once inhabited the decaying mansions in Walker's photographs.

Alston beamed at both of us and held us in suspense with his own story: his father, Melvin Purvis, was the man who shot Dillinger. He mumbled softly when he spoke, which gave the punch line an even greater boost. *Bonnie and Clyde* was in the theaters, and here was a real-life son of the G-man who captured the gangsters.

Walker was animated and lighthearted with his new friends, but I felt disconnected—was he no longer charmed by me? He seemed distant, elsewhere.

Often, before I got out of bed, I wrote to Jimmy and Tania. In New York, I depended on Mary for comfort, went to the ballet with Bernard and Leslie, and spent days visiting Alice.

Walker never again mentioned the possible job for me at the Rhode Island School of Design.

The first humid day in June drained all my energy and I collapsed like a deflated balloon. It was a Monday, Walker's day at Yale. In the noon heat, I dragged myself to the mailbox, hoping for a letter from

Jimmy. A blue envelope was all there was in the box. It said "Mr. and Mrs." on it, so Walker wouldn't mind if I opened it.

Nice invitation, I thought, just right for a party. The blue ink on the white background, and the Bodoni typeface was getting to be the class' trademark at Yale. The students must have done the printing on the school's own press. For once they got it out on time. Most years, a day or two after commencement, Hope and Alvin Eisenman gave a party in their place in the country, but this time the invitation was for a gathering at some teacher's house farther out of town.

The day of the party, Walker was printing in the darkroom. He went back to the studio after lunch, full of energy. The temperature was just right for him, hot and dry.

I came in from the garden around four to get ready. Scrubbing my nails over the kitchen sink, I heard Walker on the front steps. "Do you want some tea?" I called out to him in the hall.

"Tea—yes and a buttered English muffin with marmalade." He came in, waving his arms. "Don't talk to me, I'm still concentrating." Before I could turn around and look at him, he was gone. I made tea and brought it into the living room, left it there for him and went into the bedroom. Moments later I heard Tebaldi singing *Tosca*. Playing *Tosca* had always signaled a gala night out, when he emotionally prepared himself and took a long bath, shampooed, carefully parted his straight hair, and put on evening clothes. Was it worth it to go through the ritual for faculty and students at a cook-out? It might take a whole hour. A quick shower would do.

Tebaldi's voice filled the house while the water was running in his bathroom. No need to hurry, I'd be waiting for him as usual.

We arrived late and parked in the field next to the barn. Before Walker closed the car doors I grabbed his cardigan. He said he'd tie it around his waist so he wouldn't lose it. We started to walk in the direction of the house, where the music and voices were coming from. Walking behind him, I thought he could have wrapped a wool blanket around his middle and still looked thin. And wasn't he lucky, already tan, his hair appeared lighter, almost white. Summer was really his best time, he couldn't get enough sun.

I hated my red arms and the sharp line where the T-shirt sleeves ended. White upper arms were no things of beauty. Too bad, I should've known not to wear the new spaghetti-strap dress.

Walker stopped and looked up at the pale sky. "Soon we'll have the longest days of the year. It's close to seven and the sun's still up." He shielded his eyes with his hand and commented on the tricky light. I noticed he was still wearing his dark glasses.

"You didn't bring your cameras?" I asked.

He said he had thought about it and decided against it. His students were supposed to photograph the party, it was their assignment. "Black- and-white, of course, and no flashes."

When we turned the corner we heard shouts and squealing girls' voices. "One, two, three—go!" About twenty students in a row, holding hands, started to run into the wild lupine field and all at once tumbled down to the ground. Then they chased each other through the tall spikes of purple, pink, and white, their bare arms and legs sticking out, like children playing in a hammock. Others stood in the grass, clicking their camera shutters.

"Let's say hello to Alvin," said Walker and pulled me around some students toward a tall, lean man standing in the middle of the mowed field, waving to us with both arms. He looked younger than his age, and nothing in his gentle, humorous manner let on that he was the chairman. I had never seen him impatient or cross.

"Join us, you two," he said, smiling. "I was worried you wouldn't make it. We missed you, Isabelle. How was Zurich?"

"Great, thanks. What a day for a party. I had forgotten how beautiful the lupine is."

"Yeah. We'll have lots of pictures, they're all working away." He observed that we didn't have a drink. "The bar is on the porch, but come back, I want to see you."

We took a few steps, looking around for people we knew. "Stay here," said Walker, "I'll bring you some wine." He didn't get very far. I watched four or five students greet him and introduce him to their girls. They soon encircled him, talking, laughing. Most of them were so much bigger that Walker was hidden by their bodies in no time.

Why hadn't I seen Hope? In her own place she'd be busy with the food, but here she was free to visit with friends. I thought I'd go and find her and get a bite to eat. It was my first charcoal-broiled food this year, roasted peppers, potatoes, and chicken. But I still didn't have my wine. Where was Walker?

Everybody was eating. The sound of Duke Ellington's big band came over the loudspeakers on the porch. It was getting dark and the cameras were being put away. Walker hadn't eaten, I was sure. By now he must be weak with hunger, so bad for his stomach. He could be in the house, sometimes he lay down during a party, took a nap. Maybe upstairs in one of the bedrooms. Everybody knew his peculiar habits.

I stepped inside the house, checked the living room sofas and the window seat in the study, and looked in the kitchen. Before starting up the stairs, I knocked on the door to the bathroom. A dog barked, and there was loud rock music coming from a bedroom. All the doors were open on the second floor except one. It had a large red Do Not Disturb sign. For a moment the pounding beat drowned out the dog's barking. Whoever was in there wouldn't hear my knock. Banging and yelling were the only thing to do.

"Who is it?" The voice was that of a young boy.

"Oh, don't bother, it's OK." Walker wouldn't be up here with that music.

I left through the back door and bumped into the garbage cans, stubbing my toe. Past the jungle gym the party noises grew dimmer. I had no idea where I was going. It was nearly dark now, hard to see what was underfoot; some ferns, but mostly low weeds. There was a smell of moist earth. I came to a hedge of tall hemlocks. Peering through the feathery branches I could see no lights, nothing but underbrush and trees.

As I walked along the hedge, a rattling of chains, quite near now, made me stop and hold my breath. I heard voices, a man's low voice, then exploding female laughter. The rattling turned into a squeak-squeak, like a hinge that needed oiling. I took another couple of steps and listened. Coughing, a man cleared his throat. No—No!—It was Walker's cigarette cough, I'd know it in my sleep.

I stood still, my heart beating so fast, nothing made sense. What to do? Stay or leave? But first I had to see who was there with him. I bent down and moved a couple of yards forward along the hedge until I thought I was directly across from the voices. What was he saying? I put my head through the first layer of branches. It sounded like French—*"elle, elle"*—and then the high teasing voice—*"Regarde, plus haut"*—coming from above the tops of the hemlocks. She had to be one of his students, she sounded young.

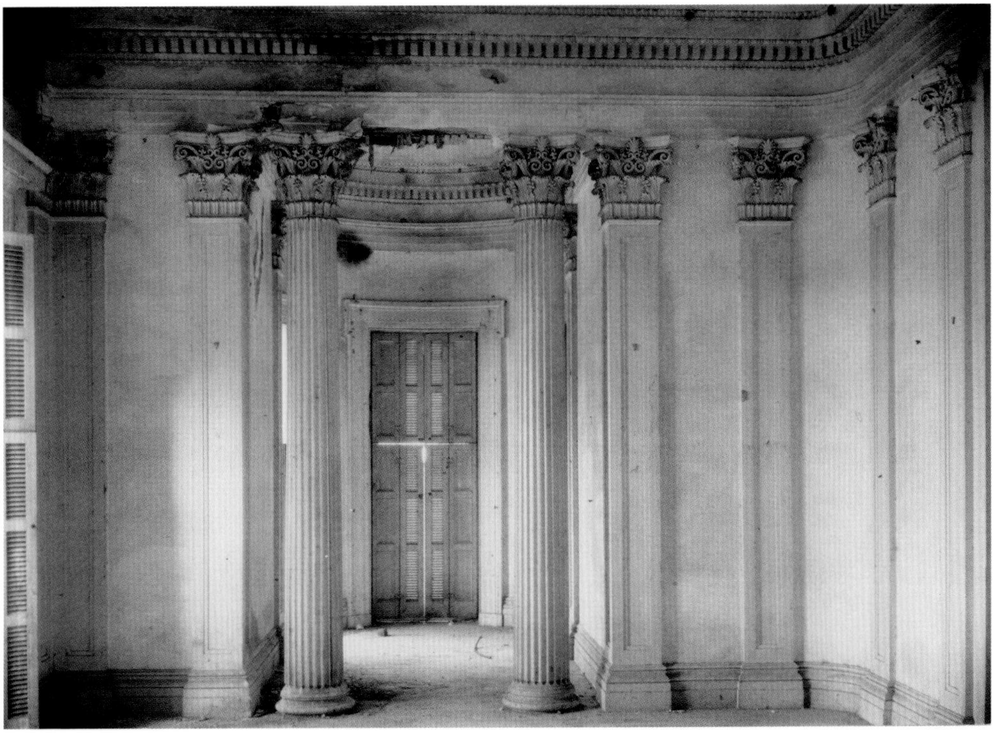

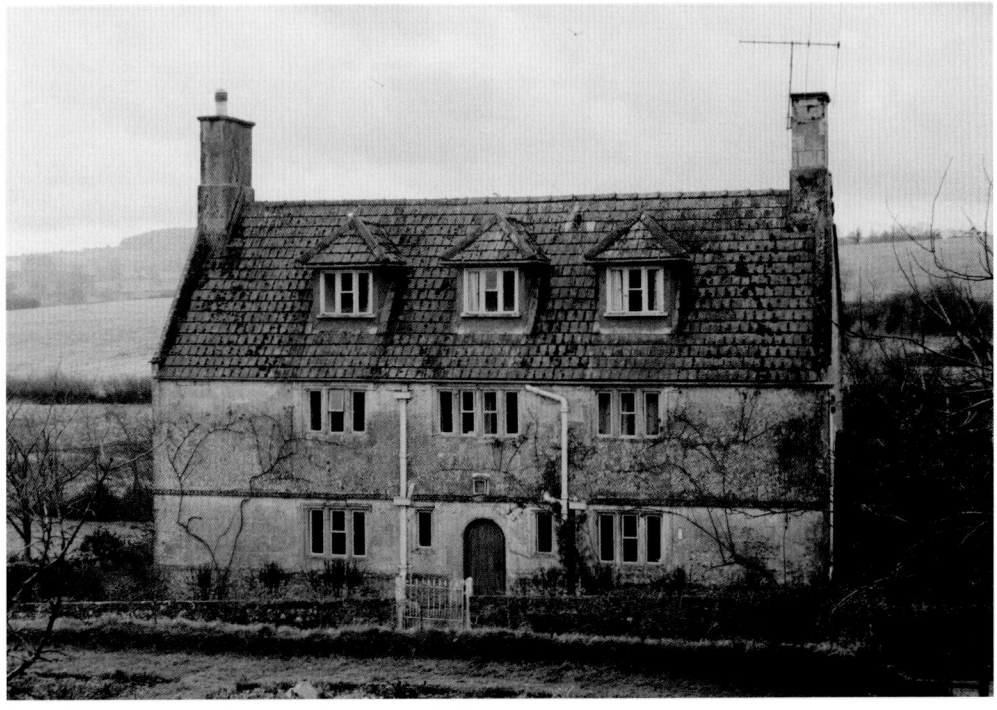

"Breakfast Room" at Belle Grove Plantation. Photograph by Walker Evans, 1935
Jimmy and Tania Stern's house, Hatch Manor, Tisbury, Wiltshire, England. Photograph by Walker Evans, 1967

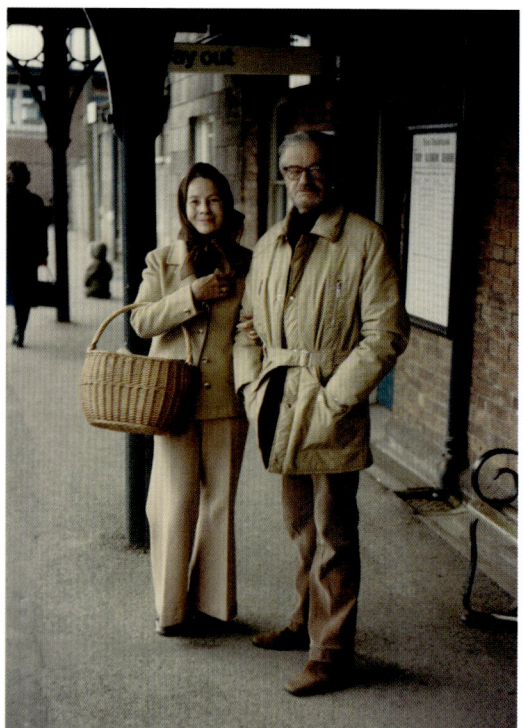
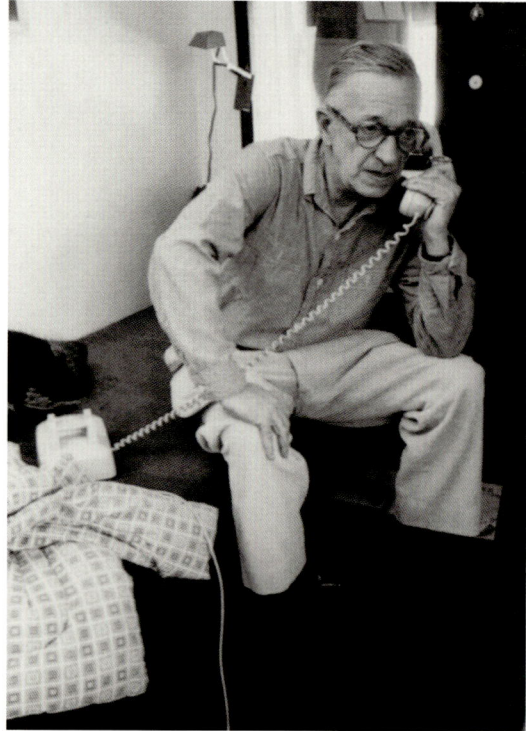
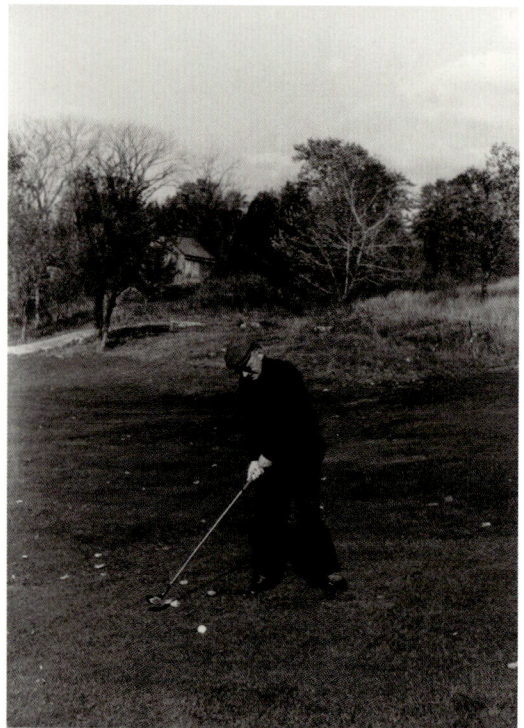
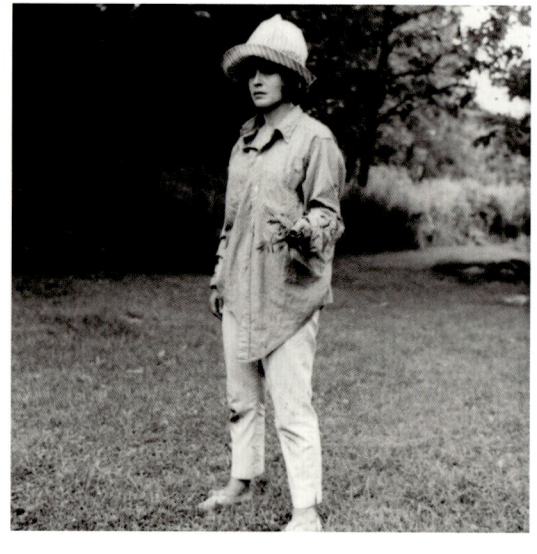

Jimmy and Tania at the Tisbury railroad station, early 1970s. Photograph by Alston Purvis
Walker in his Lyme studio, 1960s.
Walker on the Old Lyme Country Club golf course.
Gardening in Lyme, 1966. Photograph by Walker Evans

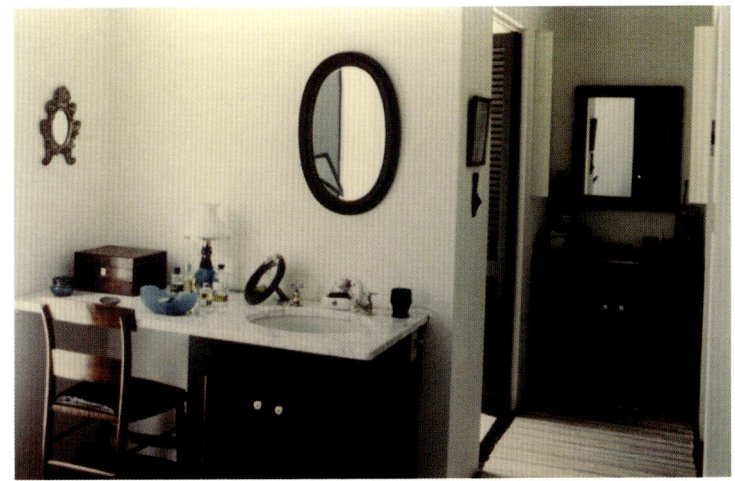

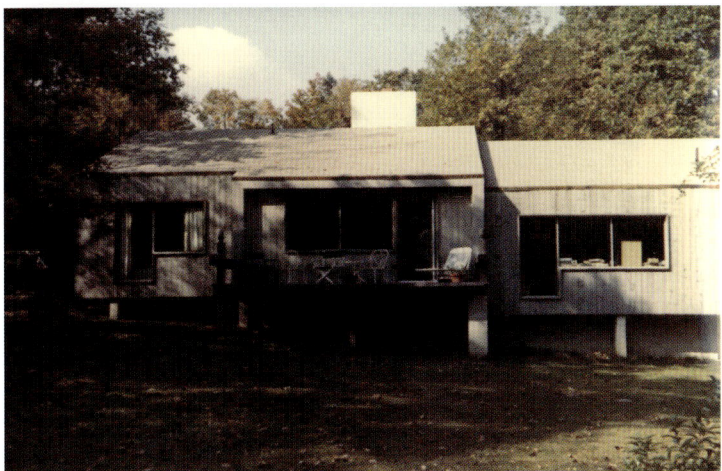

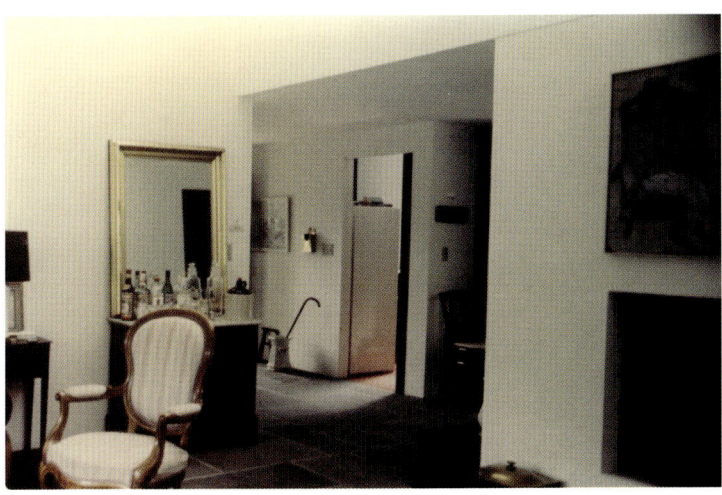

Our house in Lyme, Connecticut was designed by Robert Busser, graduate of the Yale School of Architecture, 1966:
My white marble dressing table in the bedroom. Photograph by Robert Busser
Eastern Exposure. Photograph by Robert Busser
Entry and part of living room. Photograph by Robert Busser

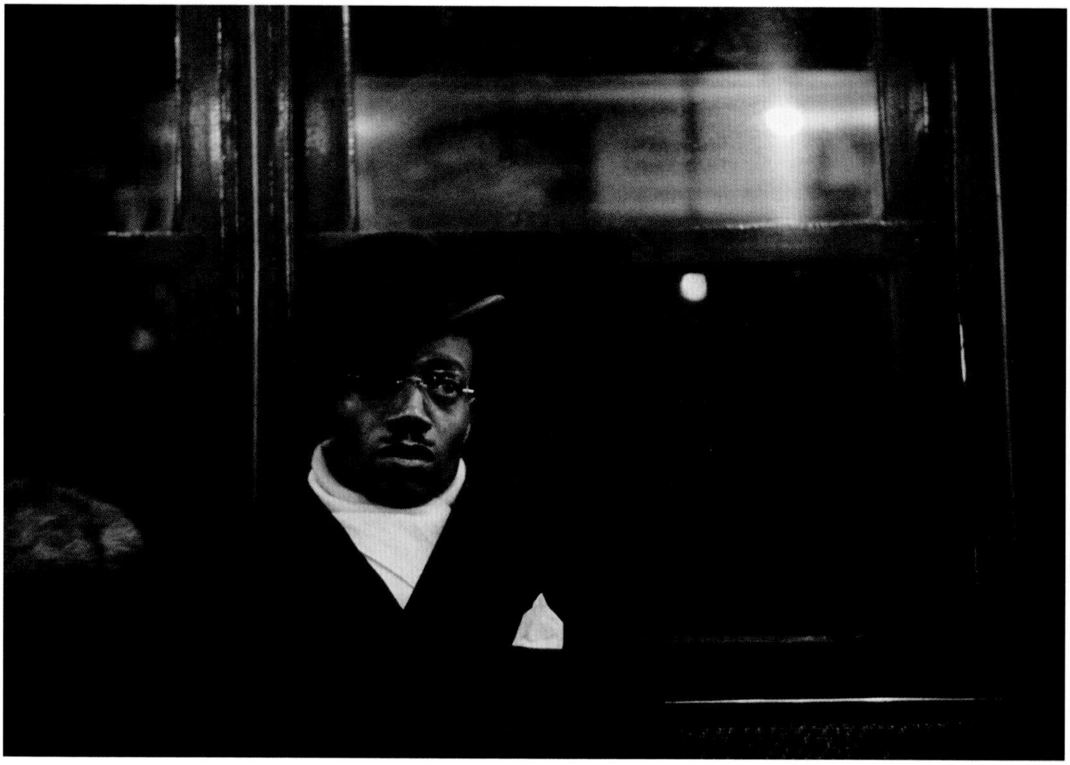

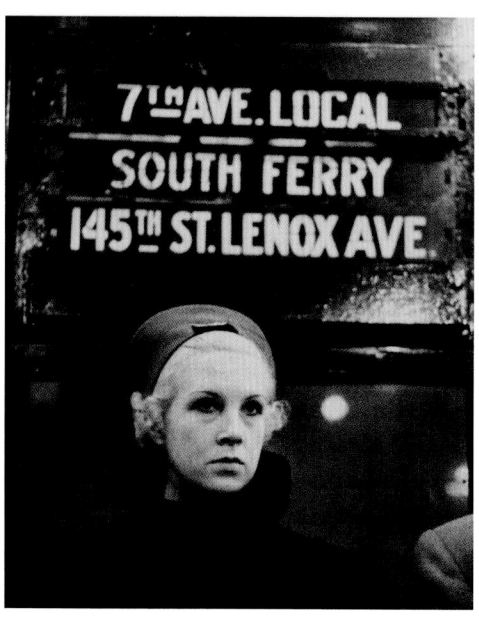
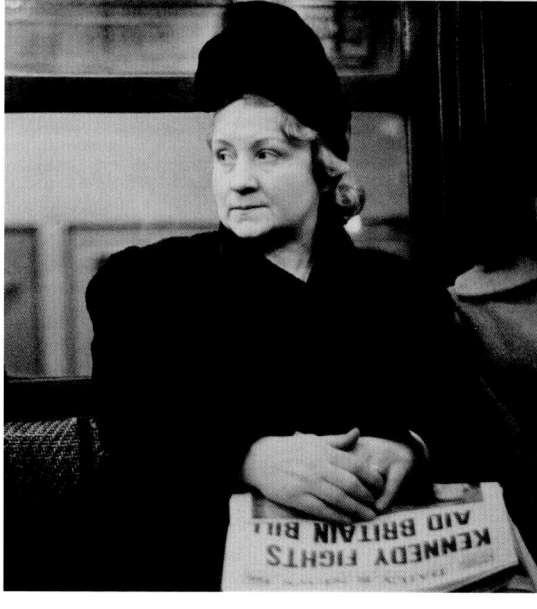

Subway Passenger, New York City. Photograph by Walker Evans, 1941
Subway Passenger, New York City. Photograph by Walker Evans, 1938
Subway Passenger, New York City. Photograph by Walker Evans, 1941

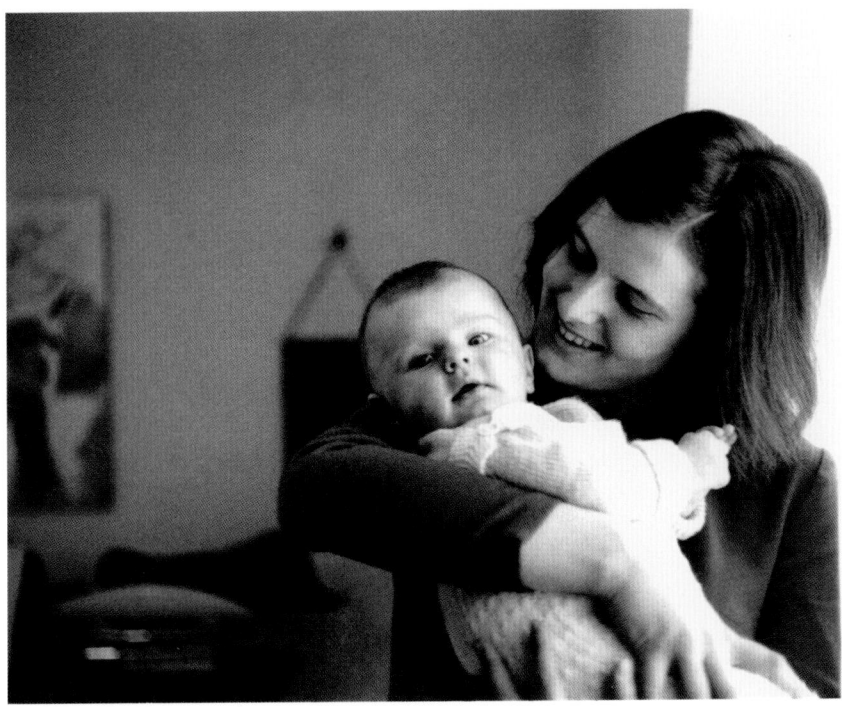
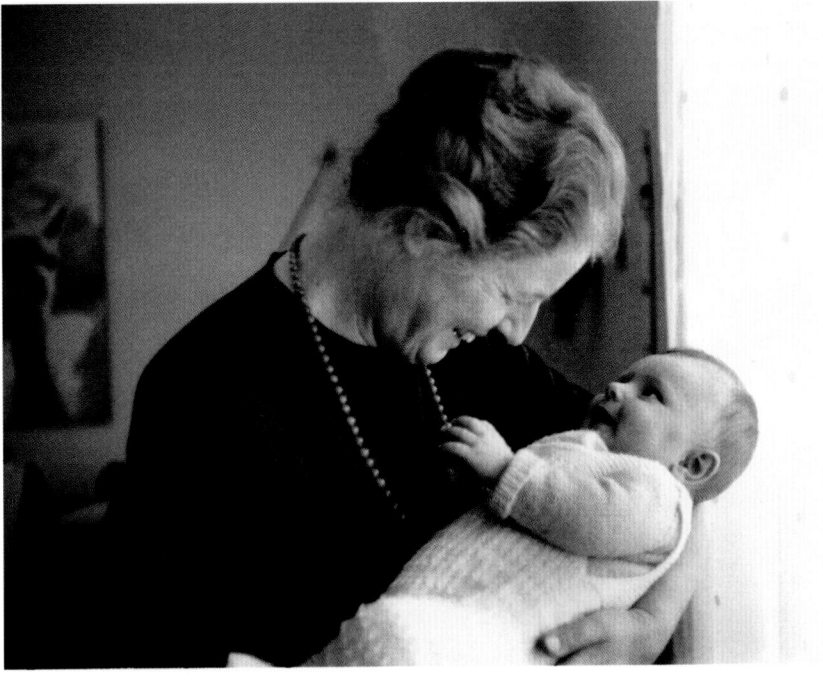

Anne-Marie and her baby, Annette, Bern, 1967. Photograph by Walker Evans
Maman and her first grandchild, Annette, Bern, 1967. Photograph by Walker Evans

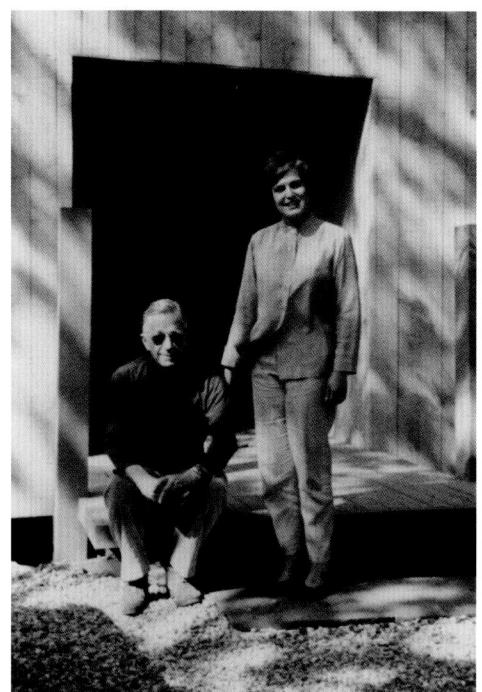
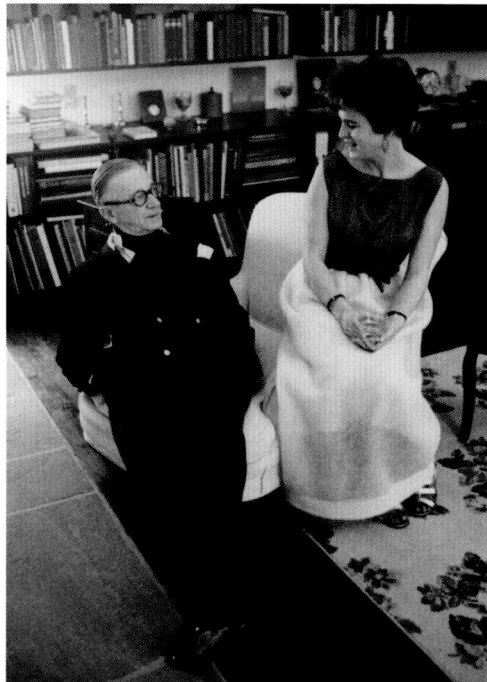
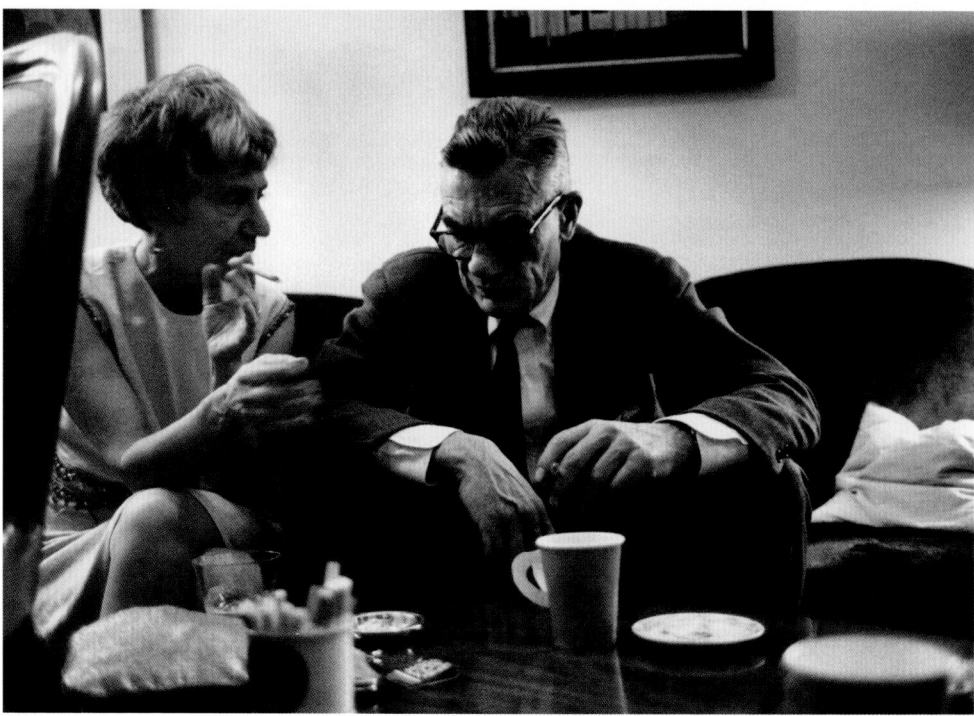

In front of our new house in Lyme, Connecticut, spring 1966. Photograph by Billie Vorhees
Waiting for guests to arrive in our new house, 1967. Photograph by Sedat Pakay
Housewarming party in Lyme, 1967. Dorothy Eisner and Jack Jessup. Photograph by John T. Hill

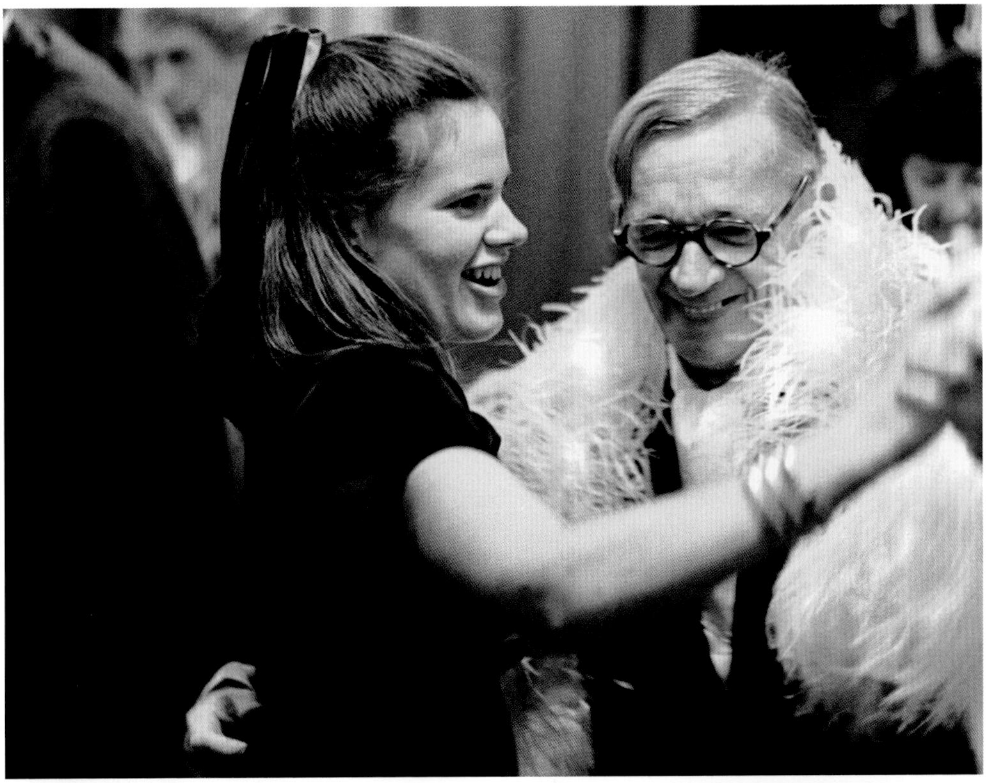

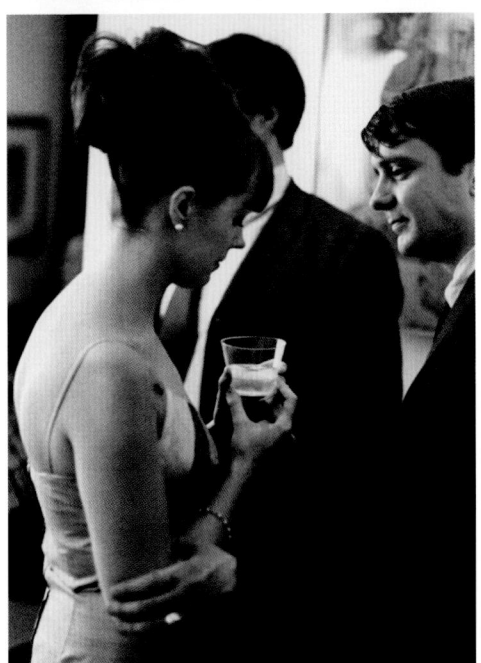
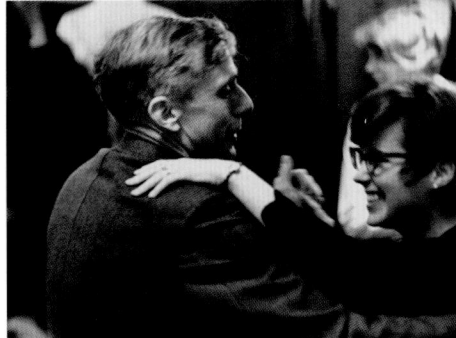
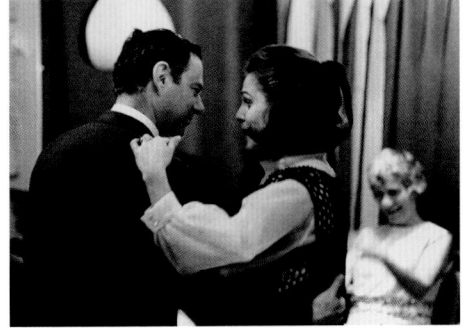

Housewarming party in Lyme, 1967:
Walker dances with Susan Mabry. Photograph by John T. Hill
Alston Purvis with Susanna Sage Wolcott. Photograph by John T. Hill
Alvin Eisenman dancing away. Photograph by John T. Hill
Dancing with Leslie Katz. Photograph by John T. Hill

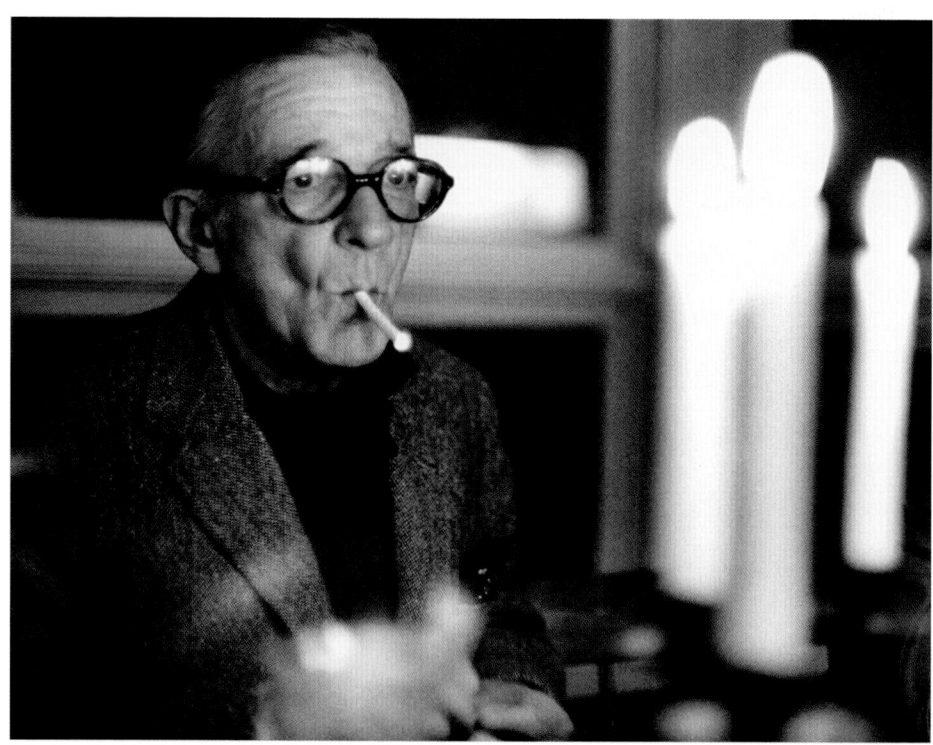

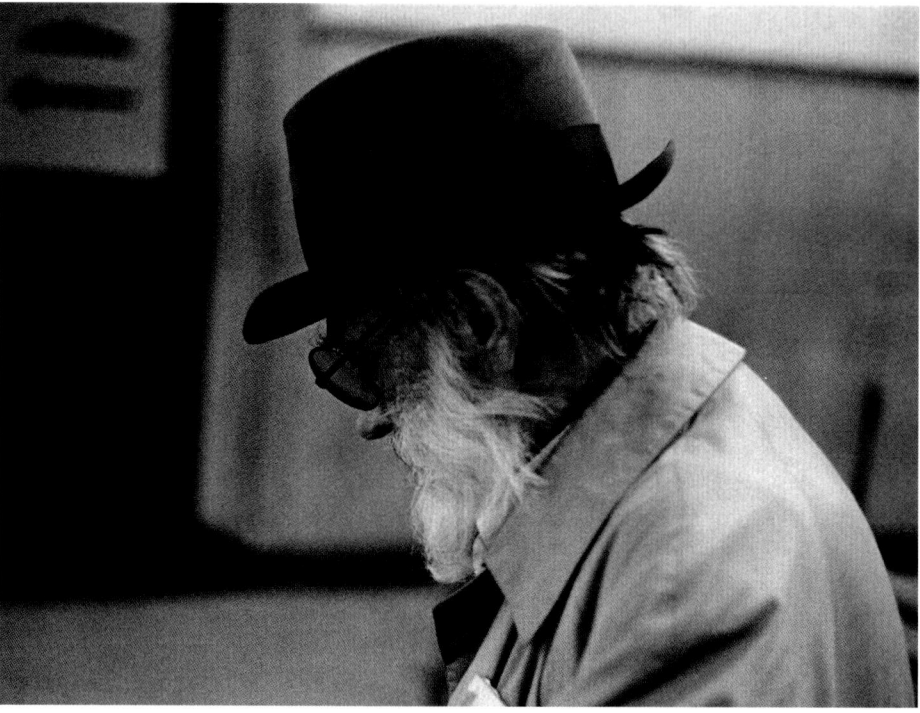

Walker, 1967. Photograph by John T. Hill
Walker the way he looked the last time I saw him. Photograph by Alston Purvis, 1974

I walked back a few steps and stood on my tiptoes. There, there—in a clearing—he had a girl on a swing, her light hair flying, someone worth watching. Higher and higher she went, until her full skirt peeled back and a pair of pale thighs came flashing over Walker's head. He was leaning against a tree, smoking. Every time the swing came forward he stretched out his arms, as if to grab her thighs. *"Belle, belle."* He said it over and over again.

I wasn't in a hurry to leave. Just once more I wanted to see the thighs, this was my chance to be a voyeur. How many times Walker had surprised me. I'd turn around and he'd be watching me as I came out of the bath, fixed my hair in front of the mirror, dressed, or took my clothes off. He'd be standing in the doorway, eyes glowing, always silent.

A few years ago I had been the girl on the swing. Now I knew there'd always be another. And few could resist. His age didn't matter; on the contrary, the girls were getting younger.

I turned away and walked back toward the house, empty. Was there something wrong with me? Most women would be angry or jealous, but all I felt was this heavy numbness. I mustn't really be alive if I can't get angry; soon I'll be in worse trouble, like a tree with all its branches cut off.

Where had I been all this time? Pretending he loved me, when fears kept me awake at night. I had been lying to myself, feeling so noble taking care of him when he was sick. But I believed it was my duty, my job, in sickness and in health—breakfast, lunch, and dinner, and tea in the afternoon. Right now, Walker was the one who didn't need help. He obviously liked his life, and his work was going well. Even last week, in the garden, I had doubts about our future. How long could I go on waiting and hoping for things that did not happen? My legs hurt. I needed to lie down in the car and forget everything.

I stopped near the back of the house and looked for the quickest way to the barn. With luck I wouldn't have to speak to anyone; the party was almost over. There were only a few cars left in the field. I walked to our rented car, opened the back door, and stretched out on the seat.

I would go to New York and talk to Dorothy. She knew Walker best, and she wasn't a feminist. She'd understand and be honest with me. I needed something more—love....

First I had to leave, be by myself and sort things out. And leaving would take time and money. Walker would be furious. He only spent money on things he liked, and there was little left over for me. In the beginning, I was sure, he wanted to take care of me, he tried, but now I must bore him. How could he be so selfish and insensitive?

Leave, don't wait, go now—hidden thoughts spun around in my head. Should I listen to my most secret wishes, escape from my prison and find a new life?

I climbed into the driver's seat. The key was under the mat. Damn it, I couldn't remember where the headlights were. I hadn't driven this car very much. Fumbling wasn't going to help. Here, I pushed the right button. No time to waste. I started the car and drove off—away from the lupine field and into the dark night.

Chapter 31: 1973

It was a cold gray day in Boston, in November 1973. My new husband's oldest daughter, Barbara, was a freshman at Yale. She had suggested we come down to New Haven for the game. I don't know enough about football to enjoy it, but with Jimmy even a football game turned into a pleasant occasion. I packed a picnic of hot soup, artichokes, sandwiches, and a bottle of wine.

It was my first time at the Yale Bowl. Walker had liked the idea of the game, but when the time came it was always too cold for him and we went home after lunch.

The big field was beginning to fill up with cars, and groups of old college friends met and greeted each other loudly, using sophomoric nicknames and telling favorite jokes even before they opened their bottles. Their tall, pretty, blond wives in fur coats, the kind who lived in John Updike's novels, moved back and forth among them, holding drinks, laughing with their girlfriends, and catching up on recent gossip.

A few of Jimmy's old classmates from Groton and Harvard came over to say hello. They wanted to meet me. I usually felt at ease after exchanging a few words with them. His friends were not the noisy rah-rah types; on the contrary, he had told me when we first met that he disliked macho men—was actually afraid of them. "I don't have enough confidence," he had said.

During lunch we concentrated on Barbara and her friends as they described their courses, activities, and new friends. Jimmy had a very open way with his five daughters. He often said he wouldn't have known how to bring up a son.

Our tickets were on the Yale side of the field, which required some tact on Jimmy's part every time Harvard scored. I wasn't able to follow the game, but I was watching the people around us, the huddles of players in their space-age uniforms, the huge crowd cheering and waving flags. According to Jimmy, today's game wasn't as exciting as games he remembered from his time as sports editor of *The Crimson*. But he liked being here with Barbara, his Yalie daughter.

The momentum picked up at the very end and Harvard won. Jimmy refrained from cheering as much as possible, but his pleasure was visible to all as we made our way back to the car.

The girls were disgruntled because they had no boyfriends to take them out to dinner. I told Jimmy about the Blessing, a Chinese restaurant most students liked; later we made a plan to go there for dinner.

We were inching our way through the traffic up York Street when I observed an odd couple on the sidewalk. An old man in a well-cut tweed coat and a brown fedora hat was being pulled along by a much younger girl with a halo of curly hair. As we came closer I knew it was Walker. I hadn't seen him in two years. His white hair hung down to his scarf, and he had a long white beard. Sad—if it weren't for his good coat he'd look like a street person. And he used to be so handsome.

I nudged Jimmy and told him quietly. He observed the unlikely pair and shook his head in disbelief. "Quick, girls, look out the window, that's Walker Evans, Isabelle's former husband."

I turned around to watch their expressions. It was easy to read their thoughts, their astonishment: How come Dad's wife, this young woman—and that old, frail man—hard to believe they were married. We know he is famous, but is he all right?

We all watched silently a while longer as the girl waited for Walker to catch up, then took him by the arm.

It was the last time I saw him.

Epilogue: A Walk With My Father, 1982

My parents moved to an old house in a village outside of Bern, and I visited them in March 1982. One morning the Föhn had caused the snow on the neighboring hills to melt overnight. My father suggested we take a walk to the highest point, a lookout nearby. The view would be especially grand today.

We set out through open farmland, past orchards and clumps of old trees. Papa was smoking his pipe.

"In most lives there are times," he said, flicking a stone out of the way with his cane, "when one's mind and emotions are fully engaged and life is more intense. For me it was the years in Berlin, witnessing the rise of Hitler—living history day by day." He cleared his throat. "I knew then that Europe would never be the same."

I asked him if that intensity also had to do with living abroad, observing everything more keenly in a foreign country. Yes, he agreed, that was certainly part of it. He turned to me and said, "Your years with Walker in New York were probably such an experience. It'll always be part of your life."

I said I'd certainly learned a lot very quickly, "but I was very unhappy and so lonely."

"Come, come," he said and took my arm. "Think of the people you met—the books you read—you grew up. It's never easy." He blew out his pipe and knocked it against the nearest tree to get rid of the ashes. The spicy smell of his Dunhill tobacco had been part of him for as long as I could remember. It was in his clothes and his desk drawers. During the war, when he was away for a long time, our house no longer smelled of his pipes, and I missed him very much.

Slowly we climbed to the top. There, surrounded by a chain of snow-capped mountains, glistening in the sun, way above the clouds like a weightless crown, were the three highest peaks: Jungfrau, Eiger, Mönch.

When we were growing up, Papa had taught us the names of our mountains, streams, and lakes, and the dates of important battles. He had spent time with us children whenever he was at home. I could count on him, always.

As we made our way to the village, through the barren fields, we felt the warm sun on our backs. Spring would soon be here.

The following photographs in the collection of the Walker Evans Archive, The Metropolitan Museum of Art are reproduced with permission (in order of appearance in the book):

1. *Caroline Blackwood, ca. 1963*
The Metropolitan Museum of Art, Walker Evans Archive, 1994 (1994.253.717.1-106)

2. *John McDonald, 1961*
The Metropolitan Museum of Art, Gift of Christie McDonald and Joan McDonald Miller, 2005 (2005.455.10(b))

3. *Dorothy Eisner Sitting Down in the Gallery of her Solo Show, 1961*
The Metropolitan Museum of Art, Gift of Christie McDonald and Joan McDonald Miller, 2005 (2005.455.8)

4. *Trash Can, New York City, 1962*
The Metropolitan Museum of Art, Walker Evans Archive, 1994 (1994.253.791.1-9)

5. *Brooklyn Bridge, New York, 1929*
The Metropolitan Museum of Art, Gift of Arnold H. Crane, 1972 (1972.742.3)

6. *Underneath the Brooklyn Bridge, New York, 1928–1929*
The Metropolitan Museum of Art, Walker Evans Archive, 1994 (1994.251.245)

7. *Interior View of Mary Frank's Bedroom, New York City, 1959*
The Metropolitan Museum of Art, Walker Evans Archive, 1994 (1994.252.173.1-20)

8. *Interior View of the Coggeshall House, Newcastle, Maine, ca. 1967*
The Metropolitan Museum of Art, Walker Evans Archive, 1994 (1994.252.114.1-9)

9. *View from the Heliker House, Cranberry Island, Maine, 1962*
The Metropolitan Museum of Art, Walker Evans Archive, 1994 (1994.252.111.1-65)

10. *Stove, Heliker House, Cranberry Island, Maine, 1967–1968*
The Metropolitan Museum of Art, Walker Evans Archive, 1994 (1994.252.115.1-86)

11. *Robert LaHotan, Cranberry Island, Maine, 1962*
The Metropolitan Museum of Art, Walker Evans Archive, 1994 (1994.252.117.6)

12. *"Breakfast Room" at Belle Grove Plantation, 1935*
The Metropolitan Museum of Art, Gilman Collection, Purchase, Ann Tenenbaum
and Thomas H. Lee Gift, 2005 (2005.100.322)

13. *Jimmy and Tania Stern's House, Hatch Manor, Tisbury, Wiltshire, England, 1967*
The Metropolitan Museum of Art, Walker Evans Archive, 1994 (1994.253.770.1-154)

14. *Subway Passenger, New York City, 1941*
The Metropolitan Museum of Art, Gift of Arnold H. Crane, 1971 (1971.646.19)

15. *Subway Passenger, New York City, 1938*
The Metropolitan Museum of Art, Gift of Arnold H. Crane, 1971 (1971.646.20)

16. *Subway Passenger, New York City, 1941*
The Metropolitan Museum of Art, Walker Evans Archive, 1994 (1994.253.574.4)

Acknowledgements

When I asked my husband Jimmy if he would mind my writing this memoir, he laughed and said, "Oh, go ahead, I have lived with Walker all these years of our married life."

Jimmy was the first one to read my manuscript, and he deserves my greatest thanks for his generous encouragement, professional and sensitive editing, and sense of humor when the going was hard. He also introduced me to Albert LaFarge, my spirited, energetic agent who helped me rework and shorten the manuscript with expertise and a light touch. Thank you, Albert.

I began writing the manuscript at the Vermont Studio Center in the winter of 1996. It was the perfect place for me, and I am grateful for this opportunity.

I would like to thank my valued readers and friends, whose criticism and suggestions provided much-needed support over an extended period of time: Betty and George Kramer, Mary and Bob Carswell, Jane Mayhall, the late James Mellow, Elenita Lodge, Rosanna Warren, Ann Cobb, Ellie Dwight, Martha Green, Alice Truax, Virginia Zabriskie, the late Bob Glynn, Linda and Ollie Wolcott, Margie Vernon, Bunny McPeck, Victoria Drake, Sallie Bass, Sunny Dupree, Joan Lee, Chris Clyde, Nancy and Laury Coolidge, Katie Ongaro, Ann LaFarge, Archie Hobson and Peter Kayafas.

The photographs are essential to the book. Jeff Rosenheim was most generous with his time and helped me select the Walker Evans photographs from the Metropolitan Museum archives. It was his idea to make prints, some of which are published for the first time, from the original negatives. I am grateful for his genuine interest in my project.

John Hill, Walker's original executor and close friend, provided some of the best photographs of Walker during his Yale years and of our life and friends in Lyme. I can't thank you enough, John.

My thanks go to Patricia Bailey, Director of the Heliker-LaHotan Foundation, for contributing Walker's photographs taken on Cranberry Island, Maine, and snapshots of Walker's visits on the island; to Alston Purvis, one of Walker's former Yale students and good friend, who contributed my favorite picture of Tania and Jimmy Stern and a late photograph of Walker, taken a year before his death; and to Sedat Pakay, a former Yale student, for his charming double portrait of Walker and me. Several delightful snapshots of Walker and friends were generously lent by Christie McDonald and Eliza Hobson. I thank them for digging around in their family archives and finding these treasures. Michaela Baldwin, my creative computer teacher, saw me through all the anxieties of a new laptop with angelic patience and good humor. Thanks, Michaela.

It is a privilege to work with the experts at powerHouse Books. I would like to thank my publisher Daniel Power, my editor Nicholas Weist, Craig Cohen, Kiki Bauer, and Sara Rosen for their understanding and visual sophistication. I feel honored to be published by powerHouse Books.

Walker's Way
My Years with Walker Evans

© 2007 powerHouse Cultural Entertainment, Inc.
Text © Isabelle Storey
Photographs by Walker Evans © Walker Evans Archive,
The Metropolitan Museum of Art
Additional photographs and artwork © Isabelle Storey, unless otherwise noted

All rights reserved. No part of this book may be reproduced in any manner in any media, or transmitted by any means whatsoever, electronic or mechanical (including photocopy, film or video recording, Internet posting, or any other information storage and retrieval system), without the prior written permission of the publisher.

Published in the United States by powerHouse Books,
a division of powerHouse Cultural Entertainment, Inc.
37 Main Street, Brooklyn, NY 11201-1021
telephone 212 604 9074, fax 212 366 5247
e-mail: walkersway@powerHouseBooks.com
website: www.powerHouseBooks.com

First edition, 2007

Library of Congress Control Number: 2007930810

Hardcover ISBN 978-1-57687-362-5

Duotone separations, printing, and binding by Midas Printing, Inc., China

Book design by Kiki Bauer

A complete catalog of powerHouse Books and Limited Editions is available upon request; please call, write, or visit our website.

10 9 8 7 6 5 4 3 2 1

Printed and bound in China